WENAMUN'S PROPHETIC MISSION

CRITICAL STUDIES IN THE HEBREW BIBLE

Editors
ANSELM C. HAGEDORN, *University of Osnabrück*
NATHAN MACDONALD, *University of Cambridge*
STUART WEEKS, *Durham University*

1. *A More Perfect Torah: At the Intersection of Philology and Hermeneutics in Deuteronomy and the Temple Scroll*, by Bernard M. Levinson
2. *The Prophets of Israel*, by Reinhard G. Kratz
3. *Interpreting Ecclesiastes: Readers Old and New*, by Katharine J. Dell
4. *Is There Theology in the Hebrew Bible?* by Konrad Schmid
5. *No Stone Unturned: Greek Inscriptions and Septuagint Vocabulary*, by James K. Aitken
6. *Joel: Scope, Genre(s), and Meaning*, by Ronald L. Troxel
7. *Job's Journey*, by Manfred Oeming and Konrad Schmid
8. *Infant Weeping in Akkadian, Hebrew, and Greek Literature*, by David A. Bosworth
9. *The Development of God in the Old Testament: Three Case Studies in Biblical Theology*, by Markus Witte
10. *"Like a Lone Bird on a Roof": Animal Imagery and the Structure of Psalms*, by Tova L. Forti
11. *A Concise History of Ancient Israel: From the Beginnings Through the Hellenistic Era*, by Bernd U. Schipper
12. *First Isaiah and the Disappearance of the Gods*, by Matthew J. Lynch
13. *The Torah Unabridged: The Evolution of Intermarriage Law in the Hebrew Bible*, by William A. Tooman
14. *The Torah and Its Documents*, by Baruch J. Schwartz
15. *The Language of Trauma in the Psalms*, by Danilo Verde
16. *Boschwitz on Wellhausen: The Life, Work, and Letters of a Jewish Scholar in Nazi Germany*, by Paul Michael Kurtz
17. *Wenamun's Prophetic Mission: Theocratic Rhetoric in Egypt and the Hebrew Bible*, by Christopher B. Hays

Wenamun's Prophetic Mission

Theocratic Rhetoric in Egypt and the Hebrew Bible

CHRISTOPHER B. HAYS

EISENBRAUNS | University Park, Pennsylvania

Library of Congress Cataloging-in-Publication Data

Names: Hays, Christopher B., 1973– author.
Title: Wenamun›s prophetic mission : theocratic Amun rhetoric and Hebrew prophecy / Christopher B. Hays.
Description: University Park Pennsylvania : Eisenbrauns, 2025- | Series: Critical studies in the Hebrew Bible ; 17 | Includes bibliographical references and index.
Summary: "Explores theological parallels between the ancient Egyptian story of Wenamun and the texts of the Hebrew prophets. It examines how Amun worshipers› theocratic claims influenced the southern Levant, encouraging scholars to reconsider the cultural context that shaped Iron Age Yahwism and the development of biblical monotheism"—Provided by publisher.
Identifiers: LCCN 2025004445 | ISBN 9781646023189 (hardback)
Subjects: LCSH: Wen-Amon. Report of Wenamun. | Amon (Egyptian deity) | God (Judaism) | Prophecy—Judaism.
Classification: LCC BL2450.A45 H39 2025 | DDC 891/.3
LC record available at https://lccn.loc.gov/2025004445

Copyright © 2025 Christopher B. Hays
All rights reserved
Printed in the United States of America
Published by The Pennsylvania State University Press,
University Park, PA 16802-1003

Eisenbrauns is an imprint of The Pennsylvania State University Press.

The Pennsylvania State University Press is a member of the Association of University Presses.

It is the policy of The Pennsylvania State University Press to use acid-free paper. Publications on uncoated stock satisfy the minimum requirements of American National Standard for Information Sciences—Permanence of Paper for Printed Library Material, ANSI Z39.48–1992.

CONTENTS

Preface and Acknowledgments..vii
List of Abbreviations ix
Note on Style and Translation.. xi
The Voyage of Wenamun xiii
Chronology of Ancient Egyptian Rulers xxi
Map... xxiv

INTRODUCTION 1

CHAPTER 1. *Wenamun* as History, Literature, and Theology 5

CHAPTER 2. *Wenamun* and the Hebrew Bible 19

CHAPTER 3. Amun and Yahweh as Theocrats............................31

Excursus: Wenamun's "Crazy Crusade" 46

CHAPTER 4. Amun and Yahweh as Sovereigns and Suzerains 50

CHAPTER 5. Wenamun as a Prophetic Messenger..................... 67

CHAPTER 6. Is Wenamun Also Among the Prophets? 75

CHAPTER 7. Wenamun and Jonah: Foolish Prophets of Serious Gods.. 84

CONCLUSION: AMUN THEOCRACY AND BIBLICAL MONOTHEISM 97

Bibliography.. 113
Subject Index 129
Ancient Source Index... 133

PREFACE AND ACKNOWLEDGMENTS

Sometimes a book is said to be "the last word" on a subject. This one is meant to be more like a first word—an invitation to further conversation. Narrowly, it invites biblical scholars to consider more closely the ancient Egyptian story of Wenamun. More broadly, it invites scholars of the ancient Mediterranean to revisit the channels of intellectual influence that gave rise to "biblical monotheism."

I'm thankful to friends who have read drafts and/or discussed the material that became this book, including: Nadia Ben-Marzouk, Brian Donnelly-Lewis, Jeremy M. Hutton, Martti Nissinen, and Thomas Schneider. Thanks also to Anselm Hagedorn, Nathan McDonald, and Maria Metzler for their encouragement and support through the process of publication in the CSHB series.

I am also grateful for the collegial support of Alphonso Groenewald and colleagues at the University of Pretoria (S.A.), where I am a research associate.

This book grows out of my relatively long history of work in both Hebrew prophetic literature and in the comparative study of Israelite and Egyptian culture. I commented in my first book, *Death in the Iron Age II and in First Isaiah*, on the relevance of Egyptian religion to understanding various aspects of the book of Isaiah. Shortly after I moved to the Los Angeles area in 2008, I got to know Kara Cooney and others on the UCLA Egyptology faculty. These scholarly relationships have developed over the years into important ones for me, and I'm grateful to many at UCLA whom I have learned from, including Jonathan Winnerman and Willeke Wendrich. Among the other colleagues to whom I'm grateful for entertaining nascent forms of the ideas that led to this book are Nick Brown, Adam Chebatah, Hong Chen, Jordan Galczynski, Brandon Keith, Elizabeth Koch, Alison McCoskey, Jeff Newman, Marissa Stevens, Kylie Thomsen, and Matei Tichindelean.

In 2022–23, I found myself in Jerusalem on an annual professorship at the Albright Institute for Archaeological Research. Even though this book was not my primary project during that time, I found it a remarkably congenial place to get work done on it. The extensive Egyptology collections at the neighboring École Biblique et Archéologique Française were a pleasant surprise and saved me a great deal of legwork. I am grateful to Bernard Didier Ntamak Songué, O.P., and the rest of its staff, as well as to Emily Johnson of the AIAR library for her help, and to Emilio Núñez and the rest of the staff of the David Allan Hubbard Library at my own institution, who were consistently willing to make acquisitions to support my research.

This book is dedicated to my colleagues on the steering committee of the Prophetic Texts in Their Ancient Contexts section of the Society of Biblical Literature—including Ehud Ben Zvi, C. L. Crouch, Julie Deluty, Esther Hamori, Martti Nissinen, Ryan Schroeder, Jennifer Singletary, Jonathan Stökl, and Hanna Tervanotko—who have formed a most collegial and enriching group with whom to discuss these matters and eat Mexican food.

Pasadena, CA
March 15, 2024

ABBREVIATIONS

ÄAT	Ägypten und Altes Testament
ABD	*Anchor Bible Dictionary.* Edited by David Noel Freedman. 6 vols. New York: Doubleday, 1992.
AEL	*Ancient Egyptian Literature.* Edited by Miriam Lichtheim. World Literature in Translation. Berkeley: University of California Press, 2019.
BASOR	*Bulletin of the American Schools of Oriental Research*
BZAW	Beihefte zum Zeitschrift fur Alttestamentliche Wissenschaft
CAD	*The Assyrian Dictionary of the Oriental Institute of the University of Chicago.* Edited by Ignace J. Gelb et al. 21 vols. Chicago: The Oriental Institute of the University of Chicago, 1956–2010.
CHANE	Culture and History of the Ancient Near East
COS	*The Context of Scripture.* Edited by William W. Hallo and K. Lawson Younger Jr. 4 vols. Leiden: Brill, 1997–2016.
CTH	*Catalogue des Textes Hittites.* Emmanuel Laroche. Paris: Klincksieck, 1971.
DLE	*Dictionary of Late Egyptian.* Edited by Leonard H. Lesko and Barbara S. Lesko. 4 vols. Berkeley: B. C. Scribe, 1982–89.
DNWSI	*Dictionary of North-West Semitic Inscriptions.* Jacob Hoftijzer and Karen Jongeling. 2 vols. Leiden: Brill, 1995.
DULAT	*A Dictionary of the Ugaritic Language in the Alphabetic Tradition.* Gregorio del Olmo Lete and Joaquín Sanmartín. Translated and edited by W. G. E. Watson. 3rd ed. 2 vols. Leiden: Brill, 2015.
EA	El Amarna Letters
FAT	Forschungen zum Alten Testament
GM	*Göttinger Miszellen*

HALOT	*The Hebrew and Aramaic Lexicon of the Old Testament.* Ludwig Koehler, Walter Baumgartner, and Johann J. Stamm. Translated and edited under the supervision of Mervyn E. J. Richardson. 2 vols. Leiden: Brill, 2001.
JAEI	*Journal of Ancient Egyptian Interconnections*
JEA	*Journal of Egyptian Archaeology*
JNES	*Journal of Near Eastern Studies*
KAI	*Kanaanäische und aramäische Inschriften.* Herbert Donner and Wolfgang Röllig. 2nd ed. Wiesbaden: Harrassowitz, 1966–69.
KTU	*Die Keilschrifttexten aus Ugarit.* Edited by Manfried Dietrich, Oswald Loretz, and Joaquín Sanmartín. Münster: Ugarit-Verlag, 2013. 3rd enl. ed. of *The Cuneiform Alphabetic Texts from Ugarit, Ras Ibn Hani, and Other Places.* Edited by Manfried Dietrich, Oswald Loretz, and Joaquín Sanmartín. Münster: Uagrit-Verlag, 1995.
LASM	Lingua Aegyptia / Studia monographica
MT	Masoretic Text
NEA	*Near Eastern Archaeology*
OBO	Orbis Biblicus et Orientalis
OEAE	*The Oxford Encyclopedia of Ancient Egypt.* Edited by Donald Redford. 3 vols. Oxford: Oxford University Press, 2001.
OLA	Orientalia Lovaniensia Analecta
SAA	State Archives of Assyria
SBLWAW	Society of Biblical Literature Writings from the Ancient World
TA	*Tel Aviv*
TLA	*Thesaurus Linguae Aegyptiae*
Wb	*Wörterbuch der ägyptischen Sprache*
ZÄS	*Zeitschrift für Ägyptische Sprache und Altertumskunde*

NOTE ON STYLE AND TRANSLATION

"Wenamun" is italicized when referring to the literary work, and in Roman font when referring to the character.

All translations from biblical Hebrew and other Semitic languages are the responsibility of the author unless otherwise noted. Readers will notice that I default to the NRSV for biblical translations where there is no reason to do otherwise.

I render the name of the god of Israel as "Yahweh." In more specialized academic writing, I prefer "Yhwh," reflecting the consonants of the Tetragrammaton (יהוה), but a vocalized form will be more readable to a wider audience.

The bibliographic choices of this volume reflect its goals. While I hope that Egyptologists find it stimulating, biblical scholars are its primary intended audience. Mercifully, the corpus of scholarship on *Wenamun* is relatively manageable, and so I have tried to incorporate it fully, for the sake of readers who would like to dig further. By contrast, a full survey of the relevant scholarship on Hebrew prophecy and Israelite religion would immediately explode the constraints of a short monograph, so I have cited only a select number of representative sources.

THE VOYAGE OF WENAMUM

Robert K. Ritner's translation of this text is presented here for reference. It is authoritative, accessible, and the most recent major translation of the story into English. The transliteration of the hieratic Egyptian text may be found on pp. 88–92 of his volume.

The translation of specific pages is discussed in the body of the volume, but here Ritner's translation is presented without alteration, apart from the addition of subheadings and notes, and the adjustment of the spelling of certain names (e.g., Amon to Amun, Tchekerbaal to Zakarbaal, and Tcheker to Tjeker) for the sake of consistency within this volume. (The spelling of names in other secondary sources has not been altered.)

The parenthetical numbering system in the text refers to the column number and line number on the papyrus, e.g., (1/1). Only one copy of *Wenamun* has survived (P. Moscow 120). It has a significantly damaged section and is missing its ending, as noted below. Photos of the papyrus have been published by Korostovtstev (1960) and updated by Schipper (2005).

***

The temple official Wenamun sets off from Thebes on a mission to secure timber
(1/1) Regnal year 5, month 4 of summer, day 16,[1] the day of departure made by Wenamun, the elder of the portal of the estate of Amun, (1/2) [Lord of the Thrones] of the Two Lands, in order to bring back the timber for the great and

---

* Text of *Wenamun* is reproduced by permission from Robert K. Ritner, *The Libyan Anarchy: Inscriptions from Egypt's Third Intermediate Period*, edited by Edward Wente, SBLWAW 21 (Atlanta: Society of Biblical Literature, 2009), 92–98.

1. Probably 1065 BCE; see discussion in chapter 2.

noble bark of Amun-Re, King of the Gods, which is upon (1/3) [the river and whose name is] Amun-user-hat.

Wenamun arrives in Tanis and receives support from rulers there
On the day when I had arrived at Tanis at the (1/4) [place where Smendes] and Tanetamun were, I gave to them the dispatches of Amun-Re, King of the Gods, and they (1/5) had them read aloud in their presence, and they said: "I shall act, I shall act in accordance with that which Amun-Re, King of the Gods, (1/6) our [lord], has said." And I spent from month 4 of summer within Tanis. Then Smendes (1/7) and Tanetamun sent me off with the ship's captain Mengebet, and I went down to (1/8) the great Syrian sea in the first month of summer, day 1.

Wenamun arrives at Dor and is robbed
I arrived at Dor, a town of (1/9) the Tjeker, and Bedor, its prince, had 50 loaves, 1 jug of wine, (1/10), and 1 haunch of beef brought to me. Then a man of my ship fled, having stolen 1 golden (1/11) [jar] amounting to 5 deben, 4 silver jars amounting to 20 deben, and a bag of 11 deben of silver, (1/12) [with the total of what] he [stole being] 5 deben of gold and 31 deben of silver.[2]

And I arose on that morning, and I went to (1/13) the place where the prince was, and I said to him: "I have been robbed in your harbor. Now you are the prince of this land. Now (1/14) you are its investigator. Search for my money! But really, as regards the money, it belongs to Amun-Re, (1/15) King of the Gods, the Lord of the Lands. It belongs to Smendes; it belongs to Herihor, my lord, and the other (1/16) magnates of Egypt. It is yours. It belongs to Warti; it belongs to Mekamer; it belongs to Zakarbaal, the prince of Byblos."

And he said to me: "Whether you are distraught or trustworthy, now look, I cannot (1/18) understand this response that you have said to me. If it had been a thief who belonged to my land who had gone down (1/19) to your ship and stolen your money, I would replace it for you from my storehouse until (1/20) your thief, whatever his name, had been found. But really, as regards the thief who robbed you, he is yours. He belongs to (1/21) your ship. Spend a few days here near me so that I may search for him."

And I spent 9 days moored (1/22) in his harbor. Then I went before him and I said to him: "Look, you have not found my money. (1/23) Please [send] me [off] with the ship's captains and those who go to sea."

[*The section of the papyrus containing lines 1/24–32 is significantly damaged. The prince tells Wenamun to be still and (perhaps) to remain at Dor, but instead*

---

2. This is the equivalent of roughly half a kilo of gold and 3 kilos of silver. See discussion below.

Wenamun sets off and makes a stop at Tyre. After that, he takes 30 deben of silver from a ship belonging to a seafaring people called the Tjeker. He then goes to Byblos, where he receives a chilly reception from the ruler, Zakarbaal. Nevertheless, Wenamun announces that he will keep the silver until his money or the thief is found.]

And he said to me: "Be silent! (1/24) [If you wish to] find your [money...] listen to my [words and do what] I [say] to you, but do not (1/25) [...] listen to [...] the place where you are. You will take possession of their boats (?), and you will be paid in full like [...] (1/26) [... until] they go to search for their thief who [robbed them...] (1/27) [... Spend the] night at the harbor. Look, [you will (?) ..."... And I arrived at] (1/28) Tyre.

And I left from Tyre at first light [...] (1/29) [...] Zakarbaal, the prince of Byblos [...] (1/30) [...] a ship, and I found 30 deben of silver in it, and I took possession of it. [I said to the ship's owners: "I have taken possession of] (1/31) your money. It will remain with me [until] you have found my [money or the thief] (1/32) who stole it. I have not robbed you, although I shall rob him. But as for you, [you] shall [...] me to [...]."

(1/33) Then they went away and I celebrated by myself [in] a tent on the seashore at the harbor of Byblos. And [I found a] (1/34) [hiding place for] Amun-of-the-Road and I placed his possessions within it. Then the [prince] of Byblos sent word to me, saying: "Get [yourself out of] (1/35) [my] harbor!" And I sent word to him, saying: "Where [should I go]? [...] I [...] go [...] (1/36) [...] If [you have a ship] to transport me, let me be taken (1/37) back to Egypt." And I spent 29 days in his harbor, [although] daily he spent time sending word to me, saying: "Get (1/38) yourself out of my harbor!"

A Byblian prophet speaks up on Wenamun's behalf
Now when he offered to his gods, the god (Amun) seized a great seer from among his (1/39) great seers, and he caused him to be in an ecstatic state. He said to him:

"Bring up the god!
Bring the messenger who bears him! (1/40)
It is Amun who has sent him.
It is he who has caused that he come."

But the ecstatic became ecstatic on that night only after I had found (1/41) a ship heading for Egypt, and I had loaded all my belongings onto it, and I had watched (1/42) for darkness to fall so that I might put the god on board in order to prevent another eye from seeing him.

And the (1/43) harbor-master came to me, saying: "Stay until morning—so says the prince!" And I said to him: "Are you not the one who (1/44) daily spent time coming to me, saying: 'Get yourself out of my harbor'? Are you saying 'Stay tonight,' (1/45) just to allow the ship that I have found to depart, and then you will come back, saying: 'Be off with you,' again?" Then he went and told it to (1/46) the prince, and the prince sent word to the captain of the ship, saying: "Stay until morning—so says (1/47) the prince!"

Wenamun meets with Zakarbaal, the ruler of Byblos
Morning came and he sent word and took me up while the god rested in the tent (1/48) where he was on the seashore. I found him (i.e., Zakarbaal) seated in his high chamber with his back set (1/49) against a window, while behind his head crashed the waves of the great Syrian sea. (1/50)

I said to him: "Amun be merciful!" He said to me: "How long has it been until today since you came from the place where (1/51) Amun is?" I said to him: "Five full months until today." He said to me: "Indeed, you are correct. Where is the (1/52) dispatch of Amun that is in your possession? Where is the letter of the First Prophet of Amun that is in your possession?" I said (1/53) to him: "I gave them to Smendes and Tanetamun."

And he became very irritated, and he said to me: "Now look, neither dispatches nor (1/54) letters, nothing is in your possession. Where is the pinewood ship that Smendes gave to you? Where is (1/55) its Syrian crew? Has he entrusted you to this foreign ship's captain just to have him kill (1/56) you and have them throw you into the sea? With whom would the god be sought? And you also, (1/57) with whom would you also be sought?" So he said to me.

And I said to him: "Is it not an Egyptian ship? Now, they are Egyptian crews that sail (1/58) under Smendes. He has no Syrian crews."

He said to me: "Are there not 20 cargo ships (1/59) here in my harbor that are in partnership with Smendes? As for that Sidon, (2/1) the other place that you have passed, are there not another 50 ships there that are in partnership (2/2) with Werketer, although it is to his house that they haul?"

And I was silent at that important moment.

(2/3) And he responded, saying to me: "On what commission have you come?"

I said to him: (2/4) "It is in pursuit of the timber for the great and noble bark of Amun-Re, King of the Gods, that I have come. What your father did, and what (2/5) the father of your father did, you shall do also." So I said to him.

He said to me: "It is they who did it, truly. (2/6) If you pay me for doing it then I shall do it. But really, mine did this commission only after (2/7)

Pharaoh, l.p.h.,[3] had caused 5 ships to be brought, which had been loaded with the products of Egypt and then were unloaded into their (2/8) storehouses. As for you, what is it that you have brought to me for my part?"

Zakarbaal asserts the power of his land and its gods
He had the daily ledger of his ancestors brought, (2/9) and he had it read aloud in my presence. They found 1,000 deben of silver and all manner of things on his ledger. (2/10) He said to me: "Were the ruler of Egypt the lord of what is mine, and I his servant as well, (2/11) would he have caused silver and gold to be brought to say: 'Perform the commission of Amun!'? Wasn't it the delivery (2/12) of royal gifts that he used to perform for my father? Now as for me myself, I am not your (2/13) servant, nor am I the servant of the one who sent you either. If I but cry out to the (2/14) Lebanon, heaven opens with the logs lying right here on the seashore! Give (2/15) me the sails that you brought to take your ships laden with your logs to Egypt. (2/16) Give me the ropes [that] you brought [to bind the pines] that I am to cut down in order to make them for you. (2/17) [...] that I am to make for you for the sails for your (2/18) ships, and the yards may be too heavy and may break, and you may die in the midst of the sea. (2/19) Look, Amun thunders in the sky only since he placed Seth at his side. Now (2/20) all lands has Amun founded. He founded them only after he had first founded the land of Egypt, the one from which you have come. (2/21) Thus virtues came forth from it just to reach the place where I am. Thus learning came forth (2/22) from it just to reach the place where I am. What is the sense of these foolish wanderings that they have made you do?"

Wenamun answers Zakarbaal and offers a deal
I said to him: (2/23) "Wrong! They are not foolish wanderings that I am on! There is not any ship upon the river that (2/24) does not belong to Amun. His is the sea and his is the Lebanon, about which you say: 'It is mine.' It is (2/25) a nursery just for Amun-user-hat, the lord of every ship. But really, he—that is Amun-Re, King of the Gods—said in speaking to Herihor, (2/26) my lord: 'Send me off!' And he caused that I come bearing this great god. Now look, you have caused (2/27) this god to spend these 29 days moored in your harbor, without your knowing whether he was here or whether he was not the one whom (2/28) he is. You are waiting to haggle over the Lebanon with Amun, its lord!

---

3. L.p.h., short for "life! prosperity! health!" (*'nḫ wḏ3 snb*), is a very common exclamation inserted after the name of pharaoh throughout Egyptian history, much as one might add "Long live the King!"

"As for your saying that the (2/29) former kings used to send silver and gold, if they had possessed life and health they would not have sent those things. (2/30) It was instead of life and health that they sent those things to your fathers. Now, as for Amun-Re, King of the Gods, he is the (2/31) lord of life and health. Now he is the lord of your fathers. They spent their lifetimes offering (2/32) to Amun. You also, you are a servant of Amun. If you say 'I shall act, I shall act' to Amun, and you accomplish his commission, you will live; you will prosper; you will be healthy; and you will be fortunate in your entire land and your people. Do not covet for yourself (2/34) the property of Amun-Re, King of the Gods! For really, a lion loves his property!

"Let your scribe be brought to me so that (2/35) I might send him to Smendes and Tanetamun, the foundations whom Amun has placed in the north of his land, (2/36) and they will have everything brought. I shall send him to them, saying: 'Let it be brought until I return to the south, and then I shall have (2/37) absolutely all your expenses brought back to you in turn.'" So I said to him.

Egypt sends goods to Byblos in exchange for timber
He placed my letter in the hand of his messenger, and he loaded the (2/38) keel, the bow-post, and the stern-post together with another 4 hewn logs, for a total of 7, and he had them brought to Egypt.

(2/39) His messenger went to Egypt and returned to me in Syria in the first month of winter, Smendes and Tanetamun having sent: (2/40) 4 jars and 1 vessel of gold, 5 silver jars, 10 articles of clothing of royal linen, 10 veils of sheer cloth of good quality, 500 mats of smooth linen, (2/41) 500 ox-hides, 500 ropes, 20 sacks of lentils, and 30 baskets of fish. And she had brought to me: (2/42) 5 articles of clothing of sheer cloth of good quality, 5 veils of sheer cloth of good quality, 1 sack of lentils, and 5 baskets of fish.

Then the prince rejoiced, and he supplied (2/43) 300 men and 300 oxen, and he assigned heralds over them to have them cut down the logs. And they cut them down, and they spent the winter (2/44) lying there. In month 3 of summer, they dragged them to the seashore.

Wenamun and the Byblians exchange barbs as he prepares to leave
The prince went out and stood by them, and he sent word to me, (2/45) saying: "Come!" Now when I was conducted near to him, the shadow of his lotus fan fell upon me, and Penamun, (2/46) a cupbearer who belonged to him, intervened, saying: "The shadow of Pharaoh, l.p.h., your lord, has fallen upon you." And he became angry (2/47) at him, saying: "Leave him alone!"

I was conducted near to him, and he responded, saying to me: "Look, the commission that (2/48) my fathers did previously, I have done it—even though you, for your part, have not done for me what your fathers used to do for me. Look, (2/49) the last of your lumber has arrived and is in place. Do as I wish and come to load it, for will it not be given to you? (2/50) Do not come to look upon the terror of the sea! Were you to look upon the terror of the sea, you would look upon (2/51) my own. For really, I have not done to you what was done to the messengers of Khaemwase, when they had spent 17 years (2/52) in this land. In their jobs they died." And he said to his cupbearer: "Take him! Let him see their tomb in which they (2/53) lie."

And I said to him: "Don't make me see it! As for Khaemwase, they were but men whom he sent to you as messengers, and he himself a man. (2/54) You do not have here one of his messengers, that you should say: 'You should go and see your fellows.' Why do you not rejoice (2/55) and have [made] for yourself a stela and say upon it: 'Amun-Re, King of the Gods, sent to me Amun-of-the-Road, his messenger, (2/56) l.p.h., together with Wenamun, his human messenger, in pursuit of the timber for the great and noble bark of Amun-Re, King of the Gods. I cut (2/57) it down. I loaded it. I equipped him with my ships and crews. I caused that they reach Egypt in order to beseech for myself (2/58) 50 years of life from Amun over and above my allotted fate.' And should it happen after another day that a messenger comes (2/59) from the land of Egypt who knows writings and he reads your name on the stela, you will receive water in the west like the gods who (2/60) are there."

He said to me: "This is a great testimony of words that you have said to me." I said to him: "Regarding the many things that you have said to me, if I reach (2/61) the place where the First Prophet of Amun is, and he sees your commission, it is your commission that will draw (2/62) profit to you."

The Tjeker arrive at Byblos in pursuit of Wenamun
Then I went off to the seashore to the spot where the logs were placed. I caught sight of 11 (2/63) ships coming in from the sea that were under the control of the Tjeker, who were saying: "Imprison him! Do not let a ship (2/64) of his head for the land of Egypt!"

Then I sat down weeping. The secretary of the prince came out to me, (2/65) and he said to me: "What's with you?" I said to him: "Do you not see the migratory birds who have already made two descents into Egypt? (2/66) Look at them going to the cool water region. Until what comes about shall I be abandoned here? Now do you not see the ones coming (2/67) to imprison me again?

Then he went and he told it to the prince. The prince began to weep because of the words that were told to him, for they were (2/68) painful. He sent his secretary out to me, bringing me 2 jugs of wine and 1 sheep. And he sent (2/69) to me Tanetniut, an Egyptian songstress whom he had, saying: "Sing for him!

Do not allow his heart to obsess upon affairs." And he sent word to me, (2/70) saying: "Eat! Drink! Do not allow your heart to obsess upon affairs. You will hear whatever I shall say in the morning."

The morning (2/71) came, and he had his assembly summoned. He stood in their midst and he said to the Tjeker: "What is the meaning of your journeys?" (2/72) They said to him: "It is in pursuit of the blasted ships that you are sending to Egypt together with our adversaries that we have come." (2/73) He said to them: "I will not be able to imprison the messenger of Amun within my land. Let me send him off, and you go after him (2/74) to imprison him."

Wenamun flees to Cyprus and seeks asylum
He had me board, and he sent me off from there at the harbor of the sea. The wind blew me to the land of (2/75) Alasiya.[4] The people of the harbor came out against me in order to kill me, and I forced my way through them to the place where Hatiba, (2/76) the princess of the town, was. I found her when she had gone out of one of her houses and was in the act of entering into her other one. I (2/77) hailed her, and I said to the people who were standing near to her: "Is there not one among you who understands the Egyptian language?" And one among them said: "I understand." I said to him: "Say to my lady: 'I have heard as far as Thebes, in the place where Amun is, that even as (2/79) injustice is done in every town, so justice is done in the land of Alasiya.' Is injustice done daily even here?"

Then she said: "Really, what is the meaning of (2/80) your saying that?" I said to her: "If the sea rages and the wind blows me to the land where you are, (2/81) will you let them greet me so to kill me, although I am a messenger of Amun? Look here, as for me, I shall be sought (2/82) for all time. As for this crew of the prince of Byblos, whom they are seeking to kill, will not its lord find 10 (2/83) crews belonging to you and kill them then for his part?" Then she caused that the men be summoned and they were arraigned. She said to me: "Spend the night." [...]

[*The text stops abruptly at the end of the second column. It is unknown how the story ends, since the rest has been lost.*]

---

4. I.e., Cyprus.

CHRONOLOGY OF ANCIENT EGYPTIAN RULERS

(All dates are BCE)
Late New Kingdom
Dynasty 20 (ca. 1186–1069)

Setnakht Userkhaure	1186–1183
Ramses III	1183–1152
Ramses IV	1152–1145
Ramses V	1145–1142
Ramses VI	1142–1134
Ramses VII	1134–1126
Ramses VIII	1126–1125
Ramses IX	1125–1107
Ramses X	1107–1099
Ramses XI	1099–1069

Third Intermediate Period
Dynasty 21 (1070/1069–946/945)

Nesbanebdjed (Greek Smendes)	1069–1043
Amenemnisut (Greek Nephercheres)	1043–1039
Pasebakhenniut I (Greek Psusennes)	1039–994
Amenemipet (Greek Amenophthis)	996–984
Osorkon (Greek Osochor)	984–978
Siamun	978–959
Pasebakhenniut II (Greek Psusennes)	959–945

* Adapted with permission from The Petrie Museum of Egyptian and Sudanese Archaeology, University College London, https://www.ucl.ac.uk/museumsstatic/digitalegypt/chronology/index.html.

High Priest of Amun in Thebes (eleventh–tenth centuries)
Piankhi
Herihor
Pinodjem I
Masahalot
Djedkhonsjufankh
Menkheperre
Smendes II
Pinodjem II
Psusennes

Dynasty 22 (946/945–ca. 735)
Sheshonq I	946–925
Osorkon I	925–ca. 890
Takelot I	ca. 890–877
Sheshonq II	ca. 877–875
Osorkon II	ca. 875–837
Sheshonq III	ca. 837–798/785[?]
Sheshonq IIIa	ca. 798–785[?]
Pamui	ca. 785–774
Sheshonq V	ca. 774–736

The Upper Egyptian Line
(During Osorkon II's reign, rule was divided between kings in Tanis and Upper Egypt.)
Horsiese	ca. 870–850
Takelot II	ca. 841–816
Padibast	ca. 830–880/800
Iuput I	ca. 816–800
Sheshonq IV	ca. 805/800–790
Osorkon III	ca. 790–762
Takelot III	ca. 767–755
Rudamun	ca. 755–735
Ini	ca. 735–730

Dynasty 23 (818–715)
Padibast II (in Bubastis/Tanis)	ca. 756–732/730
Iuput II (in Leontopolis)	ca. 756–724[?]
Osorkon IV	ca. 732/730–722
Psammus(?)	ca. 722–712

Dynasty 24 (727–715)
Tefnakht   ca. 740–719/717
Bakenrenef (Greek Bocchoris)   ca. 722–712

Dynasty 25 (747–656)
Kashta   before 746
Piye (formerly read Piankhi)   ca. 746–715
Shabako   715–700
Shabitko   700–690
Taharqo   690–664
Tanutamani   664–ca. 655

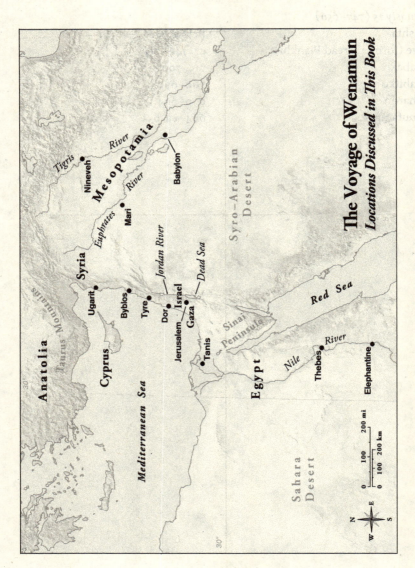

Voyage of Wenamun. Adapted by permission of Westminster John Knox Press.

Introduction

THE STORY OF WENAMUN IS an Egyptian travelogue from the turn of the first millennium BCE that is enlivened by visits to exotic ports of call, piracy, intrigue at foreign courts, verbal sparring, and attempted murder. Life had perhaps not always been so dramatic for Egypt's emissaries, but it was an era of upheaval in the ancient Near East; boundaries and powers were renegotiated in the wake of the collapse of the Late Bronze Age's "Club of Great Powers."[1] Egypt survived this transitional period, and the attacks of the "Sea Peoples" who played a role in it—but it did not survive unscathed. The Ramesside 20th Dynasty came to an end in 1069,[2] and historians mark the beginning of the Third Intermediate Period.

As with earlier "intermediate periods" in Egypt, the term reflects a decline of centralized power in the homeland and a loss of imperial control beyond it. Territories from Nubia to the Levant became independent, or even conquered parts of the Egyptian heartland. This was the same power vacuum in which the populations emerged who would later coalesce into Israel. For Egyptians, such periods of crisis raised questions about national identity, about the value of received wisdom, and about the power of the gods. Previous intermediate periods had given rise to pessimistic literature, which uncharacteristically entertained doubts about the veracity of traditional teachings and theologies.

The *Story of Wenamun* also addresses Egypt's reduced stature and the problems it causes for Egyptians, but in a different way. It tells a tale about an official of the Temple of Amun in Thebes who journeys by ship to the coast and islands of the eastern Mediterranean in order to secure timbers from the famous forests of Lebanon for construction of his god's sacred bark. At one level, *Wenamun* is a breezy tale that entertains its audience with vignettes from around the Mediterranean world—Tanis, Dor, Tyre, Byblos, and Cyprus. Along the way, Wenamun finds that Egypt can no longer snap its fingers and

---

1. The general reader can find expert and readable treatments of these events in Cline, *1177 B.C.*
2. All dates are BCE.

get what it wants in a foreign land, but his faith in Amun and his confidence in his mission are undimmed. Although Wenamun shows certain lapses in his practical competencies, his speeches are lofty and poetic. In fact, any reader of the Hebrew prophets is bound to recognize a certain kinship between these ancient texts.

Despite this, *Wenamun* has been essentially ignored by most biblical scholars, who may know only that it includes a brief appearance by an ecstatic prophet from Byblos. The present book makes the case that *Wenamun* deserves much greater attention. It analyzes the story from various perspectives and opens up new vistas of comparison between it and ancient Near Eastern prophecy.

Wenamun's confrontations with Bedor of Dor and Zakarbaal of Byblos are waged in theological terms. The very name of the main character, *wn-imn*, "Amun exists!,"[3] arguably announces the story's message, and his climactic encounter with Zakarbaal is essentially a theological debate in which the two speak like prophets. As in any cultural encounter, their speeches contain elements of the theological rhetoric of both spheres (including some that was essentially international in the period) as each man tries to assert his power over the other.

In the Hebrew Bible as well, the prophets are theopolitical commentators. They announce the success and failure of nations, often correlated with the degradation of foreign gods and the ascendancy of the national deity, Yahweh. The surviving prophetic corpora from other places, especially Nineveh and Mari, similarly carry political messages: the ambitions of Aššur, the assurances of Adad, or the comforting words of Ištar.

Because theological claims for national deities naturally came into conflict with each other, Semitic prophecy was also agonistic by nature. Theological conflicts with political implications are frequently attested in the Bible, whether between the prophets of different gods (e.g., Isa 19:11–15; Hos 2), between prophets of Yahweh (e.g., Isa 29:8–11; Jer 14:13–16), or between a prophet and opponents who are only implied (e.g., Isa 9:13–17; Jer 14:13–15; Ezek 13). Occasionally a complete prophetic debate is depicted—as in the conflicts between Elijah and the prophets of Baal in 1 Kgs 18, and between Jeremiah and Hananiah in Jer 28—but in nearly every case one can assume that a prophet is speaking against an implied opposing view.

A full overview of the book's argument appears in the concluding chapter, but in short: It begins by locating *Wenamun*'s narrative world and composition within the history of Egypt, laying out the ways in which the story is conversant with historical realities yet essentially a literary work. It goes on to

---

3. Di Biase-Dyson, *Foreigners*, 320; Winand, "Report of Wenamun," 550.

consider the story's theology of Amun's dominance and compare it with biblical theologies of Yahweh's dominance. Both *Wenamun* and the Hebrew Bible describe their chief gods as rulers who have the right to impose covenantal obligations on those who are subject to them, and both stories share in the common ancient Near Eastern trope of prophets as messengers of the gods. As with some biblical stories of prophets, the serious and humorous aspects of *Wenamun* coexist; the story of Balaam in Numbers and the book of Jonah offer comparative case studies. These comparisons shed light in both directions, on the biblical and Egyptian texts alike.

In the course of the analysis and comparison, I have generally sought to avoid speculation about the origins of specific themes and details that the texts share, and how they might have been transmitted. The final chapter, however, steps back to reflect briefly on the broader religio-historical connections and implications. *Wenamun* offers a rare direct glimpse of what was likely a broader influence of theocratic and summodeistic Egyptian rhetoric in the development of monotheizing rhetoric in the Hebrew Bible.

"Theocratic" refers to theological ideologies in which a deity is portrayed as ruler. As later chapters discuss, such rhetoric was compatible with monarchy as well as with hierocracy;[4] both kings and priests regularly participated in the cult and wielded religious power as well as political power in the ancient Near East. "Summodeism" refers to an often related form of theological rhetoric in which the state's deity is asserted as the sole ruling god, such that other deities are seen to be manifestations or derivatives of that god. In contrast to philosophical monotheism, however, summodeism does not deny the existence of the other deities as such, nor is their worship forbidden. One might say that theocracy and summodeism are, respectively, political and theological ways to describe claims for the sole power of a deity.

The term summodeism was popularized by the political philosopher Eric Voegelin, for whom it was only one of two major ancient Near Eastern forms of asserting theological supremacy as a symbol of political power in the ancient Near East. He defined "political summodeism" as "interpreting a manifold of highest local divinities as aspects of the one highest empire god," and the conglomeration of Mesopotamian city-states into empires served as his prime example. (Another example is the Babylonian theology expressed in *Enuma Elish*, in which the fifty names of other deities are ascribed ultimately to Marduk.[5]) Voegelin also, however, identified "theogonic speculation" as another means of asserting divine supremacy, in which "the other gods

---

4. We could simply use the term "hierarchy," but it has lost its priestly associations in current usage.
5. VI.121–VII.144; Lambert, *Babylonian Creation Myths*, 116–33.

originate through creation by the one truly highest god." He gives as the prime example the Memphite Theology, which emphasizes Ptah's primacy.[6]

The story of *Wenamun* reflects a Theban tradition of Amun theology in which both political summodeism and theogonic speculation were at work. Those who have followed Voegelin, notably Jan Assmann and Mark S. Smith, have often employed "summodeism" as a blanket term for both forms of rhetoric,[7] and for the sake of a streamlined presentation I adopt the same usage here.

This focus on Amun's dominance has Egyptian roots going back into the Bronze Age, and it remained more or less prominent throughout the Third Intermediate Period—that is, until the seventh century. Both textual and material evidence attest to consistent and meaningful cultural and political contacts between Egypt and Israel/Judah at this time. As the conclusion to the book lays out, Egyptian influence on Israel and Judah would have functioned both through the lingering Egyptian presence in the southern Levant, and through intermediaries such as the Phoenicians. The main episode in which Wenamun asserts Amun's rule takes place in Byblos, a Phoenician city-state with connections to both Egypt and Israel/Judah.

Wenamun was written in a time very near the origins of the ancient Israelite state—before the lifetimes of any of the biblical "writing" prophets to whom monotheism is classically attributed—and it portrays an Egyptian religious official proclaiming the dominance of a single god over the whole earth. This invites fresh reflection on the theocratic and (to a lesser extent) summodeistic tendencies in the Hebrew Bible. The analysis of "prophetic" rhetoric in *Wenamun* is not merely an interesting literary study, but suggests a new taproot for Egyptian theological influence on the prophets, and on Israelite religion in general.

To some degree, the influence surely ran in both directions. This theological conversation between the two cultures long predates the first millennium, and the Egyptian adoption of the Levantine Baal as a form of Seth is particularly relevant in a story populated by Baal-worshipers. Thus the present study also has potential implications for the study of Egyptian religion. Although Israel and Yahweh do not appear in *Wenamun*, it significantly informs our understanding of the "never-ending story" of the relations between the two cultures.[8]

---

6. Hogan, *Collected Works of Eric Voegelin*, 45–47.
7. See, e.g., Assmann, "Monotheism and Polytheism," 18; Smith, *God in Translation*, 169.
8. Ben-Dor Evian, "Egypt and Israel," 30–39.

CHAPTER 1

Wenamun as History, Literature, and Theology

WENAMUN BEGINS IN A WAY that has suggested to some an official administrative report, or an official autobiography of the sort that Egyptian officials often had recorded in their tombs, recounting the worthy service they rendered to the pharaoh and the gods. Some of the text's early interpreters expected that the tomb of Wenamun, with the text *in situ*, would eventually be discovered.

Narrative Setting

These conclusions and expectations were encouraged by the text's allusions to and broad agreement with the historical context in which the narrative is set. It is dated to "year 5," but whose year 5 is not specified. Despite reams of scholarship, the point is still disputed.[1] The story refers to events in the reign of the final Ramesside ruler, Khaemwase (Ramses XI), which were at least seventeen years in the past (2/51–53).[2] Therefore, the fifth year must be that of one of the rulers who followed him. Ramses XI reigned 1099–1069, so the story is generally thought to be set in 1065.[3]

There are two rulers mentioned in *Wenamun* who reigned in Egypt at that time. The first was Smendes (Hedjkheperra Setepenra; r. 1069–1043), founder of Dynasty 21. He seems to have controlled only the Delta, however, with power centers in Tanis (as reflected in *Wenamun* 1/3–6) and perhaps Memphis.

---

1. No one has devoted more effort to the question of *Wenamun*'s chronology than Arno Egberts, so when the former positivist concludes, "I have forsaken my belief in the historical relevance of the chronology of 'Wenamun,'" we should take him seriously ("Hard Times," 104–5).
2. Egberts, "Hard Times," 102; Redford, *Egypt, Canaan, and Israel*, 290n28.
3. For a recent review of scholarship on the chronology of the period, see James and Morkot, "Herihor's Kingship," 231–60.

5

The story repeatedly mentions him together with Tanetamun, seemingly as a ruling couple.[4]

The second ruler of the period mentioned in *Wenamun* is Herihor, a military official who became High Priest of Amun at Thebes. The last Ramessides, their power already weakened, had largely left the administration of Upper Egypt to the priests of Amun at Thebes. Wenamun is delegated by Herihor, who seems to have taken pharaonic authority for himself as Ramesside rule collapsed.[5] Eventually, rulers from Lower Egypt reestablished authority over Thebes, partly by installing women of their families as "God's Wives of Amun" there;[6] but in the power vacuum early in the Third Intermediate Period, the priests and prophets of Amun themselves seem to have controlled the region.

Herihor and Smendes thus reigned in different parts of the land, in Upper and Lower Egypt, respectively. The fact that their power was regional is reflected by the recurring formulation "where RN is" (used of Smendes and Tanetamun in 1/4 and Herihor in 2/61).[7] Wenamun's passing reference to "the other magnates of Egypt" (1/15–16) may reflect that other minor principalities also existed at the time. The story is not very forthcoming about the realities of the divided rule between Smendes and Herihor. Wenamun refers to Herihor as his lord (1/15, 25–26), but at the very outset he seeks the partnership of the Delta rulers in his project of restoring the sacred bark of Amun, and they enthusiastically accept.

The ruling ideology of Herihor and the Theban priesthood was distinctive; it is commonly characterized as a "theocracy,"[8] and was very plausibly considered radical by rulers whose power it rivalled. One could view it more basically as a hierocracy, since its rulers were also priests. This was an unusual development in Egyptian history, but in this new and less centralized order, there was room to experiment with new ways of formulating claims to power. The way the claims were expressed varied depending on the ruler and even among inscriptions by the same ruler.[9] The priestly title could take the place of, or

---

4. 1/7, 53; 2/35, 39; and presumably 1/4, where Smendes's name is restored. Tanetamun is thought to have been part of the Ramesside royal family. Egberts, "Hard Times," 97–98.

5. The chronology, reigns, and relationship of this period are murky, and deeply disputed. One ruler not discussed here (because he is not mentioned in *Wenamun*) is Pinudjem I. See James and Morkot, "Herihor's Kingship," 231–60. See also Jansen-Winkeln, "Das Ende des Neuen Reiches," 22–37; Egberts, "Hard Times," 93–108. Ultimately, these questions are not of the first importance for the present analysis, and to address them at length would be a distraction.

6. Ayad, *God's Wife, God's Servant*; Becker, Blöbaum, and Lohwasser, *Prayer and Power*.

7. See also Bedor 1/13; Amun 1/50–51; Zakarbaal 2/21–22; Hatiba 2/75–76. See Egberts, "Hard Times," 99. Usually r pȝ nty PN im, though with some variation.

8. This view was championed early on by Kees, *Das Priestertum*. On the historical reconstruction of the period, see Broekman, "Leading Theban Priests of Amun," 125–48; Kitchen, *Third Intermediate Period*. See below for additional recent literature.

9. Römer, *Gottes- und Priesterherrschaft*, 78–131.

be combined with, the royal titulary. At the level of mythological meaning, the inscriptions reflect that rulers sometimes shifted the governing metaphor from "god as father and king as son" to "god as lord and priest as servant."[10]

In conjunction with the priests' assumption of pharaonic authority, a system of oracular communications from Amun became more prominent in the period: the royal court issued rulings directly from the god, rather than from the pharaoh. These oracles are sometimes portrayed as a degradation of Egyptian religion, an effect of foreign influence, or a crisis of confidence on the part of the priest-rulers who embraced them. That is at least partly a misunderstanding; the use of oracles is better interpreted as an outgrowth of intra-Egyptian religious trends near the height of the New Kingdom empire. The practice is first attested under Thutmose III, although it did grow in popularity in the Third Intermediate Period.[11]

Malte Römer has observed, "With regard to the sovereignty of the deity, the Egyptian oracle system is comparable with the proclamations of the Old Testament God who directs the destinies of his people."[12] On the one hand, the scope and nature of the oracular statements from Amun (and other Egyptian deities) seem to have been somewhat more limited than those of Yahweh in the Hebrew Bible. On the other hand, they covered some of the same ground. The Egyptian oracles commonly involved the divine determination of guilt or innocence in judicial situations (cf. 1 Sam 14:41–42; 1 Kgs 1:50–52); others pertained to the oracular selection of high priests and later pharaohs in a process comparable to the divine selection of kings in the Bible (e.g., David in 1 Sam 16:7–13).[13]

An increase in theological rhetoric in the Third Intermediate Period has been broadly observed. In religious texts, one sees an increased emphasis on humility, and submission to the will of the god(s).[14] Aidan Dodson notes that by the 22nd Dynasty pharaohs began submitting to divine judgment like the rest of the dead, as described in the Book of the Dead.[15] A similar process is often remarked upon in the "religionization" of wisdom instructions—in early periods, the role of the gods in revealing right action was only implicit, but in

---

10. Or, to put it in a format used by theorists of metaphor, the metaphor shifted from god:king::father:son to god:priest::lord:servant. In an extreme case, Pinedjem I had two inscription types, one using each of these formulae (Römer, *Gottes- und Priesterherrschaft*, 131).

11. Černý, "Egyptian Oracles," 35.

12. Römer, *Gottes- und Priesterherrschaft*, 274: "Was diese Souveränität des Gottes angeht, steht das ägyptische Orakelwesen auf einer Stufe mit den Verkündigungen des alttestamentlichen Gottes, der die Geschicke seines Volkes lenkt."

13. Černý, "Egyptian Oracles," 35–48; Ritner, *Libyan Anarchy*, 5, and examples given throughout the volume; Römer, *Gottes- und Priesterherrschaft*, 276–77.

14. Römer, *Gottes- und Priesterherrschaft*, 279: "der bedingungslosen Demut gegenüber Gott."

15. Dodson, "Some Notes Concerning the Royal Tombs," 228.

later texts, submission to the gods is emphasized. For example, in the Instruction of Amenemope, first attested in the 21st Dynasty, the hearer is told: "You cannot know the plans of God; / You cannot perceive tomorrow. / (So) sit yourself at the hands of God" (22,5–7).

The ascendancy of a single deity was already apparent in what Jan Assmann has called the "new solar theology." It originated before the Amarna Period, by the fifteenth-century reign of Hatshepsut, with strong political and propagandistic aspects.[16] But in the late New Kingdom and Third Intermediate Period, as it developed into the form of Theban Amun theology that is the focus here, it had to wrestle with the totalizing theological claims of the Amarna Period and the tensions between totality and specificity that Amarna theology raised—immanence vs. transcendence; the one supreme god vs. the many gods, and so on.[17]

In light of all this, it is not hard to see why the theocracy of the 21st Dynasty has been compared with biblical monotheism. Jan Assmann comments that "the system imposed by Herihor in Thebes comes nearest to the Jewish variety."[18] This was the universalizing and highly theologized thought-world out of which *Wenamun* came.

Wenamun's Title and Mission

At the beginning of the story, Wenamun is called *sms[m].w ḥȝy.t n pr-imn*, "elder of the portal of the temple of Amun" (1/1). This is not a common or well-understood title.[19] There are, however, provocative indications that there was a real temple official in Thebes named Wenamun in roughly the period in question. The name Wenamun, written in the same way as in the story, appears in a list of young men assigned to the tutelage of a senior scribe in a letter from the reign of Ramses XI.[20] In another letter from the same period, the official who sent it closes by saying, "I've written to provide you with testimony (*mtr*) through the watchman (*wrš*) Wenamun."[21] The same word for "testimony" is

---

16. Assmann, *Search for God*, 193–98, 201–8, 241. German original: *Ägypten: Theologie und Frömmigkeit*; Assmann, *Egyptian Solar Religion*, 128–29. German original: *Re und Amun*, 182–84. For the remainder of this book, the later English versions are cited.

17. Hornung, *Conceptions of God*; Assmann, *Egyptian Solar Religion*, 133–210.

18. Assmann, *Mind of Egypt*, 295, 300.

19. For discussion, see Scheepers, "Anthroponymes," 31–33; Winand, "Report," 550–51.

20. P. Berlin 10494; Wente, *Late Ramesside Letters*, 44 (Černý #12); Wente, *Letters from Ancient Egypt*, 177; Schipper, *Die Erzählung*, 328–29.

21. P. Bibliothèque Nationale 198,III; Wente, *Late Ramesside Letters*, 82 (Černý #47); Wente, *Letters from Ancient Egypt*, 173.

used to describe Wenamun's speech in 2/60. Although the same title is not used, Wenamun's title in the story might also suggest a watchman or guardian role vis-à-vis a "portal."

Wenamun's mission to acquire timber also has historical precedent during the period that the story portrays. Herihor left an inscription from the Khonsu Temple in Karnak stating that "he has carpentered his bark from the coniferwood[22] of the Lebanon (*mdḥ=f wiȝ=f m ꜥš ḫnty-š*)."[23] At the start of the first millennium BCE, there was already a long history of long-distance trade around the eastern Mediterranean.[24] This can be identified in the material record already in the fourth millennium BCE, and the specific trade for Levantine timber dates from no later than the 3rd Dynasty (2686–2613 BCE), with evidence of a small Egyptian mercantile colony at Byblos.[25]

The Egyptian appetite for timbers of the Lebanon like those that Wenamun went seeking is reflected in numerous New Kingdom texts. John Baines adduces a range of examples going back to the Old Kingdom, and he rightly connects these with the well-attested motif of kings boasting of cutting the trees of Lebanon for their use—for example, Gudea of Lagash, Sargon of Akkad, and Gilgamesh,[26] and one might add various Mesopotamian rulers of the first millennium, as well as David and Solomon (2 Sam 5:11; 1 Kgs 5:6–10).

Byblos itself occupied a special place in the Egyptian worldview at that time. It shared a "deeply rooted and outstanding relationship" with Egypt from the 3rd Dynasty on: "The kings of the Old Kingdom sent votive offerings to the main temple. From the Middle Kingdom there is evidence that Byblos was not even regarded as a foreign possession, but rather as an Egyptian town."[27] New Kingdom pharaohs such as Thutmose III and Ramses II built monumental architecture there. To Egyptians, Byblos was not just a close trading partner and an almost mythical "God's Land" (*t3ntr*). It would have been a more painful loss to Egyptian rulers of the Third Intermediate Period than most of the Levantine seacoast. Thus Byblos was a singularly apt "theater" for the conflict of perspectives that plays out in *Wenamun*.

---

22. I use "conifer" for ꜥš because, although the "cedars of Lebanon" are famed from biblical translations, a significant number of Egyptologists do not think the wood in question here was cedar, but rather pine or fir. See the numerous sources cited by Leprohon, "What Wenamun Could Have Bought," 171n10.

23. Wente, *Late Ramesside Letters*, 4n13; Schipper, *Die Erzählung*, 167. On the cutting and shipping of wood in the period, see Kuniholm, "Wood," 347–49.

24. Stieglitz, "Long-Distance Seafaring," 134–42; Parpas, *Maritime Economy*, esp. 52–53, 88, 106–8; Monroe, *Scales of Fate*.

25. Ward, "Trade, Foreign," 842–45; Bardinet, *Relations économiques*.

26. Baines, "On the Background of Wenamun," 34.

27. Wimmer, "Egyptian Temples," 1080.

The theological worldview of the Egyptian texts is discussed in more detail in chapter 3, but one striking example may be offered here: the Gebel Barkal Stela dated to the 47th year of Thutmose III, thus from the late fifteenth century. In it, the pharaoh boasts:

> My Majesty crossed to the ends of Asia; I caused many ships to be built of conifer-wood from the hills of God's Land in the neighborhood of the Lady of Byblos [i.e., the Byblian goddess].... (wood) was hewn [for me in Dja]hy each and every year, from real conifer-wood of Lebanon... through the plans of my father, [Amun-Re] who allotted to me all the Asiatics.... My Majesty hewed a processional ship of conifer-wood... [trees?] on the shore of Lebanon.[28]

The bark in question may well have been for Amun's Theban temple at Karnak, just as in Wenamun's mission. Furthermore, both the stela and Thutmose's annals refer to annual impositions and taxes on the cities of Lebanon, perhaps laid out in a written document. The details of such agreements are not clear, but the same imperial expectations of submission seem to have formed Wenamun's expectations when he sets out to do his business. The idea that Amun(-Re) had granted the pharaoh power over the Levant was a deeply ingrained article of faith by the end of the New Kingdom.

The control of this maritime trade shifted significantly over time, however. The Amarna Letters of the 18th Dynasty, from the fourteenth century, show the power of Egypt over the Levant, including many of the coastal cities. But the decline of Egypt is apparent already in Ugaritic letters from the end of the thirteenth century, as Ugarit shifted its allegiances to the Hittite Empire. With the subsequent breakdown of the imperial network of Great Powers in the twelfth century, the coastal cities, especially those considered Phoenician, achieved greater independence.

This period, from roughly 1200 to 800 BCE,[29] is sometimes dubbed a Phoenician "thassalocracy" ("rule of the seas"), but arguably they did not harbor the sort of imperial ambitions to military power that the empires before them had. Rather, they sought to enrich themselves by doing business—and there was still a lot of business to be done. They continued on, largely "unruffled" by the upheavals of the period.[30]

---

28. Lines 11, 30, 32, 45. See Kilani, *Byblos*, 104–13. See also the account of Thutmose's chief treasurer: Sethe, *Eine ägyptische Expedition*, 356–63.
29. The end date reflects the rise of Neo-Assyrian power in the Levant.
30. Broodbank, *Making of the Middle Sea*, 284–85.

The remarkably rich and international nature of Mediterranean trade throughout this period is illustrated by the contents of the Uluburun shipwreck from about 1300, found at the bottom of the sea off the southwest coast of Turkey. As Cline recounts:

> In all, products from at least seven different countries, states, and empires were on board the ship. In addition to its primary cargo of ten tons of Cypriot copper, one ton of tin, and a ton of terebinth resin, there were also two dozen ebony logs from Nubia; almost two hundred ingots of raw glass from Mesopotamia, most colored dark blue, but others of light blue, purple, and even a shade of honey/amber; about 140 Canaanite storage jars in two or three basic sizes, which contained the terebinth resin, remains of grapes, pomegranates, and figs, as well as spices like coriander and sumac; brand-new pottery from Cyprus and Canaan, including oil lamps, bowls, jugs, and jars; scarabs from Egypt and cylinder seals from elsewhere in the Near East; swords and daggers from Italy and Greece (some of which might have belonged to crew members or passengers), including one with an inlaid hilt of ebony and ivory; and even a stone scepter-mace from the Balkans. There was also gold jewelry, including pendants, and a gold chalice; duck-shaped ivory cosmetic containers; copper, bronze, and tin bowls and other vessels; twenty-four stone anchors; fourteen pieces of hippopotamus ivory and one elephant tusk; and a six-inch-tall statue of a Canaanite deity made of bronze overlaid with gold in places—which, if it was supposed to serve as the protective deity for the ship, didn't do its job very well.[31]

One of the Egyptian scarabs mentioned was made of solid gold and bore the name of none other than Nefertiti, the queen of Pharaoh Akhenaten. It was, as they say, a small world.

The list of supplies sent by Smendes and Tanetamun to Byblos in *Wenamun* is reminiscent of that actual discovery (allowing for the fact that the Uluburun goods were probably headed to Egypt rather than from it):

> 4 jars and 1 vessel of gold, 5 silver jars, 10 articles of clothing of royal linen, 10 veils of sheer cloth of good quality, 500 mats of smooth linen, 500 ox-hides, 500 ropes, 20 sacks of lentils, and 30 baskets of fish. And she had brought to me: 5 articles of clothing of sheer cloth of good

---

31. Cline, *1177 B.C.*, 72–73; see also Cline and Yasur-Landau, "Musings from a Distant Shore," 126–41; Goren, "International Exchange"; Pulak, "Uluburun Shipwreck and Late Bronze Age Trade," 289–385; Pulak, "Uluburun Shipwreck: An Overview," 188–224.

quality, 5 veils of sheer cloth of good quality, 1 sack of lentils, and 5 baskets of fish. (2/40–45)

The value of the goods transported in these elite ships was enormous, so the stakes in the negotiations between Wenamun and Zakarbaal were high. Readers and hearers of the story would have recognized this. Christopher Monroe has tentatively estimated the losses from the Uluburun shipwreck—the "sunk cost," as it were—in contemporaneous terms at 12,000 Ugaritic silver shekels. To put that in perspective, he notes that a sheep was worth 1–1.5 shekels, and a typical worker's wages started at about a shekel per month: "Thus, from the common man's perspective, the Uluburun shipment would be hard to imagine: a thousand years of salary, or more wealth than one might earn in many lifetimes. It might be easier to think of 12,000 shekels as the yearly payment for the thousand workers populating a large town."[32]

Historical or Literary?

The aforementioned details suggest a historical kernel to the story, based on real figures and events. To understand, then, why it is no longer regarded as a historical document by most interpreters, it helps to begin with the circumstances of the text's discovery. *Wenamun* is only attested in one copy, which was reportedly discovered at el-Hiba (ancient *tȝy≠w-dy*), a border town between Upper and Lower Egypt, the Delta north and the Theban south.[33]

It was found in a jar with two texts that relate to scribal education, which is sometimes called a "wisdom milieu": the Onomasticon of Amenope (Golenischeff Onomasticon) and the Tale of Woe (a.k.a. the Letter of Wermai). The former text is a list of more than six hundred nouns in various classifications, "for instruction of the ignorant and for learning all things that exist." The latter is the story, in epistolary form, of a priestly official who is expelled from his position in the Heliopolis temple of Re-Atum due to warfare in the country; he recounts his mistreatment as he wanders Egypt and implores the royal court to restore his stature.[34] Like *Wenamun*, it is written in a lively Late Egyptian style and exists only in a single copy, but unlike *Wenamun* it is rather sloppily written.[35]

---

32. Monroe, "Sunk Costs," 19–33.
33. The papyrus was purchased on the antiquities market by Russian Egyptologist Vladimir Golenischeff, who reported where he had been told it was found. Schipper, *Die Erzählung*, 4–5.
34. Caminos, *Tale of Woe*, 70–80; and Quack, "Ein neuer Versuch zum Moskauer literarischen Brief," 167–81.
35. Caminos, *Tale of Woe*, 3.

Both the find spot and the collection of texts suggest that *Wenamun* is not an official or monumental text. Nor is there any evidence that it became canonical, in the sense of being copied over a period of time.

The conversation about the nature and origins of *Wenamun* has swung back and forth over time. Vladimir Golenischeff, who purchased and published the papyrus, took it to be a genuine administrative document. Max Müller judged already in 1900 that it was "obviously embellished," but based on an actual report; he breezily attributed the imprecisions to the fact that that author was one of "the amiably dissolute Egyptian people."[36] (His comment should give a modern reader pause about the judgments of the early periods in our fields, even those of leading scholars.) The fact that its paleography was characteristic of a later period was noted already by Georg Möller in 1910,[37] but the argument that the story was an administrative report endured on the basis of the theory that the existing papyrus was a copy.[38] Jaroslav Černý buttressed the case at midcentury by pointing out that *Wenamun* is written on the vertical fibers of the papyrus like an administrative document.[39] This was an influential view for some time, notably adopted by Hans Goedicke in his 1975 monograph.[40]

The view that *Wenamun* is an administrative report has not fared well more recently, however. Miriam Lichtheim expressed doubts in 1976,[41] and Wolfgang Helck's brief entry in *Lexikon der Ägyptologie* demurred,[42] suggesting that *Wenamun* was instead a work of fiction intended to assert Amun's international authority. John Baines made a particularly helpful intervention entitled "On *Wenamun* as a Literary Text." On the matter of the papyrus's form, he adduced examples of parallels among literary as well as nonliterary manuscripts, and concluded that Wenamun's layout is not similar to that of normal business documents or significant administrative texts. Thus: "The manner

---

36. Müller, "Der Papyrus Golenischeff," 28–29: "Der Verfasser schmückt offenbar etwas aus ... da er nicht immer erfolgreich war, hatte er allen Grund, ein wenig auszuschmücken, zu rühren, zu unterhalten und seine Loyalität, sowie die Schwierigkeiten der Reise, ins hellste Licht zu setzen. Der interessante Bericht wurde dann mehrfach als Litteraturstück abgeschrieben, wie so viele Reiseberichte der alten Zeit. Ich glaube also, alle Angaben über die fremden Länder als verlässlich betrachten zu können. Die Daten machen freilich den Eindruck, flüchtig nach dem Gedächtnis gegeben sein und nur approximativen Wert zu uesitzen. Aber dafür gehört ja der Schreiber dem liebenswürdig liederlichen Ägyptervolk an. Das Itinerarium eines Babyloniers oder Palästinäers hätte vielleicht anders ausgesehen, mit genaueren Daten und Distanzen u.s.w. Unser Verfasser hat aber gewiss darin seines Bestes gethan; mehr kann man von einem ächten Ägypter kaum erwarten."
37. Möller, *Hieratische Lesestücke*, 2:29.
38. Korostovtsev, *Puteshestvie Un-Amuna*, 16–17.
39. Černý, *Paper and Books*, 21–22.
40. Goedicke, *Report*, 4–7.
41. *AEL* 2:197.
42. Helck, "Wenamun," 1215–17.

of inscription does not point to any particular genre for *Wenamun*."[43] He also contradicted the claim that its language was reminiscent of Late Ramesside administrative documents.[44] Significantly, Baines appended his comments on the form of the papyrus to a study that focused much more on the literary characteristics of the story, particularly its use of dialogue and argument. His analysis reflects a growing consensus that the story's fictional nature is apparent on internal considerations alone.[45] As scrutiny has grown, it has become clear that there are serious problems in the historical details of the story.[46]

Another clear indication that the story is not an administrative document but a work of fiction is that it does not glorify any Egyptian ruler, nor does it reflect well on its protagonist (see esp. chapter 7). There is simply not any plausible, self-interested motivation behind its presentation of its characters. This may sound cynical to some, but it will be straightforward for anyone acquainted with official first-person Egyptian texts. Scarcely any specific administrative texts are adduced as comparisons with *Wenamun*,[47] and the autobiographical texts are completely different in tone. Egyptian autobiographies are characterized by "a general reticence around presenting the negative and the subjective."[48] As Lichtheim has written, "Words were potent, hence had to be weighed; formulations that pleased became valued clichés; and to sum up one's life and person meant stressing achievements and virtues."[49] While Wenamun indulges in some of the self-praise that characterized such autobiographies, the rest of the story is written in an entirely different literary register: lively, conversational, funny, and neither cliché nor reverential toward its main character.

---

43. Baines, "On *Wenamun* as a Literary Text," 209–33.
44. Baines ("On *Wenamun* as a Literary Text," 215) calls it "'pure' Late Egyptian" with a few archaizing exceptions. On the literary features of *Wenamun*'s grammar, see Jay, "Examining the 'Literariness' of Wenamon," 287–303. On the difficulties of differentiating the literary registers of literary texts from monumental discourse, see Moers, "Vom Verschwinden der Gewissheiten," 41n206.
45. In addition to the various studies cited elsewhere in these pages, others who have emphasized the literary nature include Egberts, "Wenamun"; Moers, "Travel as Narrative," 43–61; Sass, "Wenamun and His Levant," 253; Manassa, *Imagining the Past*, 82, 163. As Schipper's method acknowledges, the literary and historical levels are not mutually exclusive (*Die Erzählung*, 325–33).
46. See, e.g., Winand, "Report," 543–49.
47. Baines ("On *Wenamun* as a Literary Text," 216) makes brief reference to the late Ramesside letters from a certain official Dhutmose about his journeys in Nubia, but these have nothing of *Wenamun*'s narrative drama or conversational flair. See Wente, *Letters from Ancient Egypt*, 185–210. See also below on 21st Dynasty letters (chapter 5); while these reveal specific similarities of terminology and phraseology, they are clearly not of a similar literary genre as a whole.
48. Stauder-Porchet, Frood, and Andréas, *Ancient Egyptian Biographies*, 2.
49. Lichtheim, *Ancient Egyptian Autobiographies*, 2. The greater individualism in the New Kingdom and afterward does not begin to account for these differences. See the later autobiographical texts in *AEL* 3:11–24.

In sum, the story may be a literary legend built around a historical figure, much as the later Aramaic tale and wisdom instruction of Ahiqar may have been based on a real Neo-Assyrian wise man.[50] But those who have emphasized *Wenamun*'s literary character as a tale are on the right track. Gerald Moers, José M. Galán, and others have now argued cogently that the text is part of a genre of fictional travel literature that also included stories such as The Shipwrecked Sailor, Sinuhe, and A Tale of Woe.[51] Others such as The Doomed Prince and The Capture of Joppa are sometimes also compared.

The debates about *Wenamun*'s relationship to history are brought into focus in the variety of ways in which it is treated by Phoenicianists. Some, such as Glenn Markoe, J. Brian Peckham, Hélène Sader, and most recently Marwan Kilani, mine the story extensively for historical information,[52] whereas it receives a brief and measured treatment by Carolina López-Ruiz[53] and is completely absent from Josephine Quinn's *In Search of the Phoenicians*.[54]

Date and Purpose of Composition

The theory that *Wenamun* is a literary work does not invalidate the quest for its historical context; even fictional stories usually make more sense when we understand the circumstances of their authors.

Wenamun is now most often dated to the second half of the tenth century, in the reign of Sheshonq I of the 22nd Dynasty. Benjamin Sass made an important contribution to this dating of the text, observing the growing awareness of its literary and ideological features and its late paleography. He writes that "*Wenamun* was composed in the 22nd Dynasty on the background of Sheshonq I's Palestinian campaign.... [It] may be a subtle literary counterpart to Sheshonq's official report, carved on the wall at Karnak and directed at the king of gods." In other words, the assertion of Amun's power over the Levant was meant to support, ideologically, the famous Egyptian raiding campaign into Palestine in the late tenth century (1 Kgs 14:25–26; 2 Chr 12:2–9). Yet *Wenamun* would have been a very subtle bit of royal propaganda indeed, in that it says almost nothing about royal power. Sass is forced to address this

---

50. A tablet from Uruk (albeit copied later, in 165 BCE) identifies a man named Aba-enlildari who was a courtier of Esarhaddon, and mentions that the Arameans called him "Aḫûqari" (Lindenberger, "Ahiqar," 479–507).
51. Moers, *Fingierte Welten*, 19–105; Galán, *Four Journeys*, passim.
52. Markoe, *Phoenicians*, passim; Peckham, *Phoenicia*, 55–58; Sader, *History and Archaeology of Phoenicia*, 13, 27, 34–36, 39, 77, 81, 99, 126, 144–45, 252, 272, 275; Kilani, *Byblos in the Late Bronze Age*, passim.
53. López-Ruiz, *Phoenicians*, 283–85.
54. Quinn, *In Search of the Phoenicians*.

problem, but concludes that the story's theological emphasis explains why "the laudation of the god is spelled out, *whereas Sheshonq's praise is sung without words.*"[55]

Building upon earlier arguments for a late tenth-century date, Bernd Schipper was able to suggest a *Sitz im Leben* for *Wenamun* that makes better sense of its theological nature: "It dates from the transition from the 21st to the 22nd Dynasty, when the prince of Herakleopolis, Sheshonq [I], as the new pharaoh, wanted to reunite Egypt domestically, and in particular had to bring the theretofore-independent center of the Theban high priests under control."[56] He connects the papyrus to the Amun temple built in el-Hiba by Sheshonq I, which would have been in competition with the Theban Amun hierarchy.[57] While Amun continued to be the chief deity of the land, Thebes and its priesthood posed a longstanding political problem for any pharaoh who wanted to unite the lands under his rule. While Schipper's theory will continue to be debated, it neatly accounts for the papyrus' find-spot, and it is provisionally adopted here.

Schipper's view, which takes seriously the story's pro-Amun perspective, stands in some tension with past work by Jan Assmann and others, who believe that *Wenamun* was meant to satirize the Theban worldview itself. The reader has already encountered Theban ideology in the aforementioned Gebel Barkal Stela of Thutmose III, with its account of cutting the timbers of Lebanon and its emphasis on the lordship of Amun over the whole earth in a manner reminiscent of Manifest Destiny.

The pharaohs may have succeeded in curbing the political power of the Theban priests, but the dominance of their god, Amun, continued to be emphasized in various ways by the 22nd and 25th Dynasties. It is exemplified by texts like the hymn that begins the Funerary Decree for Princess Neskhons,[58] from the middle of the tenth century, which Pascal Vernus has called the official "credo" of the theocratic Amun state.[59] It calls Amun-Re not only "lord of all the gods" (*nb nṯr.w nb.w*), but also the one "creator of every god within himself" (*ḫpr ntr nb im⸗f*), and "singularity of singularities who made the things that exist" (*wʿ wʿ.w ir wnn.w*). It appropriates to Amun the solar theology formerly used for Aten: "Great solar disk, with streaming rays,

---

55. Sass, "Wenamun and His Levant," 251; emphasis added.
56. Schipper, *Die Erzählung*, 332: "Sie datiert in den Übergang der 21. zur 22. Dynastie, als der Fürst von Herakleopolis, Scheschonq, als neuer Pharao Ägypten innenpolitisch wieder vereinen will und dazu insbesondere das bis dahin unabhängige Zentrum der thebanischen Hohenpriester unter Kontrolle bringen muß." Pages 1–40 provide a helpful review of scholarship.
57. Schipper, *Die Erzählung*, 319–24.
58. For the decree and the hymn, see Ritner, *Libyan Anarchy*, 143–58.
59. Vernus, "Choix des textes," 103–4.

presenting himself so that everything might live" (*itn wr ḥꜣy sty.wt diꜥf sw 'nḫ ḥr nb*).⁶⁰

Such an ambitious theology was naturally susceptible to extremism, and indeed long before Wenamun's time one may see a precursor of the sort of theocracy that the Theban priests practiced: It shared certain features with the borderline-monotheizing Atenism of the Amarna Period.⁶¹ As Assmann has noted:

> The parallels between [the Amun hymn that begins the Funerary Decree for Princess Neskhons] and the Great Hymn of Akhenaten are striking. Both the Theban state and the Amarna state were theocracies, the former ruled solely by god, the latter representing a coregency in which god was responsible for the preservation of the cosmos and therefore not concerned to intervene in human affairs by oracular agency. Both theocracies were based on what was essentially a monotheistic religion, with more emphasis on "mono" in Amarna, and more on "theistic" in Thebes.⁶²

It is often said that the backlash against Akhenaten and his religious innovations shows that the promulgation of a single god was controversial. But as chapters 3 and 4 note, theocratic and summodeistic theological rhetoric had its origins in Egypt before the Amarna Period, and it continued in the later New Kingdom, with descriptions of Amun-Re taking the place of those of Aten. The hymn in the Funerary Decree for Princess Neskhons shows its endurance. Amun's centrality and authority continued to be emphasized in various ways by the 22nd and 25th Dynasties.

Conclusion

The narrative of *Wenamun* is set in the middle of the eleventh century and has some characteristics resembling an administrative report or an autobiographical tomb inscription. It identifies rulers of the period such as Herihor and Smendes, who did indeed acquire timbers from Lebanon for their temple furnishings, as part of an active Mediterranean sea trade. There is even evidence that an official named Wenamun was operating in Thebes at the time. However, paleographic, linguistic, and above all literary considerations have led

---

60. Ritner, *Libyan Anarchy*, 146, 151 (translation adapted).
61. Shaw, *Oxford History of Ancient Egypt*, 154–55.
62. Assmann, *Mind of Egypt*, 306.

more recent scholars to conclude that the story was written about a century later. Its style and content diverge from administrative and autobiographical texts. Nevertheless, it shows a deep awareness of the historical milieu and the distinctive theological currents of the times. Because of the beauty and apparent seriousness with which Wenamun expresses these theologies, we will have to return to the question of the author's view of its main character and his god. Much of the rest of the book tries to answer that question.

CHAPTER 2

Wenamun and the Hebrew Bible

IN LIGHT OF THE IMPORTANCE of Amun in the story, it makes sense to review the past scholarship on the deity, especially in relation to the Hebrew Bible. This chapter goes on to survey what is known about the story's interaction with its Levantine context, especially through the use of Semitic loanwords, and the cultural connections between Byblos and Israel that might also encourage the conclusion that there was an exchange of theological ideas that formed a matrix for similarities in their religious proclamations.

Amun and the Hebrew Bible

The complex and enigmatic Amun has lurked on the margins of comparative scholarship for some time, and various scholars have recognized that he deserved the attention of biblical scholars. Until quite recently, however, there had been no sustained consideration of his relationship to Israelite religion since Kurt Sethe's ambitious 1929 study, which is still widely cited in Egyptology.[1] Sethe associated Amun and Yahweh primarily through the idea that Amun represented the wind of the primordial chaos, so that he was analogous to the רוח אלהים, the spirit of God on the face of the waters in Gen 1:2. From this he drew very large conclusions; as G. A. Wainwright summarized, "Sethe considers that Amun was, or might have been, the original from whom Yahweh was derived."[2] The Egyptological side of the argument associating Amun with wind has not held up well, however, and the comparative sections read as something of a timepiece today, though scholars continue to seek similar equivalences.[3]

---

1. Sethe, *Amun und die acht Urgötter*, especially his epilogue "Amun und Jahwe" (pp. 119–22/§§255–60).
2. Wainwright, "Some Aspects of Amūn," 139.
3. See, e.g., Hoffmeier, "Some Thoughts," 39–49.

Egyptologists have had a longstanding (if sporadic) interest in comparing Amun theologies and biblical theologies. One thinks first of Jan Assmann; his discussions of Amun and Aten teem with details inviting comparison between Egyptian and Israelite religion, even if they leave much unstated.[4] There is also Malte Römer's rich and provocative comparison of Amun and Yahweh as oracle-givers, which deserves more attention.[5]

Among biblical scholars, the significance of Amun for understanding the Bible has mostly been overlooked or underestimated.[6] Some of the reticence may be attributable to "the anxiety of influence," since the priority of Amun to Yahweh is almost axiomatic, given the historical evidence for each.

Significant contributions to the discussion were made by Othmar Keel and Christoph Uehlinger, whose analysis of small glyptics (seals and amulets) revealed a powerful awareness of Amun in the Levant, one that endured long after his dominance throughout the Egyptian empire of the Late Bronze Age:

> Even though the area in Canaan formerly under Egyptian rule was cut into small parcels of land as nation-states developed at the end of the second millennium, with each assigning a central role to that nation's own god who was now front and center—Yahweh in Israel and Judah, Milcom in Ammon, Chemosh in Moab, possibly Qaus in Edom—it would still seem that Amun-Re the Egyptian god who had been in the background and was involved in everything, did not lose his importance immediately and probably never lost it completely.[7]

They lamented, in closing their study, that "the significance of the god Amun, as well as his cryptographically written name in the glyptic art of the first millennium, has never been the subject of systematic research."[8] Some scholars have pursued the question, though generally in limited ways.[9]

---

4. For example, in Assmann's *Search for God*, explicit comparisons to Yahweh, Israel, and the Bible are found only on pp. 18, 158, 169, 199, 212–13, and 236. Similarly, see Assmann, *Death and Salvation*, 10–11, 414–17.

5. Römer, *Gottes- und Priesterherrschaft*, 272–83.

6. For the scant results, see the entries on Amun in various major reference works, e.g.: Assmann, "Amun"; Lewis, "Amun"; Azzoni, "Amon." Tattko ("Amun," 1:1067) writes, "Amun has several functions, e.g., those of a judge and a savior, similar to those of the biblical God, but a direct correspondence between Amun and YHWH is difficult to establish."

7. Keel and Uehlinger, *Gods*, 138. I cite the English translation for accessibility, but this comment is unchanged in the newest (German) edition: Keel, Uehlinger, and Lippke, *Göttinnen, Götter und Gottessymbole*, 156.

8. Keel and Uehlinger, *Gods*, 405.

9. E.g., Strawn, *What Is Stronger?*, 90; Liwak, *Israel in der altorientalischen Welt*, 176–77.

Since then, hundreds of additional seals have been discovered in Jerusalem at Gihon and the City of David that include extensive Egyptian motifs, as well as some that have usually been called "Phoenician," but are better described as part of an international artistic *koine*.[10] Some of these name Amun and other Egyptian deities. Keel concluded that "Jerusalem at this time was part of a much wider network than is usually assumed."[11] When it comes to the smaller Levantine nations in the Iron II, this is often described as "foreign influence," but it might be better to treat it as a sign of somewhat cosmopolitan culture interchange.

More recently still, Michael Hundley devoted a significant portion of his book *Yahweh Among the Gods* to the analysis of Egyptian religion, and noticed similarities between the theologies of Amun and those of Yahweh: "Like Marduk, Aššur, and Amun, [Yahweh] is a one-stop shop god who aggregates the skill set of all the gods into a single person."[12] But in the end, Hundley concludes that whereas "Marduk and Aššur rhetoric in particular may have influenced Yahweh rhetoric,"[13] the "connections with Amun may be more indirect."[14]

That is an eminently understandable conclusion given the status of the question. Nevertheless, there seem to have been more direct connections at times between biblical authors and Egyptian theologies. In a recent article, I have shown that the authors of Isa 45 alluded to Amun's theologies in a pejorative way with their reference to a "God who hides himself" (45:15).[15] Yahweh, they asserted, was not a hidden god like Amun: he "did not speak in secret" (45:19). This anti-Amun prophecy immediately follows an oracle in support of Cyrus, and was meant to endorse Persian plans to invade Egypt in the late sixth century.

Our focus here is on an earlier period, however, considering *Wenamun* in relation to the origins of Hebrew prophecy. The present study will show that Amun has in common with other deities (most prominently Baal/Hadad) that early Yahwistic theologians assimilated some of his characteristics while simultaneously rejecting others, along with the god himself; Mark S. Smith has called this process "convergence and differentiation."[16] The assimilation of Amun-like rhetoric is the flip side of Isa 45's rejection: it shows how, from an

---

10. Keel, "Paraphernalia of Jerusalem Sanctuaries," 315–42.
11. Keel, "Paraphernalia of Jerusalem Sanctuaries," 318.
12. Hundley, *Yahweh Among the Gods*, 219.
13. Hundley, *Yahweh Among the Gods*, 312.
14. Hundley, *Yahweh Among the Gods*, 312n28.
15. Hays, "Hidden God," 1–17.
16. Smith, *Early History of God*, xii–xiii; cf. Smith, *Origins of Biblical Monotheism*.

earlier period, biblical authors likely adopted theological rhetoric typical of Amun and used it for Yahweh.

It has been unremarked upon, so far as I can see, that the pro-Amun rhetoric of Wenamun is strikingly similar to biblical Yahwistic rhetoric—especially that of the Hebrew prophets. Given that *Wenamun* is one of the few Egyptian texts that has attracted significant attention from scholars of the Hebrew prophets, it is surprising that the speeches of Wenamun, Bedor, and Zakarbaal have not been analyzed in a sustained way from this comparative perspective.[17] Rather, prophets scholarship has focused almost exclusively on the episode of the ecstatic prophet. The rest of the story is omitted from Martti Nissinen's excellent sourcebook *Prophets and Prophecy in the Ancient Near East*,[18] and although the whole story is translated in standard compendia intended for audiences beyond Egyptology—such as *ANET*, *COS*, Lichtheim's *Ancient Egyptian Literature*, and Simpson's *The Literature of Ancient Egypt*—in none of these places is any comparative comment made about the speeches. The same is true of recent studies by eminent comparative scholars.[19]

What is the relationship between *Wenamun* and prophecy? Its prophetic characteristics are sometimes recognized in passing. After listing a number of Egyptian texts that have been considered prophetic, Stökl comments,

> I concur with most assessments that none of the above texts are prophetic. In the "prophecy" of Neferti, no attempt is made to link the predictive message to a deity, and in the other texts *apart from the Wenamun narrative*, the deity speaks directly to the addressee, which again means that these texts do not operate on the concept of prophecy as

---

17. One interesting exception is Gordon, "He Is Who He Is," 27–28. Gordon posits exceedingly briefly that Wenamun's indignant comment in 2.27–28, *nn* (=*in*) *bn sw pȝ nty wnw=f*, should be compared with the biblical divine dictum *'hyh šr 'hyh* ("I am who I am"; Exod 3:14). However, the meaning of Wenamun's question is not entirely clear. Ritner offers, "[you have caused this god to spend these 29 days moored in your harbor, without your knowing] whether he was here or whether he was not the one whom (2/28) he is." And then he offers in a footnote: "Literally, 'Is he here (or) is he not the one who he is?'" (*Libyan Anarchy*, 99n9). Lichtheim takes the phrase as referring to Amun's past glory: "Is he not he who he was?" (*COS* 1.91; followed by Moers, *Fingierte Welten*, 271; and Schipper, *Die Erzählung*, 330). Wente is different again, seemingly taking it as an allusion to the presence of the statue of Amun-of-the-Road that Wenamun has brought: "You have made this great god spend these twenty-nine days moored in your harbor, without your knowing whether he, who has been there, was present or not" (in Simpson, *Literature of Ancient Egypt*, 121); cf. Winand, "Report," 550: "without knowing whether he was there, or not, he who was present." All in all, Gordon's comparison is not very cogent.

18. Nissinen, *Prophets and Prophecy*. This is also the only part of the story mentioned in Nissinen's broader *Ancient Prophecy*, 105–6, 171, 181–82.

19. To mention only two: Schipper (in *Die Erzählung*) makes no nod to the prophetic-rhetorical connections noted here. And in *God in Translation*, Mark S. Smith discusses *Wenamun* only in terms of its allusions to the Baal-Seth equivalence.

understood here. These texts, therefore, should not be included in a study of the historical phenomenon "prophecy" such as this one.[20]

This accurate comment suggests that *Wenamun* merits further analysis as a prophetic text, but it does not receive it—Stökl too discusses only the passage about the ecstatic prophet, rather than the lengthier theological speeches. He judges *Wenamun* to be simply a portrait of a "non-Egyptian environment": "The fact that a Semitic term is used in Egyptian texts suggests that there was no Egyptian term to refer to this kind of specialist."[21] But as we will see, Wenamun's rhetoric has deep roots in native Egyptian theology.

The recent monograph by Bernd Schipper deserves special comment. It is a treasure trove, thanks to its broad review of the literature and its insights on the text from multiple methodological perspectives. It is sure to cast a long shadow over scholarship on the book for some time. Ultimately Schipper's interest is to locate the text within the history of Egypt, and his arguments for the late tenth-century dating that others had proposed more briefly are convincing.[22] In his analysis of *Wenamun*'s basic nature, Schipper advocates for the term *Theopolitik*, which is well-chosen—but whereas his study leans toward the *politik*, this one leans toward the *Theo*.[23] These are complementary perspectives. Since Schipper does not touch on the similarities to prophetic literature identified here, the present study has the potential to deepen and nuance his conclusions.[24]

On the Egyptological side, a recent essay by Alan B. Lloyd, "*Heka*, Dreams, and Prophecy in Ancient Egyptian Stories," concludes that prophecy "is integral and fundamental to the agenda" of texts from the Middle Kingdom to the Demotic Setna Cycle, and is "fully represented and over a considerably greater timespan" than revelation by dreams—yet he passes over *Wenamun* without comment.[25] Most of *Wenamun* is simply not on the radar for the study of prophecy.

In light of all this, the present book is meant to serve as a conversation-starter, in particular to invite biblical scholars who work on prophecy or the development of Israelite religion to take another look at *Wenamun*. That is also

---

20. Stökl, *Prophecy*, 15; emphasis added.
21. Stökl, *Prophecy*, 15–16.
22. Moers, "Travel as Narrative," 54; Sass, "Wenamun and His Levant," passim.
23. Schipper, *Die Erzählung*, 299–324.
24. And thus I accept his invitation to "Widerspruch und Diskussion" (Schipper, *Die Erzählung*, 328).
25. Lloyd, "*Heka*, Dreams, and Prophecy," 71–94; quotations from p. 88. It should be noted that (1) Lloyd was using *ḥkȝ* as a keyword to identify and connect the texts in question, and it does not occur in *Wenamun*; and (2) as the previous point reflects, he was not working with a definition of "prophecy" that scholars of Hebrew and ancient Near Eastern prophecy would recognize.

why, in its approach to documentation, it focuses on introducing the secondary literature on *Wenamun* more than that on the Bible. The latter is in any case too extensive to review in a brief book like this one.

I perceive significant hope that *Wenamun* can be added to these conversations. After all, fifty years ago even historians of the ancient Levant did not pay much attention to *Wenamun*—Guy Bunnens observed that it seemed to be "a preserve of Egyptologists"[26]—whereas now it is discussed in nearly any history of the period. Hopefully fifty years from now it will also be more integral to scholarship on the history of religion and theology.

Wenamun's Knowledge of the Exotic Levant

The prophetic themes in *Wenamun* are not surprising, in that the author is attuned to Semitic terminology, phraseology, and even broader literary conventions. The scene of the ecstatic prophet inspired to speak up on behalf of Amun is the most heavily studied example of this. He is called an ꜥḏd ꜥꜣ n.y=f ꜥḏd.w (1/38–39[27])—and although ꜥḏd is legible in Egyptian as something like "child" or "page,"[28] it instead appears to be a calque of a West Semitic term, with ꜥḏd ꜥꜣ rendering "great prophet."[29]

The term ꜥdd for a diviner is attested in various Semitic texts. In the Zakkur Stela, from eighth-century Hamath (Syria), the ruler Zakkur says that in the midst of his distress the god Baal-šamayn answered him by means of two types of divinatory experts, ḥzyn and ꜥddn.[30] ḥzyn is cognate with the common Hebrew term for "seer" (ḥzh), and ꜥddn is understandable for a diviner. Synonymous nominal pairs such as the ḥzyn and ꜥddn in the Zakkur Stela are very characteristic of Semitic literature. The interpretation of ꜥddn as "prophets" is strengthened by cognates such as Ugaritic ꜥdd, "herald," and possibly Hebrew ꜥd, "witness." The biblical prophets named Oded (ꜥ[w]dd; 2 Chr 15:1, 8; 28:9), Iddo the grandfather of Zechariah (ꜥdw; Zech 1:1), and "ꜥdyhw son of Isaiah" (ꜥdyhw bn yšꜥyhw), who is attested on an Iron Age bulla from the Ophel, may

---

26. Bunnens, "La mission d'Ounamon," 1.
27. Line numbers correspond to the presentation of Ritner, *Libyan Anarchy*, 87–99.
28. *Wb* 1, 242.11–17; *DLE* 1:98.
29. Ebach and Rütersworden, "Der byblitische Ekstatiker," 17–22; see also Cody, "Phoenician Ecstatic," 99–106.
30. Nissinen, *Prophets and Prophecy*, 253–57 (No. 137 = *KAI* A.12). To head off any confusion, the Zakkur of this stela, who worships Baal, is not the Zakarbaal of Wenamun; Hamath (modern-day Hama, Syria) was an inland city a little less than 100 km from the coast, and about twice that far north of Byblos.

well all share in this naming tradition.[31] While the underlying Semitic term has been disputed, it is in any event a Semitic loanword.[32]

Quite a number of other Semitic loanwords are also present in *Wenamun*.[33] There are proper names such as Zakarbaal (*Tkr-Bʽr*, a theophoric name meaning "Baal has remembered/summoned"[34]) and Lebanon (*rbrn*[35]), which one would expect to be transliterated. The name of the captain of Wenamun's ship, Mengebet (*Mngbt*), may also be Semitic.[36] But in addition, Wenamun speaks of "crews" or "partners" (*ḫbr*[37]) in shipping ventures involving vessels of Syrian design (*mnš.w*),[38] and he "draws near" (*q[r]ṯı̓*[39]); Zakarbaal sits in

---

31. A standard analysis of the name Iddo connects it to the root *ʽ-d-h* II, "to adorn," rather than *ʽ-d-d*, "to proclaim," or *ʽ-w-d*, "to bear witness" (see *HALOT*, ad loc.), but an interpretation of these prophetic names as referring to the witness or herald of Yahweh would make more sense.

32. The more established argument is that the scribe of *Wenamun* used the usual glyph for /ḍ/ (i.e., the cobra, Gardiner I10) to represent the phoneme /d/, even though the Eg. ḍ > Semitic d equivalence is not expected (Cody, "Phoenician Ecstatic," 102–4). By contrast, Görg (followed by Hoch), proposed that it is instead *ḥzyn*, the other term from the Zakkur Stela, that is cognate with *ʽdd(t)*, since (1) ḍd can occur as a group-writing for ḍ; (2) Eg. ḍ > Semitic z is a normal equivalence; and (3) the equivalence Eg. ʾ > Sem. ḥ is possible (Görg, "Der Ekstatiker von Byblos," 31–33; Hoch, *Semitic Words*, 86–87, #106). This modification to the argument conforms the data to expected phonological equivalences, but does not seem to have attained broad acceptance. For example, it is noted but not endorsed by Schipper, *Die Erzählung*, 184–85.

33. As noted briefly by Hoch, *Semitic Words*, 477; Görg, "Fremdformen im Wenamun," 69–72; and see further below. By contrast, I have seen no concrete support for John Baines's contextual assumption that the characters are meant to be speaking Akkadian ("On *Wenamun* as a Literary Text," 228).

34. Semitic *zkrbʽl*. No king named Zakarbaal is attested in surviving monumental inscriptions, but its literary plausibility as a royal name in the period and region is attested by the discovery of the royal name *zkrbʽl* (*mlk ʾamr*), "Zakarbaal (king of Amurru)," on three roughly contemporaneous bronze arrowheads: Starcky, "La flèche de Zakarbaʽal," 179–86; Bordreuil, "Flèches phéniciennes inscrites," 16–40. These were discovered in the Beqaa Valley, nearer to Hamath (where the king Zakkur of the Zakkur Stela ruled), so they do not seem to relate directly to the dynasty that ruled Byblos at the time of *Wenamun*, but in any case the name is a very plausible West Semitic formulation; one need only compare the common Hebrew PN Zechariah, *zkryh(w)*. The name *zkrbʽl/skrbʽl* is also attested in Phoenician and Punic texts of the fifth and fourth centuries BCE (Krahmalkov, *Phoenician-Punic Dictionary*, 172, 344). Sader suggests that if Zakarbaal were a real king, he must have ruled in the end of the eleventh century, since he does not fit into what is known about the tenth-century dynasty (*History and Archaeology of Phoenicia*, 35).

35. Semitic *lbnn*. Weinstein, "Lebanon," in *OEAE* 2:285. Kilani has sought to connect *rbrn* to a different Semitic term: "New Tree Name in Egyptian," 43–52.

36. *Wenamun* 1/7. Theories about the derivation vary; cf. Görg, "Zu einem semitischen Personennamen," 24–26; Schneider, *Asiatische Personennamen*, 36–37.

37. *Wenamun* 1/59. WSem *ḫbr*; *DNWSI*, 345–47. Hoch, *Semitic Words*, 240 #333; also Katzenstein, "Phoenician Term *ḥubūr*," 2:599–602; Markoe, *Phoenicians*, 33, 96.

38. *Wenamun* 1/7, 23, 46, 55, 58; Basch, "Le navire *mnš*," 99–123.

39. *Wenamun* 1/21–22; 2/45, 27, 77. Hoch, *Semitic Words*, 297–98 #431.

his "upper room" (ꜥ.t[40]); speaks of "gifts" (mrk[41]) from past pharaohs; sends Wenamun a ram (ꜣyr[42]); and summons his assembly (mwꜥḏ[43]). Various items in the lists of goods that are exchanged are Semitic loanwords,[44] and the term for the ecstatic state that the Byblian prophet reaches (hꜣw.t; 1/40) has been connected to West Semitic ḥt(h) and Akkadian ḫattu, "fear," though this is not certain.[45]

At the level of phraseology, there are other similarities. For example, Zakarbaal's "day-books of his fathers" (ꜥ.[t] hꜣ[r]w nꜣy⸗f ity.w; 2/8) evoke the "Book of the Annals (sēper dibrê hayyāmîm) of the Kings of Israel/Judah" (1 Kgs 14:19, 29, etc.).[46] Numerous other examples come up in the analysis of prophetic rhetoric below.

In light of the foregoing, Semitic etymologies may be proposed for two additional personal names: bdr, the name of the ruler of Dor, has never been explained with much conviction,[47] and may simply be a calque of Semitic b dr, "[the one] in Dor."[48] The writing of the city name Dor is identical to that of

---

40. *Wenamun* 1/48; cf. Heb. *ʿăliyyāh*; Judg 3:20, 23–25; 1 Kgs 17:19.23; 2 Kgs 4:10; etc. This association is widely accepted by translators and commentators, though see Ward, "Late Egyptian ꜥ.t," 329–35.

41. *Wenamun* 2/12. Usu. *brk*; cf. WSem. *brkh*, DNWSI, 202; Gen 33:11; Josh 15:19; Judg 1:15; 1 Sam 25:27; 30:26; 2 Kgs 5:15, etc. Despite the irregular spelling, this is a relatively common spelling of an even more commonly attested loanword. See Hoch, *Semitic Words*, 104–5, #129; and TLA. There is an older theory that the phrase should be read as *fꜣy mlk*, "königlichen Geschenken," with *mlk* deriving from the Semitic root; see Goedicke (*Report*, 79) with citations to literature going back to Erman in 1900. Moers maintains this older theory (*Fingierte Welten*, 104–42), and although Ritner does not remark on it, his "delivery of royal gifts" seems to reflect the same understanding (if not simply a double translation of *mrk/mlk*).

42. *Wenamun* 2/68; Semitic *ꜣyl*, "sheep, ram," Deut 32:14, etc. (cf. Ugaritic *ảl*; Akk. *ālu*). Hoch, *Semitic Words*, 17 #1. Interestingly, HALOT considers this an Egyptian loanword into Semitic.

43. *Wenamun* 2/71. Hoch, *Semitic Words*, 126 (#161). DNWSI, 604; Exod 30:36, etc.

44. E.g., Hoch, *Semitic Words*, #84, 198, 353.

45. Görg, "Der Ekstatiker," 33. See CAD Ḫ, 151. For example: *ḫattum ša DN [ina muḫḫ]išu liššakin* "May the terror of DN be laid upon him" (*Mémoires de la Délégation en Perse* 10 p. 85:6; cf. MDP 11 p. 13:5; and MDP 28 p. 31:6). This equation is less secure. There is also *ḥittāh ʾĕlōhîm*, "fear of God" in Gen 35:5, and *ḥt*, "fear," may occur at least once in a West Semitic inscription (Deir ʿAlla I.9), but these are from the relatively commonly geminate root *ḥ-t-t*, which does not suggest equivalence with *hꜣw.t*. I suggest tentatively that, although /ḥ/ and /h/ were normally distinguished in pronunciation, the Byblian ecstatic's *hꜣw.t* could have functioned for an Egyptian audience as a wordplay here on the similar-sounding *hꜣw.t*, "appearance, manifestation," a term very commonly used of manifestations of the divine.

46. Redford, *Pharaonic King-Lists*, 100; Redford, *Egypt, Canaan, and Israel*, 330.

47. For a review of proposals about the derivation, see Scheepers, "Anthroponymes," 38–41. He concludes that the best Semitic etymology proposed at that time connected it to Ug. *bdl*, "substitute, reserve personnel" (DULAT, 214). That term was at least loosely contemporaneous with *Wenamun* and used in the same region, but it is not really a term for a ruler, even a substitute one.

48. This is only a small variation on Goedicke's theory deriving it from Eg. *pꜣ(-n)-Dr* ("the one of Dor") "in Semitic guise": *Report*, 29 and n. 33. He rightly comments, "We might be justified in wondering whether the name does not include the name of Dor."

Bedor's name apart from the prefixed *b-* (Gardner G29), and the man determinative instead of the city determinative.

Furthermore, it is conceivable that even the much-disputed[49] name *Wrktr* for a ruler (2/2) is to be understood as an Egyptian-Semitic hybrid: *wr-ktr*, "Great One of the Crown," on the model of common Egyptian compound titles such as *wr-swn.w*, "Chief Physician," *wr-m33*, "Chief Seer," and *wrt-ḥk3w*, "Great-of-Magic/Great Sorceress."[50] In this period, *wr* was a common title for a foreign ruler in Egyptian, and its presence in the later title *wr(.t)* for Ḥatiba, the female ruler of Cyprus (2/76), means that the masculine form here would not be surprising.[51] Although the term *wr*, "ruler," is written with Gardiner A19 elsewhere in the text, and here it is spelled out in group writing,[52] this is possible for a hybrid term loaned back into Late Egyptian.[53] Egyptian-Semitic hybrid names were created by earlier Egyptianizing Levantine rulers, such as *wr n ḫ3s.t 'qrt nkmd*, "the prince of the land of Ugarit, Niqmaddu."[54] Names like "[the one] in Dor" and "Great One of the Crown," which are almost comically simple, would not be out of place in the sort of humorous wisdom fable that *Wenamun* turns out to be.[55]

The author of *Wenamun* was not the first to use all these terms in Egyptian—some of them were clearly also used in nonliterary contexts—but taken as a whole they do give the story a Semitic and Levantine flavor.[56] This technique is consistent with the author's adoption of Semitic prophetic rhetoric. Even the syntax of the Byblians may have been intended to mark their foreignness.[57] It would not be at all surprising to find linguistic

---

49. For past scholarship, see Green, "*m-k-m-r* und *w-r-k-t-r*," 115–19.
50. On *ktrt*, "crown," in Punic (in addition to Hebrew כתר), see Krahmalkov, *Dictionary*, 247. For discussion of previous proposals, see Schipper, *Die Erzählung*, 176, 190–91.
51. Lorton, *Juridical Terminology*, 60–63; Matić, "Why Were the Leaders?," 73–89.
52. *w3-r-k3-ti-r*, 𓅱𓂋𓎡𓏏𓂋.
53. As Hoch notes, "Sometimes even native words were written in group writing, so it would be mistaken to assume (as has happened) that everything written in this fashion is of foreign origin" (*Semitic Words*, 5n14). The presence of the name *wry*, apparently in Semitic, on a Bronze Age arrowhead may be evidence of this loan (Golub, "Personal Names," 35). The name *Wrt* in 1/16 ought to be brought into the conversation as well, since it is written very similarly to *Wrktr*. No such figure ever appears in the story, and conversely neither *Wrktr* nor the *wr.t* of Cyprus is mentioned in this list of authorities. *Wrt* may refer to one of them.
54. Lorton, *Juridical Terminology*, 63; Schaeffer, *Ugaritica* III, 164–68.
55. See esp. Moers, *Fingierte Welten*, 89–96.
56. Breyer makes a similar observation from an Anatolian comparative perspective: "Kleinasiatisches Lokalkolorit," 33–40.
57. Satzinger, "How Good Was Tjeker-Ba'l's Egyptian?," 171–76. This point has been disputed by Egberts, "Double Dutch in The Report of Wenamun?," 17–22. Di Biase-Dyson entertained this theory ("Linguistic Insights into Characterisation," 51–64), before eventually deciding it was too uncertain (*Foreigners*, 334–35).

code-switching used to characterize foreigners, a technique used in biblical literature as well.[58]

All in all, *Wenamun* very plausibly has elements of an exotic travelogue, in that it seeks to represent the flavor of foreign cultures to an Egyptian audience.[59] Consistent with these Levantine features, many facets of the story's dialogue between Wenamun and the Levantine rulers also resonate with West Semitic prophetic rhetoric.

Prophecy in Byblos and the Bible

All this suggests the benefits of analyzing *Wenamun*'s theological rhetoric in comparison with the Bible's. A few words are in order, however, about the warrant for connecting the two via the Phoenician culture of Byblos, where the crux of the story takes place.

Phoenicia, of course, was precisely a commercial and cultural hub. There is ample warrant in the historical and material records to posit contacts and similarities between Byblos and Jerusalem. The cultural relationships between Phoenicia and Israel/Judah are so well established that a sketch should suffice here.

Israel and Judah adapted their alphabet from Phoenicia.[60] Pottery evidence shows that Israel traded with Phoenicia from the eleventh century on. As time went on, Phoenicia served as a hub for the intensive trade among Egypt, the Mediterranean, and Israel/Judah, and this is apparent in the material record.[61] In the biblical histories, Phoenicians are said to have built the first Jerusalem Temple (according to 1 Kgs 5–7), and the Byblians are specifically named in 1 Kgs 5:18 as the stonemasons and cutters of timbers for the project. King Hiram of Tyre is credited with overseeing the project, and remembered as having conducted a shipping business with Solomon (1 Kgs 9:26–28; 10:11).[62] In addition to these well-established connections with Tyre and Byblos, it has even been argued recently that Phoenician Dor, which had extensive trading

---

58. For further discussion and literature, see Hays, *Origins*, 160–71. Note especially Power, *Significance of Linguistic Diversity*.
59. So also Winand, "Report," 552.
60. See Sanders, *Invention of Hebrew*, 90–120.
61. For a recent overview of scholarship, see Gilboa, "Southern Levantine Roots," 31–53. See also Mazar, *10,000–586 B.C.E.*, 514; Faust and Weiss, "Judah, Philistia, and the Mediterranean World," 71–92; Holladay, "Judeans (and Phoenicians) in Egypt," 405–38.
62. Like Zakarbaal in *Wenamun*, the name Hiram (*Ḥîram*) has clear historical connections. It is a shortened version of the Phoenician RN Ahiram (*'Aḥîram*), attested as the name of a king of Byblos on an inscribed sarcophagus discovered there (*KAI* 1).

relations with Egypt, became an Israelite capital city in the ninth century.[63] The realities behind specific biblical and historical claims can be debated, but the generally close cultural relations between the Phoenician cities and nearby Israel cannot.

At a literary level, the derivation of the Hebrew alphabet from a Phoenician precursor marks the two cultures' shared intellectual heritage. It is possible that Phoenician prophecy was as important a precursor as the Phoenician alphabet was. No prophetic texts from Phoenicia or the Iron Age Levantine seacoast have survived, but that is certainly an accident of preservation. The surviving references to prophecy in extrabiblical West Semitic texts from the Iron Age are very few in general, and this is consistent with the loss of most of the Phoenician and Levantine Iron Age textual tradition, thanks to the use of papyri and other soft writing media.[64]

Nevertheless, we know—not only thanks to Mari and Nineveh, but tantalizingly from the fragmentary Deir 'Alla inscriptions, Amman Citadel Inscription, and Zakkur Stela—that national boundaries were not sharp cultural boundaries when it came to prophecy. Hebrew prophecy is surely the surviving corpus of prophetic literature closest to Phoenician prophecy in time and/or space. Thus, if one asks what Phoenician prophecy in the period might have been like, it offers us the best analogy that we have. The Mari evidence (eighteenth century BCE) and the Neo-Assyrian prophetic corpus (from the Mesopotamian heartland) are more distant from Iron Age II Phoenicia.

The period of the early Iron Age is a particularly difficult one to analyze thanks to the relative shortage of texts, but the present comparative analysis of *Wenamun* continues to connect the dots among the prophets who functioned in the period.

Conclusion

Egyptologists have shown more interest in comparisons between Amun and Yahweh than biblical scholars have. Among scholars of the Hebrew prophets, *Wenamun* has been studied almost exclusively for the brief episode of the

---

63. Gilboa, Sharon, and Bloch-Smith, "Capital of Solomon's Fourth District?," 51–74. They argue that the reference to "Naphath-dor" in a list of Solomonic territories in 1 Kgs 4:11 actually reflects an Omride conquest of the area. Gilboa elsewhere observes that trade with Egypt at Dor, specifically, dropped off in the period she attributes to Israelite control: Gilboa, "Dor and Egypt in the Early Iron Age," 247–74. While trade is not equivalent with cultural contact, this may suggest indirect mechanisms of contact (e.g., via the Phoenicians).

64. *Wenamun*'s testimony to this material reality was already noted by Breasted, "Report of Wenamon," 100–109.

Byblian ecstatic prophet. Helped by analyses of small glyptic artifacts, however, a new wave of religio-historical scholarship has emphasized the ongoing presence and influence of Amun in the Iron Age Levant, and the points of comparison between Amun theologies and Israelite religion. The story of Wenamun's debates with Zakarbaal of Byblos is a particularly rich example of the cultural exchange between the cultures they represent. The story includes many instances of Semitic terms and phrases borrowed into Egyptian. Historically, Byblos and other Phoenician cities were hubs in an economic and cultural network that included both Egypt and Israel/Judah, and indeed one finds shared theological motifs in the rhetoric of all three cultures.

CHAPTER 3

Amun and Yahweh as Theocrats

THE PLOT OF *WENAMUN* IS driven by conflicts about lordship, ownership, and trading ships. The tale introduces the reader to some of the details and machinations of Mediterranean shipping in the Third Intermediate Period, including petty theft (1/10–32); the control of ship crews (1/57–2.2); and the exchange of diplomatic "gifts" (2/6–13). Throughout the story, politics, economics, and theology are intertwined as various parties vie to establish hierarchies.

Wenamun's journey is presented from the beginning as a sacred mission from the god Amun (1/2–4). The desired reaction to this claim is demonstrated at the outset by Smendes and Tanetamun, rulers of Lower Egypt in Tanis, when they receive Wenamun's "dispatches of Amun-Re, King of the gods." They immediately reply, "I shall act! I shall act in accordance with that which Amun-Re, King of the gods, our lord, has said!" (1/5–6: *iry[≠i] sp-sn m p3 [i]-dd 'Imn-R' ny-sw.t ntr.w p3[y]≠n [nb]*).[1] The repetition of the phrase "I shall act!" is certainly emphatic; it gives this utterance the quality of an oath.[2] It is quite similar to Hatshepsut's reaction when an oracle of Amun confirmed her coronation: "O my father, who devises everything that exists, what is it that you desire to happen? I shall certainly act according to your plans."[3] The simple and "proper" answer of Smendes and Tanetamun contrasts with the more complicated reactions to Amun later in the story.

---

1. In the translations and analyses that follow, I have been informed in my understanding of the text by various recent translations of *Wenamun*, including: Lichtheim (*COS* 1.41, pp. 88–93); Ritner (*Libyan Anarchy*, 87–99); and Edward Wente (in Simpson, *Literature*, 116–24). Nevertheless, I have also in some cases diverged from these translations.

2. From a Semitics standpoint one might note, for example, the repeated phrases in the divorce and marriage language of Hos 2:2, 21–22 (MT). On repetition in Egyptian oaths, including examples with *sp sn*, see Wilson, "Oath in Ancient Egypt," 129–56, esp. 139, 141, 145n102, and the summary on 156: "Under juridical inquiry the witness might be subjected to repeated oaths; even the pharaoh might feel it necessary to confirm his oath by repeating it." Also, in a later period, Massa, "Temple Oaths in Ptolemaic Egypt," 7, 28n100, 40, 67.

3. Assmann, *Search for God*, 193; Lacau and Chevrier, *Une chapelle*, 1:97–101.

Their promise to act in accordance with the word of a deity is also precisely the desired response to divine announcements delivered by Hebrew prophets. In the biblical literature, audiences are repeatedly admonished:[4] "be careful to act according to that which Yahweh your God has commanded you" (Deut 5:32); "act according to all that I have commanded you" (Jer 50:21); "keep my commandments and my statutes, in accordance with all the law that I commanded your ancestors and that I sent to you by my servants the prophets" (2 Kgs 17:13); "be careful to act in accordance with all the law that my servant Moses commanded you . . . meditate on it day and night, so that you may be careful to act in accordance with all that is written in it" (Josh 1:7–8). As with Smendes and Tanetamun's oath, these injunctions occur at crucial junctures of the stories, signaling their importance.

Wenamun seeks this same sort of quick submission from everyone he encounters. From the beginning of the story, he is quick to invoke the deity's authority as soon as things go wrong: no sooner does he reach his first port of call, Dor, than a man of his own ship (*wʿ rmṯ n tȝy⸗i byr*; 1/10) steals 5 *deben* of gold and 31 *deben* of silver and flees. This is the equivalent of roughly half a kilo of gold and 3 kilos of silver, respectively[5]—enough to feed nearly 310 people for one month, or over 25 people for a whole year. As R. J. Leprohon observes, "The ancient Egyptian audience immediately would have made the connections [with] what would undoubtedly have been enormous funds for them."[6] It was seemingly enough for him to purchase the wood outright, so this great loss threatens to make it impossible to complete his mission.[7]

Wenamun goes to Bedor, prince of Dor, and demands that he investigate and catch the thief: "Search for my money!" (1/14). He goes on to assert that the money "belongs to Amun-Re, King of the Gods, the Lord of the Lands" (1/14–15). In this same initial assertion, Wenamun expands on the hierarchy of authorities under Amun, who are also, in a subordinate way, responsible for the lost silver: "It belongs to Smendes; it belongs to Herihor, my lord, and the other magnates of Egypt. It is yours. It belongs to *Wrt*;[8] it belongs to Mekamer; it belongs to Zakarbaal, the prince of Byblos!" (1/15–16).

At a practical level, Wenamun's rhetoric of belonging is intended to emphasize the economic stakes and relationships involved. There have been various analyses of Wenamun's fiscal claim in light of ancient Near Eastern law and

---

4. The Hebrew phraseology behind these biblical admonitions varies somewhat.
5. An older and smaller standard of the *deben* might still have been in use in this late period; see discussion at Schipper, *Die Erzählung*, 173.
6. Leprohon, "What Wenamun Could Have Bought," 174.
7. Bunnens, "La mission d'Ounamon en Phénicie," 6.
8. On this title, see chapter 2 (27n53).

customs.⁹ There is fairly broad agreement that there was a principle accepted in ancient Near Eastern law that if a traveling merchant was robbed while on his route, and the thief was not caught, the town where the crime was committed, and thus its ruler, could be held financially responsible. This is enunciated more clearly in various Bronze Age law collections and diplomatic documents.¹⁰ Wenamun seems to be threatening Bedor "that severe diplomatic reprisals would result from these sources should Dor fail to honour its obligations."¹¹

The problem with that argument is that the thief was, as we have noted, identified as "a man from Wenamun's own ship"! Wenamun is trying to hold Dor accountable for thievery by a man in his own employ. We do not know, from the ancient Near Eastern legal sources, whether they even foresaw such an eventuality, but Wenamun certainly seems to be pressing his luck. Bedor's incredulous response reflects that: "Look, whether you're slow-witted or a fast-talker, I don't understand what you're saying to me" (1/17).¹² Or, as a number of past translations have rendered the alternatives he presents: "Are you serious, or are you joking?"¹³

Bedor affirms the legal principle, while denying that he and his people are responsible: "If it had been a thief who belonged to my land who had gone down to your ship and stolen your money, I would replace it for you from my storehouse until your thief, whatever his name, had been found. But really, as regards the thief who robbed you, he is yours. He belongs to your ship. Spend a few days here near me so that I may search for him" (1/18–20). Bedor is essentially dismissing Wenamun's claim, without directly saying so. Wenamun is put "on hold." The text of the next section is somewhat damaged, but nine days

---

9. This has been remarked upon by Westbrook, "International Law in the Amarna Age," 28–41; Campbell, "Cuneiform Legal Presence," 1–10; Brinker, "Are You Serious?," 89–101; Liverani, *Prestige and Interest*.

10. LH 23 (Roth, *Law Collections*, 85); EA 313; and two treaties between Ugarit and Carchemish, RS 17.230:4–23 and RS 17.146:6–27.

11. Green, "Wenamun's Demand for Compensation," 116–20.

12. *iw=f dd n=i (i)n dns=k (i)n mnḫ=k ḫr ptri bw-ir=i ꜥm n tꜣy wšb.t i-dd=k n=i* (1/17–18). This comment is clearly very colloquial, and thus has proven difficult for translators to render. (*TLA* offers a survey of about a dozen translations.) Ritner argues that "the term *dns* typically has negative nuances ('burdened, irksome'), while *mnḫ* is uniformly positive. Previous translations have reversed the nuances." The adjective *dns* in fact has a very similar semantic range to Heb. *kbd*, spanning from "important, weighty" (and thus powerful) to "heavy, burdened." My translation ("slow-witted") acknowledges Ritner's point and associates it with the brain-addling connotations of *kbd* in Exod 8:11, 28; 9:34; 10:1; Isa 6:10; Zech 7:11. As for *mnḫ*, it does denote excellence and skill, including in speech, and is sometimes associated with magic.

13. The major translators who have rendered it this way include Lichtheim, Hornung, Wente, Schipper, and Edel. And despite the previous note, it is a reasonable way to convey Bedor's question in colloquial terms.

pass without any progress, so he returns to Bedor and is told to "Be silent!" about his complaint (1/21–23).

These exchanges introduce one of the subtexts of the story: Egypt had lost much of the control and influence over Levantine cities such as Dor that it had during its New Kingdom imperial period in the late Bronze Age. This new reality was immensely frustrating to an Egyptian emissary like Wenamun, but it only seemed like a "world upside down" from the Egyptian perspective. Others benefited—and as a number of the encounters suggest, Wenamun's era was arguably "far from being a time of barbarism and anarchy," but rather one in which certain rules were carefully followed by all.[14]

Wenamun is completely unfazed by his apparent lack of actual power. His legal claims may not hold water, but he has resort to a more fundamental theological claim: he constructs a theopolitical hierarchy with Amun at the top; Egyptian rulers second; and local potentates, including Zakarbaal, in a subordinate position. Therefore Wenamun has to argue ambitiously that *regardless* who the thief was, Bedor ought to reimburse him because "*everyone* belongs to the household of Amun, King of the Gods, Lord of the Lands."[15] And since Wenamun is a Theban representative of Amun, this positions him as an ultimate human authority.

Amun's unparalleled right to rule is emphasized in the story's use of terminology: despite the mention of Egyptian rulers such as Smendes and Herihor, Amun is the only one called "king" (*nsw*) in the text, and his title *nb n n3 t3.w* ("Lord of the Lands") is reminiscent of the title *nb t3.wy* ("Lord of the Two Lands"), which was given only to pharaohs.[16] "The two lands" was a long-standing term for Upper and Lower Egypt, so the use of the plural *t3.w* as opposed to the more classical dual *t3.wy* implies a wider scope of rule, including foreign lands such as the states of the Levant. The message is clear: the god is king.[17]

Wenamun does once refer to "*former* kings" (*ny.w-sw.t ḥ3w.tyw*) in 2/29. And the term *pr-ꜥ3* is also used once by Zakarbaal of a past pharaoh (2/7). But in the present, the ruler of Egypt is just a chieftain (*ḥq3*; 2/10).

The story's emphasis on Amun and theological concerns is also reflected by a simple count of the occurrences of words in the text. "Amun" is the most-used noun in the story, with 30 occurrences, followed by *nṯr*, "god," with 19.

---

14. Bunnens, "La mission d'Ounamon," 16: "Loin d'être une époque de barbarie et d'anarchie, l'époque d'Ounamon semble soucieuse de soumettre les relations internationales à des règles admises par tous." So also Baines, "On the Background of Wenamun," 35.
15. Brinker, "Are You Serious?," 97.
16. Di Biase-Dyson, *Foreigners*, 325; Winand, "Report," 552.
17. On the assignation of royal titles to Amun in the Third Intermediate Period, and a nuanced discussion of its relationship to human kingship, see Winnerman, "New Observations."

The only words that occur more often are common pronouns, particles, and prepositions, and the verbs *iry*, "do," *dd*, "say," and *rdi*, "give, cause."[18]

This same theological emphasis explains, better than real historical conditions, the much-remarked fact that the "Lady of Byblos," the city's deity who is mentioned in New Kingdom texts, does not appear in *Wenamun*.[19] It is not likely that the socioreligious character of Byblos actually changed so much over a century or two as to marginalize this significant goddess. Rather, much like the biblical texts that elide the existence of other deities because of their total emphasis on Yahweh, *Wenamun*'s total emphasis on Amun and its literary representation of reality naturally call for a minimization of the roles of other deities. Schipper comments on what he sees as the "astonishing monosyllabicity with respect to the Syrian/Palestinian deities. The city goddess of Byblos, Baalat-Gebal, is not mentioned with a single word and instead the god Amun is emphasized several times."[20] But that is the point of the story: to emphasize Amun at the expense of Levantine deities. This is like remarking that the book of Jonah doesn't have much to say about Assyrian deities.

Amun Among the Gods

The theological tenor of *Wenamun* rises as the story unfolds. If it were merely an account of securing timber for a sacred bark, it would be a relatively simple story. If we set aside all the setbacks and verbosity, the steps involved in that business negotiation are basically as follows:

> Wenamun arrives in Byblos and asks for the timber without producing any payment or gift, and without any hint of them;
> Zakarbaal refuses to supply the wood on such terms;
> Wenamun states that counter-gifts can be sent from Egypt;
> Zakarbaal sends to Egypt a request for payment/gifts, together with a "sample" of seven beams;
> Payments/gifts arrive from Egypt;
> Zakarbaal declares that he is satisfied, and supplies the wood.[21]

---

18. Winand, *Le voyage d'Ounamon*, 75.
19. Kilani, *Byblos*, 221, 230; Schipper, *Die Erzählung*, 185–86.
20. Schipper, *Die Erzählung*, 221: "Diesem Detailreichtum hinsichtlich der Realien steht jedoch eine erstaunliche Einsilbigkeit bezüglich der syrisch-palästinischen Gottheiten gegenüber. Die Stadtgöttin von Byblos, Baalat-Gebal, wird mit keinem Wort erwähnt und stattdessen der Gott Amun mehrfach betont." Although the speeches of Zakarbaal are briefer than those of Wenamun, they are no less subtle or creative; calling them "monosyllabic" seems an overstatement.
21. Adapted from Liverani, *Prestige and Interest*, 250.

Arguably, this business transaction is all that Zakarbaal is concerned with throughout the exchange. However, Wenamun's errors compound themselves in an escalating series, as his loss of the letters and silver that might have secured the timber lead him to resort to a kind of extreme theological discourse that might have made sense in Egypt, but was bound to alienate outsiders.

And whereas the ruler of Dor responds to Wenamun only in practical terms (so far as the text is preserved), in Byblos he encounters a leader, Zakarbaal, who is willing to spar with him on theological grounds.

The background of this encounter is not as clear as it might be, thanks to damage in the papyrus that affects 1/25–30. Certain things can be discerned from it, however: Wenamun says that he found a ship with "30 *deben* [ca. 3 kg] of silver in it," and "took possession of it." He says to the ship's owners: "[I have taken possession of] your money. It will remain with me [until] you have found my [money or the thief] who stole it!" (1/30–32). Although the identity of the ship's owners has not survived, seemingly lost in a break in the papyrus, we can infer from the later pursuit by the "men of Tjeker" that it was theirs.

The Tjeker are counted among the Sea Peoples, and are named in Ramses III's Medinet Habu inscriptions. In *Wenamun*, Dor is said to have been one of the cities of the Tjeker (1/8–9), but they may have originated elsewhere.[22] There are various theories about their associations and geographic origins, but it is better not to overinterpret such an exonym; as with the use of "Philistines" in the Bible (a term derived from another group of Sea Peoples, the Peleset), these terms appear to have been applied loosely by other cultures. And despite their reputation, there is no evidence in the story that the Tjeker are "pirates," as they are sometimes called in studies of *Wenamun*; they are in fact victims of theft.[23]

Wenamun finishes his speech by insisting, "I have not robbed you, although I shall rob him!," referring to the one who stole from him (1/32). He then pitches a tent and hides the silver along with "Amun-of-the-Road," a statuette of the god.

It is not entirely unusual for Wenamun to bring a statuette with him. Certain Amarna Letters attest to rulers sending divine statues temporarily to other courts around the Near East, and the finds from the Uluburun shipwreck in the Late Bronze Age included a gilded bronze goddess statuette of a type that was also attested for Amun in the Third Intermediate Period. From it and

---

22. To head off any confusion: although the term used for the Tjeker (*Tkr*) is transliterated in the same way as one of the elements in the name of the Byblian ruler Zakarbaal (Eg. *Tkrbʿr*), the hieratic writing differs significantly, and thus this is a phonological coincidence. The two are not related.

23. Bunnens, "La mission d'Ounamon," 12.

similar statues preserved in better condition, we probably even have some idea what Amun-of-the-Road looked like.[24] Wenamun says of the hiding place, "I placed *his* [i.e., Amun's] possessions within it," so he really doesn't miss a beat in arguing for his rectitude: even the stolen silver rightly belongs to Amun.

Wenamun is initially a *persona non grata* at Byblos; one may infer that word of the disputes swirling around Wenamun has already reached the city. The local ruler Zakarbaal repeatedly tries to send him away (1/34–38). (Presumably it would be unbecoming to do business with a foreigner who pays in stolen silver.[25]) This goes on for 29 days. We recall that Wenamun was also made to wait for days for an audience with Bedor, and this is a type of diplomatic humiliation attested from various Amarna Letters. For example, in EA 138 the dethroned king of Byblos, Rib-Hadda, who had become a fugitive in neighboring Beirut, writes to the pharaoh, "Within ten minutes after my arrival in Beirut, I sent my son to the palace of the ruler(ship). Four months he has not seen the face of the king! . . . I wrote to the king; he did not listen to my word. Right now, I am dwelling in Beirut like a dog (and) my word is not heeded!"[26] In Rib-Hadda's period, Egypt was clearly more powerful; now the Levantine rulers turn the tables on the Egyptian representative and make *him* wait.

A meeting is finally instigated by a message from a Byblian ecstatic prophet: "Bring up the god! Bring the messenger who bears him! It is Amun who has sent him. It is he who has caused that he come" (1/39–40). Wenamun further sets the tone by greeting Zakarbaal in the name of Amun: *sfty imn*, perhaps meaning "May Amun be merciful!" (1/50).[27] It has been debated whether this is a rendering of a standard Semitic greeting, and there is some biblical support for that conclusion, most intriguingly in the greeting of Joseph to Benjamin when the former is vizier over Egypt: "God be gracious to you (*yḥnk*), my son!"[28] Furthermore, the Priestly Blessing that included Num 6:25—"may

---

24. British Museum EA60006, made of silver and gold and 24 cm high, is particularly reminiscent in size and workmanship of the Uluburun goddess statue, and a solid gold Amun statue at the Met is also of a similar size (267.1412; 17 cm high). Both are attributed to the region of Thebes in the Third Intermediate Period. Schipper notes that it probably had a protective function (*Die Erzählung*, 182). We may add that this function was probably not entirely supernatural; the very presence of such an elite artifact was sure to signal the wealth and power of its bearer.

25. So Liverani, *Prestige and Interest*, 101.

26. EA 138:75–78, 94–97; Rainey, *El-Amarna Correspondence*, 709. See also EA 3:13–14; 29:111–14; 36:18; Bunnens, "La mission d'Ounamon," 11–12.

27. Taking *sfty* as a modal prospective from *sf*. For other alternatives, see Di Biase-Dyson, *Foreigners*, 299n119.

28. Other texts that may have reflected a greeting formula invoking divine mercy include Isa 30:19; Amos 5:15; Mal 1:9. The verb "to be merciful" is commonly expressed with two Hebrew roots: רחם and חנן; the former never appears as an imperative or modal, but the latter is very commonly said of God, especially in psalms: Pss 4:2; 6:3; 9:14; 25:16; 26:11; 27:7; 30:11; 31:10; 41:5, 11;

Yahweh make his face to shine upon you, and be gracious to you (*yḥnk*)"—seems to have had wide currency, and might have been used as a greeting.[29] Nevertheless, even if this was a standard greeting formula in Byblos, Wenamun uses it to reassert Amun's rule.

Zakarbaal is not impressed. As the debate heats up, he further theologizes it, using Amun and Seth to symbolize the dispute between Egypt and Byblos. In contrast to Wenamun, he does not call Amun "lord" or "king," but simply by his name. There is also an edge to his opening question to Wenamun: "How long has it been until today since you came from the place where Amun is?" (*wr r pꜣ hrw m-dr iw꞊k n pꜣ nty 'Imn m*; 1/50–51; cf. 2/78). Although "the place where Amun is" can refer to a temple or palace, the ominous inference from this statement is that Wenamun has now come to a place *where Amun is not*. Amun, he implies, is not omnipresent—and he is not the lord of Byblos. "How long has it been?" may also imply that Wenamun is out of touch with the diplomatic realities of the present.

Wenamun does not seem to take the hint that Amun and he both lack authority in this context, and he goes on to make his demands. Like Bedor, Zakarbaal seems somewhat incredulous about Wenamun's demands without letters of authorization or offers of compensation—he is not playing by the rules of the game! And so he flatly denies Wenamun's claims: "I am not your servant, nor am I the servant of the one who sent you!" (2/12–13).

Zakarbaal goes on to assert his own control over the Lebanon in ways that resonate with both Egyptian and Levantine myth. "If I but cry aloud to the Lebanon, heaven opens with the logs lying right here on the seashore!" (2/13–14; *iw꞊i ꜥš sgp r pꜣ Rbrn i.ir tꜣ p.t wn iw nꜣ ḫt.w d[y] ḫꜣꜥ [ḥr] sp.t [n.t] pꜣ ym*). At a basic level, of course, he is asserting his control over the resources of his land. The phrasing alludes to an older ideology expressed in a hymn to Ramses V, in which the pharaoh cries out to the Lebanon so that it yields up its gifts.

> Because of you, the Nine Bows will come to Egypt
> with royal gifts (*fꜣy mrk*) for your might.
> You will cry out to Lebanon (*ꜥš꞊k sgp r pꜣ Rbrn*) and it trembles.[30]

51:3; 56:2; 57:2; 86:3, 16; 119:29, 58, 132; 123:3 (all MT versification); also Isa 33:2; Job 19:21. There is also the common biblical name Hananiah, which means "Yahweh has been merciful."

29. This is one of the only biblical texts with preexilic extrabiblical attestations, in the Ketef Hinnom silver amulets, and the same formula is used in Ps 67:1. A similar expression of divine benevolence seems to be found (in broken context) in *KTU* 1.10 i:12: *yḥnnn*, perhaps with Baal as subject (see ll. 5–6). See Smoak, *Priestly Blessing*.

30. Moers, *Fingierte Welten*, 140–42; Winand, "Report," 553, with some further literature; Gardiner, *Library of A. Chester Beatty*, 42.

Here the roles are changed—the local ruler Zakarbaal now claims the formerly pharaonic power to command the Lebanon.[31]

Amun vs. Seth-Baal

It becomes clear very quickly that Zakarbaal's theological confidence is based on Baal, as his name already indicates. In this Egyptian story, Baal is called Seth, because in Egyptian religion Seth was associated with foreign lands and equated with their gods, especially the Levantine Baal.[32] In Middle Egyptian, Baal's name takes the Seth-animal as a determinative,[33] and when the Levantine Hyksos of the Second Intermediate Period were said to be worshipers of Seth, this seems to have referred to Baal as well.[34]

Zakarbaal is boasting of his ability to call down the blessings of his own gods, especially Baal/Seth. Used by itself, the Egyptian verb ꜥš is commonly used in invoking or supplicating deities.[35] Its role in invoking divine witnesses to treaties has been noted (see further, chapter 4).[36] In a long tradition of extra-biblical West Semitic texts, the verb *q-r-ʾ* is used identically to ꜥš in references to calling on the gods. It is widely attested at Late Bronze Age coastal Ugarit, in the Hebrew Bible, and in Iron Age inscriptions, including one from Byblos itself, in which Yaḥawmilk king of Byblos says, "I call on my Lady, the Mistress of Byblos" (*qrʾt rbty bʿlt gbl*).[37]

The same literary motif appears in the Hebrew Bible, and provides some strikingly similar scenes to the one in *Wenamun*. The invocation of deities became a motif in prophetic conflicts, as illustrated by the contest between Elijah and the prophets of Baal in 1 Kgs 18 to see which deity will answer with fire from heaven. The other prophets call on Baal without effect, after which:

> Elijah mocked them, saying, "Cry out (*qrʾw*), for he is a god; either he is meditating, or busy, or he is on a journey! Or perhaps he is asleep and will wake up!" Then they cried with a loud voice (*wyqrʾw bqwl gdwl*) and cut themselves with knives and spears, according to their custom, until the blood gushed out over them. (1 Kgs 18:27–28)

---

31. Weinstein, "Lebanon," 2:286.
32. Schipper, *Die Erzählung*, 195–96; Te Velde, "Seth"; Te Velde, *Seth*, 109–51; Loprieno, *Topos und Mimesis*, 73–84.
33. *Wb* I.447.
34. Te Velde, *Seth*, 121.
35. Cerný, "Egyptian Oracles," 43.
36. Morschauser, "Crying," 317–30.
37. *KAI* 10:7–8; the Ugaritic and biblical texts will be familiar to knowledgeable readers; see *DULAT* and *HALOT*, s.v. *q-r-ʾ*.

True gods, in both Egyptian and biblical contexts, are able to make things happen when called upon. In the Bible, Yahweh's power to open up the heavens with blessings is alluded to in Deut 28:12; Ps 78:23; Isa 45:8; and Mal 3:10. In the same way, Zakarbaal brags to Wenamun that he can call down the divine blessings of wood from the heavens.[38]

This, then, is a religious motif shared by both cultures involved—one that Wenamun can be trusted to understand. But Zakarbaal's boast that he can summon the mighty Baal in this way is an affront to Wenamun's confidence in Amun as the true "king of the gods."

Zakarbaal goes on to insult Wenamun directly. Although the text is partly broken, Zakarbaal seems to suggest that the Egyptian could not get the mighty conifer logs of Lebanon home on a ship even if Byblos provided them: "The yards (supporting the sails) may be too heavy and may break, and you may die in the midst of the sea" (2/18). His comments relate to the dispute earlier in the text (1/54–2/2) about who is really running the ships that made Mediterranean commerce work: Zakarbaal is asserting that Egypt is not competent in maritime matters. Zakarbaal's comment probably had a basis in fact, insofar as most of the major powers of the Iron Age essentially outsourced their Mediterranean shipping to the coastal cities, especially Phoenicians.[39] This exchange is highly analogous to the insult to Judah's horsemanship made by an Assyrian official to the men of Hezekiah in Isa 36:8–9, meant to undermine the morale of Jerusalem as the city is under siege: "Come now, make a wager with my master the king of Assyria: I will give you two thousand horses, if you are able to put riders on them." The assumption is that Judah does not have enough competent equestrians to do so. The Assyrian goes on: "How can you repulse a single captain among the least of my master's servants, when you rely on Egypt for chariots and for horsemen?"

Having undermined Egypt's claims to power, Zakarbaal comes to the point in a very direct way: "Look, Amun thunders in the sky only since he placed Seth at his side!" (*mk i-ir ʾImn ḫrw m tꜣ p.t iw di=f Swtḥ m rk=f*; 2/19). Seth was a deity associated with storms and thunder in Egypt since the Old Kingdom,[40] and the cross-cultural awareness of the motif of Baal/Seth thundering is

---

38. More generally, the debate about which deity is the source of blessings and goods is the center of the pro-Yahweh/anti-Baal speech of Hos 2, which accuses Israel of not understanding: "She did not know that it was I who gave her the grain, the wine, and the oil, and who lavished upon her silver and gold that they used for Baal" (Hos 2:10 MT).

39. For an overview, see Markoe, *Phoenicians*, 26–40. For the example of the Neo-Assyrian employment of Phoenician maritime expertise, see Fales, *Guerre et Paix en Assyrie*, 130–33.

40. Te Velde, *Seth*, 85, 90, 102–3. He argues against an older view of Seth's origins as more intra-Egyptian: Zandee, "Seth als Sturmgott," 144–88; Wainwright, "Some Aspects of Amūn," 139–53.

already attested in the Amarna Letters—notably EA 147, in which Abdimilki of Tyre writes of the pharaoh that he "has given his voice in the sky like Ba'al, and all the land was frightened at his cry."[41] Albright deemed it practically a direct translation from Egyptian.[42] The direction of influence in this case is not quite so clear, however, since thunderstorms were surely more common on the northeastern Mediterranean coast than in Egypt.

Since *Wenamun* is set in the 21st Dynasty and probably written in the 22nd Dynasty, it fits well into what is known about the Egyptian reception of Baal-Seth. After the Hyksos period, Baal-Seth was mentioned less during the 18th Dynasty, but then gradually grew in popularity again, seemingly thanks to traders in contact with the Levantine coast, because of Baal's role as a controller of the sea.[43] Seth seems to have absorbed from Baal the myth of combat with the sea,[44] and on the New Kingdom Year 400 Stela, found at Tanis, he is portrayed in a human form, and in dress characteristic of Levantine portrayals of Baal. This reflects an incorporation of Baal-Seth into Egyptian imperial theological rhetoric in the 19th and 20th Dynasties.[45] For example, Ramses II not only claimed to be "beloved of Amun" his father, but also called himself Seth/Baal, and boasted that the Hittites said to him: "You are Seth—Baal in person; the dread of you is a fire in the land of Hatti."[46] The mighty pharaoh was Baal.[47]

Even in the 21st–22nd Dynasties, Egyptians and Levantine states would have remembered when Egypt thundered in the person of Baal-Seth. But no more—according to Zakarbaal, Baal now thunders for himself and for Byblos. His point is that Amun of Thebes is no longer powerful enough to rule without accepting Baal of Byblos as at least an equal and coregent. The power of the pharaoh is reduced, and this growing conflict of interest between Egypt and the Levant is surely one reason that Seth names and temple-building declined in Egypt after the 20th Dynasty. Seth became a reminder of Egypt's weakness vis-à-vis foreign nations, just as he did after the Hyksos period.

The thundering motif is one of a number of examples of *Wenamun*'s shared phraseology with the text The Contendings of Horus and Seth from the

---

41. EA 147:13–15: *id-din ri-ig-ma-šu i-na sa-me ki-ma* ^{d}IŠKUR *ù 'tar'-gu₅-ub gáb-bi* KUR-*ti 'iš'-tu ri-ig-mi-šu*; Rainey, *El-Amarna Correspondence*, 742–43. Noted earlier by Gressmann, "Hadad und Baal," 198–99, 203–10.
42. Albright, "Egyptian Correspondence," 198.
43. See Te Velde, *Seth*, 122–23.
44. E.g., Baal's battle with Yam in the Ugaritic Baal Myth.
45. See further Allon, "Seth Is Baal," 15–22.
46. *AEL* 2:67, 71.
47. This was part of a wider adoption of Levantine deities; Ramses II exceptionally called himself "beloved of Anat" and referred to her as "mother." Cornelius, *Many Faces of the Goddess*, 85.

20th Dynasty (Ramses V; mid-twelfth century). This invites reflection on the reason for the intertextual relationship between these two texts.[48] The Contendings is a myth about the competition between Horus and Seth for divine kingship. Horus triumphs through a series of challenges in which he proves his wits and wisdom, in contrast to the foolish Seth.[49] At the end of the story, the gods seek some sort of consolation prize for Seth:

> Then Ptah ... said: "What shall be done for Seth? For see, Horus has been installed in the position of his father Osiris." Said Re-Harakhti: "Let Seth, son of Nut, be delivered to me so that he may dwell with me, being in my company as a son, and he shall thunder in the sky and be feared."

The myth has often been analyzed as a political allegory.[50] Most commonly, scholars have perceived an allusion to pharaonic power over the North and South of Egypt, but in light of Seth's equation with the Levantine Baal it is also quite susceptible to being read as an allegory about Egyptian superiority to the Levant, and it seems natural to conclude that the author of *Wenamun* alluded to it repeatedly for just this reason. At the very least, this mythological conflict has been applied to a new region. In The Contendings, Seth thunders only with the permission of Re-Harakhti, an expression of the New Kingdom pharaohs' imperial power. But Zakarbaal says that the Levantine states now have all the thunder. He is undermining Wenamun, as he and his courtiers do throughout the story.

Multiple aspects of Zakarbaal's statement also find echoes in biblical prophetic rhetoric—again, the main evidence we have for Iron Age prophecy in the Levant. His boast about Seth's thunder has especially close biblical cognates in the prophets and beyond, since Yahweh took over the storm-god persona otherwise occupied by Baal in the West Semitic pantheon. Yahweh

---

48. The aforementioned phrase used for Zakarbaal's "crying aloud" (*ꜥš sgp/sgb*) appears at least 15 times in the 20th Dynasty text The Contendings of Horus and Seth (Ramses V; mid-twelfth century)—according to the *TLA*, which lists some 174 occurrences of *ꜥš* alone without *sgb/sgp*. Since Horus was the god of Egyptian kingship and Seth was equated with Baal, it is possible to interpret that story as a contest between Egypt and the Levant. Thus the author of *Wenamun* may have intended to allude to the mythological story of that conflict.

49. Goedicke, "Seth as a Fool," 154; Te Velde, *Seth*, 65.

50. Griffiths, *Conflict of Horus and Seth*. For a survey of past interpretations, see Oden, "Contendings of Horus and Seth," 352–69. The idea that The Contendings is about the unification of North and South under pharaonic rule is grounded ultimately in the idea that it is an *Urgeschichte* of Egypt's original formation as a state, but the Chester Beatty Papyrus on which it is found is from the end of the New Kingdom, when different concerns may well have been in view. See Assmann, *Search for God*, 134–41.

frequently brings thunder (Heb. *qwl/rʿm*; Exod 9:23–34; 1 Sam 2:10; Job 40:9; Ps 29:3) as Seth/Baal is said to in *Wenamun*. Yahweh also sends lightning (often called "fire of God/Yahweh"), including the aforementioned Elijah contest (1 Kgs 18:38; 2 Kgs 1:12; Num 11:1; Job 1:16).

Even Zakarbaal's introductory *mk . . . ʾImn* in the exclamation "Look, Amun thunders in the sky!" is similar to the common oracular opening *hnh yhwh* ("Behold, Yahweh . . ."; Isa 19:1; 22:17; 24:1; 26:21; 62:11; 66:15; Amos 6:11; Mic 1:3).[51] It has been argued that Zakarbaal's use of *mk* here is archaizing and meant to be ironic—in much the same way that the King James-ism "Behold!" sounds archaic to contemporary English speakers.[52]

Isaiah 19:1 nicely combines these two rhetorical features, the mirative introductory particle and the storm-god imagery, in an oracle about Egypt:

> See, Yahweh (*hnh yhwh*) is riding on a swift cloud
>   and comes to Egypt;
> the false gods of Egypt will tremble at his presence,
>   and the heart of Egypt will melt within it.

Isaiah's message here is similar to Zakarbaal's: the gods of Egypt are nothing compared to the storm gods of the Levant. One can see that these sorts of claims could be employed by either side, since later Egyptian hymns turn the tables on the Levantine storm-gods, saying that "Heaven and earth quake in fear for [Amun] in his stormcloud"[53] and that Amun "thundered towards the earth from his storm-cloud."[54] Amun, who was not originally a storm-god, absorbs Seth/Baal's characteristics.

Zakarbaal is a bit more collaborative than Isaiah, however: he emphasizes that Amun and Seth *could* stand side by side, as allies.[55] And he continues by granting Amun his status as primordial creator, and Egypt as the origin of craftsmanship and knowledge: "Now all lands has Amun founded (*grg*). He

---

51. This list could be multiplied greatly by including *hnh*-formulae without the proper divine name *Yhwh*: from the book of Isaiah alone, Isa 3:1; 8:7; 10:33; 13:9, 17; 28:16; 30:27; 35:4; 40:9; 43:19; 48:10; 49:22; 51:22; 65:17–18; 66:12. Such constructions are not so easy to find in NW Semitic inscriptions; the general lack of prophetic oracles in NW Semitic texts contributes to this lacuna.

52. Winand, "L'ironie," 105–10.

53. *nwr n=f p.t t3 m igp=f*; Great Amun Hymn from Hibis, cols. 11–12. Klotz, *Adoration of the Ram*, 87. In his discussion on p. 91, he notes: "Such an expression is somewhat unusual in Egyptian texts."

54. *sgb.n=f m t3 m igb=f*; Urk. VIII, 138b. See discussion at Klotz, *Adoration*, 64.

55. It is possible that Isaiah also envisioned an alliance, but that depends on one's assessment of Isa 19:23–25, which has a remarkably positive vision of Egypt. It is usually taken to be later than the preceding parts of Isa 19, but this is not certain. The issue cannot be addressed here.

founded them only after he had first founded the land of Egypt, the one from which you have come" (2/20).

Again, the later Hebrew prophets use similar rhetoric. The description of Yahweh as founder of the earth is highly characteristic: Jer 10:12; 33:2; 51:5 (*kwn*); Isa 48:13; 51:13, 16; Amos 9:6; Zech 12:1 (*ysd*). Furthermore, prophetic texts like Amos 9:7 and Isa 19:18–25 mention Yahweh working in the histories of other nations.[56] These biblical authors use these international claims to assert the universal lordship of Yahweh, but Zakarbaal has something else in mind—he goes on to argue that Byblos, having absorbed these divine blessings via Egypt, is their true telos: "Thus craftsmanship (*mnḫ[.t]*) came forth from it *just to reach the place where I am*. Thus learning (*sbꜣ*) came forth from it *just to reach the place where I am*!" (2/21–22). The terms the author put in Zakarbaal's mouth have a range of meanings—I have preferred Lichtheim's rendering of *mnḫ.t* (𓏠𓈖𓐍𓏏𓏛) as "craftsmanship" (*COS* 1.41:91) because it seems to be a fairly direct reference back to the boasts about maritime expertise: Egypt may have invented culture, but Byblos's technology is now the state of the art.

Thus a dispute that began over a demand for materials unfolds into a clash of worldviews expressed in theological terms. Wenamun and Zakarbaal, each crafty with words in his own way, vie to assert the dominance of their nations and their gods.

Conclusion

Wenamun sets out on his voyage from Thebes with the expectation that those he meets will readily submit to the decrees of Amun. He meets with success in Lower Egypt, but once he is on the open waters of the Mediterranean, things start to go wrong. He is robbed by one of his own crew, and the local rulers of the coastal cities will not honor his demands. He feels compelled to resort to extreme measures, both practically (by stealing silver from another ship) and theologically (by summoning the bravado to make imperialistic claims on Amun's behalf). This leads to a negotiation with the ruler of Byblos that is couched as a theological debate. The central question is whether Egypt (symbolized by Amun) or Byblos (symbolized by Baal) has the power to command

---

56. The abrupt shift from Isaiah's cursing of Egypt in 19:1–15 to the vision of a community of nations at the end of the chapter (e.g., 19:24: "On that day Israel will be the third with Egypt and Assyria, a blessing in the midst of the earth") usually causes biblical scholars to assign them to different authors, and this is probably correct; however, it is interesting that an aspirational vision of equality follows an effort to put the Egyptian gods in their place, as in *Wenamun*.

the resources of the Lebanon. The rhetoric of the two men shows an array of theological ideas and debates that were shared not only between Byblos and Egypt, but have extensive echoes in the biblical text as well. Prominent among these is the question of which deity controls the awe-inspiring power to thunder.

Excursus: Wenamun's "Crazy Crusade"

The speeches by Zakarbaal and Wenamun in 2/10–37 form a theological crux. In the long-running debate about the broader meaning of the story, much depends on the interpretation of this exchange. Is the story a satire about a foolish religious extremist on a crazy mission,[1] or is it a sincere assertion of Amun's universal authority?

At the core of the exchange is a repeated phrase that sheds light on those questions. Zakarbaal ends his speech by asking, "What is the sense of this foolish journey (*mšꜥ śwgꜣ*) that they have made you do?" (2/22)—and Wenamun begins his by protesting, "Wrong! It is not a foolish journey (*mšꜥ śwgꜣ*) that I am on!" (2/23). Since *mšꜥ* is also the common term for a military campaign, one could translate "crazy campaign," or even, in light of the overtly religious justification for the mission, "crazy crusade."

It has not been noted that the author's use of *śwgꜣ* (𓊃𓅱𓎼𓄿𓀸)[2] appears to extend the story's rumination on ecstatic prophecy beyond the earlier episode in 1/38–40. The verb *śwgꜣ* means "to be silly, foolish, or stupefied,"[3] and a related noun refers to an immature child.[4] The verb *śwgꜣ* is also used in the Hymn to Hapy of the gushing overflow the Nile flood, which "makes the fields drink"[5]—in this image, the hymn's author seems to portray the fields as drunk with water. This already is suggestive of divinatory practice, since prophets in

---

1. E.g., Osing, "Die Beziehungen Ägyptens," 39.
2. This term is transliterated as *swgꜣ* by Ritner and others, because /s/ and /š/ had fallen together by this stage of the language.
3. *Wb* 4, 76.8: "töricht sein"; cf. *DLE* 2:22.
4. *Wb* 4, 76.9–10: "unmündiges Kind"; thus Winand, "Report," 546: "childish enterprises." As discussed above, the crucial term for the ecstatic prophet in *Wenamun*, ꜥḏd, is very close to the term for "child," so it might have created a double entendre in which all the prophets in the story are being belittled as childish.
5. The Hymn to Hapy 9,6 // §7,5; translation by Lichtheim, *AEL* 1:207.

the ancient world seem sometimes to have used alcohol to commune with the divine and loosen their lips;[6] but the connection is even more explicit.

The term *šwgꜣ* leads us into an interesting and significant set of Semitic cognates used to refer to uncontrolled and unstable things, particularly raving prophets. The Akkadian verb *šegû(m)* similarly means "to be wild, rage," and is applied to rabid dogs and other wild animals, and by extension to angry spouses and political rebels—people who are deemed mad and unstable.[7] It is also equated with the technical prophetic term *maḫû/muḫḫû* ("to be ecstatic"/"ecstatic prophet"),[8] which has well-known attestations in both Mari and Nineveh.[9]

Akkadian *šegû(m)* was used from the Old Babylonian period onward, and *šwgꜣ* appears in the New Kingdom and is consistently written in group writing, meaning that it was likely understood as a foreign word. Thus we may proceed with the hypothesis that *šwgꜣ* is a loanword from Semitic.[10]

Akkadian *šegû(m)* is also cognate with Hebrew *š-g-ʿ*,[11] which is used contemptuously and mockingly of the prophets.[12] One of these scenes also involves a political rebellion, when Elisha sends a disciple to anoint Jehu king, and the other officers ask, "Why did that madman (*mešuggāʿ*) come to you?" (2 Kgs 9:11). In seeking to deflect the question, Jehu answers, "You know the sort and how they babble." Jeremiah 29:26 refers to the right of a priest to install "officers in the house of Yahweh to control any madman (*ʾîš mešuggāʿ*) who prophesies, to put him in the stocks and the collar." And Hos 9:7 laments the days in which the nation is hostile to prophecy and cries, "The prophet is a fool, / the man of the spirit is mad (*mešuggāʿ*)!" Forms of *š-g-ʿ* are also used of divinely inflicted madness in the covenant curses of Deut 28:28, 31. Again, all of this correlates nicely with Zakarbaal's message to Wenamun, that his mission is both crazy and a transgression of political power.

---

6. The Hebrew prophets sometimes allude to prophets and diviners as drunk (Isa 19:11–15; 28:7; Jer 23:9). The Mari letter ARM 26 207 alludes to giving diviners something to drink, but it is not clear whether this refers to alcohol; see Nissinen, *Prophets and Prophecy*, 41–43; Nissinen, *Ancient Prophecy*, 182–83; Stökl, *Prophecy*, 49–50. For Egyptian divination involving alcohol, see Bryan, "Hatshepsut," 93–123; Hays, "'Those Weaned from Milk,'" 61–89.

7. (AHw. 1208f; CAD Š/2, 260a); per CAD, the root is used of mad dogs and wives who fly into a rage and kill their husbands. At Mari, in a letter from Kibri-Dagan regarding a rebellion (ARM 3 18: 15), we get: *kīma kalbim šagêm ašar inaššaku ul idi*, "Like a mad dog, I do not know whom he will bite."

8. Freedman, *Tablets 41–63*, 18. (No. 43 r.5–6).

9. For an overview, see Nissinen, *Prophets and Prophecy*, 6–7.

10. I am grateful to Thomas Schneider for his correspondence on this point. The earliest attestations of *šwgꜣ* are in pAnastasi V and VII. It is not related to *swgg*, "to ruin," or *sgi*, "to marvel at."

11. Tawil, *Akkadian Lexical Companion*, 388–89; HALOT, s.v. שׁגע.

12. Parker, "Possession Trance and Prophecy," 282–83.

Although the functional similarity among Akk. *šegû*, Heb. *š-g-ʿ* and Eg. *śwgȝ* is clear, the assertion that they are cognate requires comment from a phonological standpoint. The correspondence Eg. /ś/ = Semitic /ṯ/ = Hebrew and Akkadian /š/ was normal prior to the first millennium,[13] and it is not surprising that the sharing of the term reaches that far back, since many Egyptian and Semitic terms were transmitted early on.[14] However, as reflected by the later Coptic form, the root of *śwgȝ* is *s(w)g*.[15] This is not a serious problem for the theory, however, since weak verbs were commonly reanalyzed to create biforms that coexisted in Semitic languages; examples in the case of II-weak and III-weak biforms include בוז/בזה "to despise" and גור/גרה "to attack, stir up strife." Examples of II-weak and geminate biforms include מוש/משש "to feel, grope"; צור/צרר "to bind, confine, besiege"; צור/צרר "to attack"; and רום/רמם "to rise, exalt oneself."[16]

In the Semitic languages, it appears *šegû(m)* was similarly received in various ways. There appear to have been *intra-Semitic* developments that led to not only *šgʿ*, but also Heb. *šgh*(=*šgy*)/*šgʾ*/*šgg*. As is recognized in *HALOT*, etc., these latter three are all triforms: *šgh/šgʾ* meaning "to stray, stagger, do wrong," or in the causative Hiphil form, "to lead astray"; and *šgg* meaning "to make a mistake, go astray." The root *šgy* is also attested in Phoenician, where it refers to wild beasts just as *šegû* does in Akkadian, and there are also cognates in various forms of Aramaic.[17] Given that the Egyptian system did not systematically use trilateral roots, it is even more likely that a weak verb such as *šegû(m)* would have been reanalyzed upon reception, rendering *s(w)g*.

The likelihood that Hebrew speakers viewed the aforementioned Hebrew roots as related is demonstrated when Isaiah uses *šgh* three times of false and misleading prophets, in much the same way that *šgʿ* is used:[18]

But these are also muddled (*šgw*) by wine and dazed by liquor:
    Priest and prophet are muddled (*šgw*) by liquor;
They are confused by wine; They are dazed by liquor;

---

13. Quack, review of *Egyptian Proper Names*.
14. Noonan, *Non-Semitic Loanwords*, 306–7, 314–15.
15. The element *gȝ* is simply group writing for the g sound.
16. Reymond, *Intermediate Biblical Hebrew Grammar*, 38; see 39–46 for numerous related examples.
17. *HALOT*, ad loc.; *DNWSI*, 1108–9. Notably, *š-g-ʾ* occurs with the sense of "lead astray" in Official Aramaic, in Aḥiqar 137. Forms of *š-g-ʿ* do not seem to appear in the existing corpus of NW Semitic extrabiblical inscriptions.
18. Ezekiel 34:6 uses the same verb to describe the misled people: "My sheep were scattered [*yšgw*], they wandered over all the mountains and on every high hill; my sheep were scattered over all the face of the earth, with no one to search or seek for them."

They are muddled (šgw) in their visions; They stumble in judgment. (Isa 28:7, NJPS)

Isaiah revels in wordplay on similar-sounding words, and so may have meant to evoke more than one of the aforementioned meanings of šgʿ/šgh/šgʾ/šgg.[19]

An alternative to the etymological connections proposed here would be to analyze Egyptian śwgȝ as related to swḫȝ (the causative of wḫȝ, meaning "to make a fool of"), but this /ḫ/ > /g/ shift is not characteristic in Egyptian, nor is this theory followed in the newly published *Egyptian Root Lexicon*.[20] The theory of a Semitic connection is preferable, especially since śwgȝ is Late Egyptian, *Wenamun* is set in a West Semitic linguistic context, and the story has numerous other Semitic loanwords in it.

To bring the discussion full circle, this usage to describe the raging or drunken confusion of prophets fits with prophetic practice in the ancient Near East, and also with the Hymn to Hapy's use of śwgȝ to describe the inundation's "inebriation" of the fields. It appears that in *Wenamun*, Zakarbaal is similarly insulting Wenamun by saying that he is acting drunk, and that his prophetic declarations on behalf of Amun are false and empty.[21]

The fact that Wenamun immediately picks up on and responds to Zakarbaal's insult is another indication that the two men are not speaking on different levels, but rather seem to understand each other reasonably well.[22] This has not always been recognized. Assmann has written: "In Wenamun's report of his travels in the eleventh century B.C.E., the appearance of a Syrian ecstatic is described with all the trappings of the exotic," and he uses this observation as proof that the Egyptians viewed prophecy as foreign even in this period.[23] And yet Wenamun and Zakarbaal have no trouble understanding each other, and they sound so similar—and Wenamun is for the most part announcing theologies that were well known in connection with Amun in Egypt. Perhaps the two cultures had more in common than is often granted.

---

19. Roberts, "Double Entendre in First Isaiah," 39–48.
20. śwgȝ is not connected to any Egyptian verbal root: Satzinger and Stefanović, *Egyptian Root Lexicon*, 363.
21. Although Zakarbaal is known to employ ecstatic prophets himself, he is not exactly in awe of his own prophet's words in support of Wenamun either.
22. Pace Schipper (*Die Erzählung*, 268) who remarks that whereas Zakarbaal seems to be commenting on Wenamun's lack of practical preparedness when he calls the mission "crazy," "Wenamuns Antwort auf einer ganz anderen Ebene liegt" ("Wenamun's answer is on a completely different level").
23. Assmann, *Search for God*, 154.

CHAPTER 4

Amun and Yahweh as Sovereigns and Suzerains

IT IS TO BE EXPECTED that when competing systems of viewing the world encounter each other, they may vie for supremacy and generate conflict. As Gerald Moers has written, Wenamun's and Zakarbaal's ideological worlds overlap, but "the representation of one world places a question mark behind the other."[1] Only one of these worldviews can be true; the other must be false. Having been challenged by Zakarbaal, Wenamun seeks to assert Amun's sovereignty, and his right to impose duties on the ruler and inhabitants of the land. These ideas will be familiar to students of Hebrew prophecy and biblical law, especially in relation to ancient Near Eastern treaties and loyalty oaths.

After denying that his mission is mad, Wenamun responds to Zakarbaal by contradicting his claims for Seth-Baal entirely, and asserting Amun's lordship over the entire region: "There is not any ship upon the river that does not belong to Amun. His is the sea and his is the Lebanon, about which you say: 'It is mine'" (2/23–28). Even Amun's sacred barge, Amunuserhat, is "the lord of every ship" (*p3 nb n im.w nb*; 2/25)!

This is radical language from the standpoint of a Mediterranean political economy which, at that point, required cooperative work—but it was also largely in keeping with totalizing Amun theologies that developed during the New Kingdom, especially in the wake of the Amarna Period (see chapter 1). Gerald Moers has argued that the statue of Amun that Wenamun brings along is "a metaphor for the New Kingdom concept of 'Amun' himself."[2] He is symbolically bringing Amun's rule to the Levant.

There is a disjunction, however, between that older era, when such claims were plausible, and the current situation in the story. Indeed, one of its basic "running jokes" is that Wenamun consistently comes up with theological

---

1. Moers, *Fingierte Welten*, 270: "Wenamuns und Tjekerbaals Welten stehen vielmehr unvermittelt nebeneinander, während die Repräsentation der einen das Fragezeichen hinter der je anderen Welt markiert."
2. Moers, "Travel as Narrative," 54; Moers, *Fingierte Welten*, 272.

claims based on outdated assumptions, only to be regarded quizzically by his Levantine interlocutors. Even Hans Goedicke, who regards the whole exchange with Zakarbaal as a good deal more friendly than many interpreters do, calls Wenamun's speech to Zakarbaal "a remarkable piece of sophism."[3]

It is not feasible to present here a full picture of Amun theology as it flourished in the New Kingdom,[4] but a limited number of examples in the pages that follow illustrate key points of continuity.

The New Kingdom hymn to Amun from P.Leiden I 350 is particularly relevant for understanding the ideology Wenamun expounds, in that it also expresses Amun's ownership of the trees used for his sacred bark:

> Every region is in awe of you [Amun],
> even those in the Underworld praise your majesty;
> Your name is exalted and your power mighty,
> Euphrates and the circling ocean dread you;
> [Hapy?] makes offering to you when he arrives on earth
> and among the islands in the Great Green Sea [i.e., the Mediterranean].
> Deserts and mountains descend to you,
> and [fertile] land lies in fear of you.
> ...
> Coniferous trees grow tall for you (*srwd n≠k ꜥš*)[5] ...
> to decorate your splendid bark, Userhat.
> Mountains of stone flow down to you
> to elevate the gates [of your sanctuary].
> Nile-ships and ships of the open sea are out on the waters
> (*mnš.w ḥr ym ḥry.[t] ḫr-mt[r]w*)
> laden and headed for your presence. ...
> There is no god who is so far-reaching [as you],
> the entire [earth] is your domain.[6]

This hymn is found on the recto of a papyrus whose verso contains an actual ship's log. If this reflects a connection between the hymn's theologies and the actual practice of trade, then it could hardly be more relevant to the case at hand:[7] it expresses the imperial ideology that empowered New Kingdom

---

3. Goedicke, *Report*, 88.
4. See further Sethe, *Amun*; Assmann, *Egyptian Solar Religion*, passim.
5. Despite the identical consonants with the verb ꜥš discussed earlier, this term for the Lebanese trees is written differently, and is unrelated.
6. Foster and Hollis, *Hymns*, 68. For the Egyptian text, see Mathieu, "Études de métrique égyptienne," 136–37.
7. Janssen, *Two Ancient Egyptian Ship's Logs*; Vinson, "Boats (Use of)."

Egypt's control of the Mediterranean and its resources. *Wenamun* also shows some influence from administrative scribal practices.[8]

This theology of Amun's lordship was repeatedly expressed and widely propagated, not only in the New Kingdom in texts such as the Cairo Hymns to Amun (P.Boulaq 17), but also in later Amun hymns such as those from the temple in Hibis built by Persian emperors:

> [His] titulary is from the mountains to the sea as Amun-who-endures-in-everything,
> this noble god who began the world through his plans.
> nḥb(.t)[⸗f] m ḏw.w r nwn [m] ʾImn-mn-m-ḫ.t-nb
> nṯr pn šps šꜣꜥ tꜣ m sḫr.w⸗f[9]

Taken together, this evidence shows the endurance of Amun theocracy, its transmission to foreign nations, and even its employment there.

Divine Kings and Their Property

Having asserted Amun's ownership, Wenamun goes on to demand: "You are prepared to haggle over the Lebanon with Amun, its lord?" (2/28).[10] This has quite specific biblical cognates, since Yahweh, too, is portrayed as having lordship over the Lebanon (Isa 35:2; 60:13; Ezek 31:15–16); as dominating it (Isa 2:14; 10:33; Ps 29:5–6); and even as having planted its famed cedars (Ps 104:16).

Wenamun also cautions Zakarbaal: "Do not desire for yourself the property of Amun-Re, King of the Gods!" (2/33–34: m-ir mr n≠k nkt n ʾImn≠Rʿ [ny-sw.t] nṯr.w). In the Hebrew Bible, the property of Yahweh is also jealously guarded; beyond the general prohibitions of covetousness,[11] there is an entire category of spoils that are specifically designated as Yahweh's property—that which is ḥerem, traditionally rendered "dedicated to the ban." Various biblical narratives illustrate the seriousness of this prohibition. Saul forfeits his right to reign Israel most directly by violating the terms of the ban after a battle against Amalek (1 Sam 15). And Josh 7 tells the story of Achan, a military man who keeps

---

8. As noted in chapter 1, *Wenamun* was written down the length of a roll of papyrus, like a ship's log or other administrative document; this is unusual among literary texts, which are more typically written across the scroll, and it has sometimes been taken as evidence that *Wenamun* is a historical document. That is unlikely for reasons already discussed, but it may reflect that the scribe had a background writing administrative texts. See Spalinger, "Wenamun," esp. 192–97.

9. Great Amun Hymn, cols. 4–5; see Klotz, *Adoration*, 74–75.

10. Lichtheim, *COS* 1.41 (p. 91).

11. Heb. ḥmd; e.g., Exod 20:17; Deut 5:21.

some of the spoils of war after the fall of Jericho. In the story's denouement, he confesses: "When I saw among the spoil a beautiful mantle from Shinar, and two hundred shekels of silver, and a bar of gold weighing fifty shekels, then I coveted them and took them. They now lie hidden in the ground inside my tent, with the silver underneath" (Josh 7:21). Then "all Israel" stones him to death and burns him and his household (7:25–26).

Wenamun gives Zakarbaal a warning about coveting Amun's posessions when he adds, "A lion loves his property!" (*y3 m3i mr 3ḫ.t=f*; 2/34).[12] Yahweh, too, was portrayed as a lion who loves his property and territory in Isa 31:4:

> As a lion or a young lion growls over its prey,
>   and, when a band of shepherds is called out against it,
> is not terrified by their shouting
>   or daunted at their noise,
> so Yahweh of hosts will come down
>   to fight upon Mount Zion and upon its hill.

Yahweh is similarly portrayed in Jeremiah as a lion that scares away his opposition (49:19; 50:44).[13] In Amos he inspires fear with his roar (1:2; 3:8), and in Hosea he is a lion who savages his prey (5:14; 13:7–8) but also leads his people like a pride (11:10).

In Ezekiel one sees a contest of power analogous to that between Zakarbaal's Byblos and Egypt, when Ezekiel delivers this word from Yahweh to the pharaoh:

> You consider yourself a lion among the nations,
>   but you are like a dragon in the seas;
> you thrash about in your streams,
>   trouble the water with your feet,
>   and foul your streams. (Ezek 32:2)

Here, as in *Wenamun*, Egypt imagines itself as a lion; Ezekiel and Zakarbaal both try to put the lion in its place.

Lion iconography was commonly used for the pharaoh during the Late Bronze Age Egyptian imperial period, and it continued on mass-produced goods from close to the time of *Wenamun*—the Iron I–IIA (21st and 22nd

---

12. This passage is discussed in Strawn, *What Is Stronger?*, 205. See also Schipper, *Die Erzählung*, 198–99.

13. Often, however, these images of the leonine Yahweh are reversed, so that Israel and Judah are the prey (Jer 25:38; Lam 3:10; Hos 5:14; 13:7–8; Amos 3:8).

Dynasties). Othmar Keel has argued that such iconography reflects the adaptation of Egyptian culture to that of its territories, which he calls "de-Egyptianization," in the period of imperial rule over the Levant.[14] Based on their rough workmanship, these goods were initially thought to have been made in the Levant, but more recently Stephan Münger has argued that they were made in Egypt.[15] If so, they were still brought in large numbers to the Levant, where more than two hundred have been excavated at sites throughout ancient Israel and Judah—literally from Dan to Beersheba (and beyond). Wherever the artifacts were made, they indicate the prominent role of leonine imagery in the discourse of power between Egypt and the Levant in the Iron Age.

Amun's dominion and ownership are the keys to Wenamun's reasoning, and these totalizing claims also resonate with the Yahwistic rhetoric of the Hebrew Bible, such as Exod 19:5 ("the whole earth is mine") or Deut 10:14–15 ("heaven and the heaven of heavens belong to Yahweh your God, the earth with all that is in it"). It scarcely needs to be stated that lordship over the earth is a common assertion of the Hebrew prophets and other theologians (Josh 3:11, 13; Ps 97:5; Isa 6:3; 37:16, 20; Mic 4:13; Zech 4:14; 6:5; 14:9).

A very similar dispute to Wenamun's, over the ultimate ownership of territory, plays out in Ezekiel's oracle against the pharaoh in 29:3–10, and again one sees how the same rhetoric was used on both sides. The pharaoh is portrayed as saying, "My Nile is my own; I made it for myself" (29:3). And in response, Yahweh says, "The land of Egypt shall be a desolation and a waste. Then they shall know that I am Yahweh. Because he (i.e., pharaoh[16]) said, 'The Nile is mine, and I made it,' therefore, I am against you, and against your channels, and I will make the land of Egypt an utter waste and desolation" (29:9–10). As in *Wenamun*, these theological claims are ultimately expressions of imperial aspirations. As in the Exodus story, Yahweh's power and dominion confront that of pharaoh and the Egyptian gods. On the human plane, one sees similar *royal* rhetoric in the Bible, such as Ben-hadad of Aram's assertion to Ahab of Israel that, "Your silver and gold are mine; your pretty wives and children also are mine" (1 Kgs 20:3). Similarly, in Ezek 18:4, Yahweh asserts that "all lives are mine," and in Ps 50:9–10, Yahweh says, "I will not accept a bull from your house, / or goats from your folds. / For every wild animal of the forest is mine, / the cattle on a thousand hills." The message to the human audience is

---

14. Keel, *Studien zu den Stempelsiegeln*, 232.

15. Münger, "Egyptian Stamp-Seal Amulets," 381–403. He is followed by Schipper, who judges that these items should be understood as reflecting intra-Egyptian cultural developments (*Die Erzählung*, 300–308, 331).

16. See 29:2–3. The Versions correct this to 2ms ("you said"), but the shifting perspective is relatively normal in prophetic address.

that an animal sacrifice will do no good because the animals already belong to Yahweh.

It is not surprising, then, that in monotheizing texts such as the latter portions of Isaiah, this doctrine is extended to its logical, universal extreme. It envisions Yahweh enthroned over heaven and earth as its creator:

> Heaven is my throne,
> and the earth is my footstool...
> All these things my hand has made,
> and so all these things are mine.[17] (Isa 66:1–2)

This again has precedents in Amun theology, as in the hymn to Amun-Re from P.Cairo 58032:

> [Amun] reaches the ends of eternity, circles about the sky,
> traverses the place below to brighten the world he had created.
> The god who fashioned himself on his own,
> who created heaven and earth to his desire.

Such divine-enthronement language is of course widespread in the ancient world; taken by itself, it would not be remarkable. However, in the context of the broader picture of this give-and-take between Egyptian and Levantine theological rhetoric, it provides yet another point of contact.

The same can be said for other aspects of Wenamun's speech that are not distinctively characteristic of biblical texts, yet would be fully at home there. One might return, for example, to Wenamun's claim that Amun is "King of Gods" (*ny-sw.t ntr.w*; 2/25, 30). This is not a Levantine rhetorical feature as such, since Amun(-Re) is called the same in Egypt,[18] but it is another way in which the theological claims of the two cultures clearly overlap. Although one might expect the title "King of the Gods" to be more at home in polytheistic texts,[19] numerous biblical texts assert Yahweh's reign over the gods: Ps 95:3 calls him "a great King above all gods"; Deut 10:17 and Josh 22:22 call him "God of gods." His ascendance in power is the focus of Ps 82: "God has taken his place in the divine council; in the midst of the gods he judges" (82:1). And having found the other gods lacking, he announces, "You are gods, children of the Most High, all of you; nevertheless, you shall die like mortals, and fall

---

17. So 𝔊 (καὶ ἔστιν ἐμά), supported by 𝔗 and 𝔖. MT/1QIsa[b] ויהי. 1QIsa[a] והיו.
18. For various titles, see Leitz, *Lexikon der Ägyptischen Götter*, I.321, etc.
19. The same epithets occur for various Egyptian deities, and a similar rhetoric of divine kingship is well attested in Mesopotamia; see Lambert, *Babylonian Creation Myths*, 248–78.

like one of the princes" (82:6). The psalmist closes with an announcement of Yahweh's rule: "Rise up, O God, judge the earth, for you have inherited all the nations!" (82:8). And he also judges the gods of other nations in Exod 12:12; Num 33:4; Jer 46:25; and Zeph 2:11. (In Hebrew and other Semitic languages, "judging" [*špṭ*] can denote a ruling function as well as a juridical one.)

In sum, Amun and Yahweh are spoken of in strikingly similar terms as divine sovereigns and the rightful lords of the whole earth. While these claims were certainly made widely in the ancient Near East, they are consistent with the observation of a shared theological outlook that was part of the conversation between Egypt and the Levant already in the time of *Wenamun*. Many of the same forms of rhetoric continued in the eras when the Hebrew prophetic and historical literature were formed.

Treaty and Covenant Motifs in Wenamun and the Bible

One of the privileges of a powerful king in the ancient Near East was to dictate the terms of treaties and oaths to vassals and other subordinates. The more powerful party was known as the suzerain,[20] and the treaties as suzerainty treaties. An early major corpus of these treaties comes from the Hittite Empire of the Late Bronze Age, and another collection of loyalty oaths issued by the Neo-Assyrian Empire has also survived.

Biblical covenants are often compared with suzerainty treaties. In Deuteronomy, for example, Yahweh takes on the role of the human ruler and the laws are analogous to the stipulations of a treaty. These covenants, with their divine suzerain, are sometimes considered unique and special adaptations of a secular form, but Wenamun shows some of the same slippage between the human and divine. The diplomatic/treaty associations of *Wenamun* have occasionally been observed, but not the classic covenantal language with which they are so closely connected.[21]

In the midst of his speech to Zakarbaal, Wenamun reminds the Byblian ruler that there was a tradition of the Levant being subject to Egypt: he opens with a curt demand to supply the timber as "your father did, and . . . the father of your father did" (2/4–5). Later, he reiterates: "[Amun] is the lord of your fathers (*nb nꜣy⸗k ity.w*). They spent their lifetimes offering to Amun" (2/31–32). And indeed Egypt had dominated the Levant as part of its New Kingdom empire, as attested by the Amarna Letters and by ample evidence of Egyptian garrisons and settlements in the area.

---

20. This was a French term for a feudal lord, and etymologically related to "sovereign."
21. E.g., Goedicke, *Report*, 7; de Spens, "Droit internationale et commerce," 105–26.

Such reminders about past subjugation are standard language in suzerainty treaties; for example, Hittite treaties regularly begin with historical prologues summarizing a history in which the forefathers of the current vassal king were loyal to the Hittite emperor, and impressing on him the importance of doing likewise. In a treaty with Tuppi-Teššup of Amurru, Mursili II impressed on the Amorite the importance of paying tribute as his forefathers had:

> Aziru, your [grandfather], became the subject of my father.... [and] did not become hostile.... I have now made you swear an oath to the King of Hatti and the land of Hatti, and to my sons and grandsons. Observe the oath and the authority of the King.... The tribute which was imposed upon your grandfather and upon your father shall be imposed upon you: They paid 300 shekels of refined gold by the weights of Hatti, first-class and good. You shall pay it likewise. You shall not turn your eyes to another. Your ancestors paid tribute to Egypt, [but] you [shall not pay it].[22]

Similarly, Suppiluliuma I ordered Niqmaddu II of Ugarit: "As previously your forefathers were at peace with Hatti and not hostile, now you, Niqmaddu, shall thus be hostile to my enemy and at peace with my friend."[23] These sorts of injunctions to continue past faithful actions are a key aspect of the treaties' ideology.[24]

In the Amarna letters, also from the Late Bronze Age, Phoenician kings express this same intergenerational submission to Egypt and its rulers. For example, in EA 118:39–44, Rib-Hadda of Byblos writes: "Look, as for me, it is my intent [t]o serve the king according to the manner of my fathers, so may the king send his regular troops and may he pacify his land."[25] And in EA 150:33–37, Abi-Milki of Tyre: "[I]n the stre[et I will pro]claim. I will give lumber and wine. The king, my lord, [g]ave to my fathers, to my fathers (and) the gods. To the king, my lord, have I sent."[26] Other letters from larger powers express hopes for intergenerational friendship with Egypt (e.g., Karaduniash in EA 8:8–12; Mitanni in 27:9–12). We consider below what role actual treaties may have played in Egypt's international relationships.

---

22. CTH 62; Beckman, *Hittite Diplomatic Texts*, 55–56.
23. CTH 46; Beckman, *Hittite Diplomatic Texts*, 119.
24. For another example, Tudhaliya II of Hatti says to Sunaššura of Kizzuwatna, "Formerly, in the time of my grandfather, Kizzuwatna came into the possession of Hatti" (*CTH* 41, 131; Beckman, *Hittite Diplomatic Texts*, 14).
25. Rainey, *El-Amarna Correspondence*, 626–27.
26. Rainey, *El-Amarna Correspondence*, 760–61.

This same sort of covenant language, with its emphasis on memory and the tradition of submission from the time of the fathers/ancestors, is frequently adopted in biblical covenants as well. For example, Deut 6:1–3 commands "you and your children and your children's children" to "fear Yahweh your God all the days of your life, and keep all his decrees and his commandments... so that it may go well with you, and so that you may multiply greatly in a land flowing with milk and honey, as Yahweh, the God of your fathers, has promised you." Comparable rhetoric about multigenerational loyalty can be found in Deut 1:11, 21; 4:1; 12:1; 27:3; Josh 18:3; 24:2, 6; and 1 Sam 12:7.

Even the direct-genitive construction of the Egyptian phrase *nb nȝy=k ity.w* ("lord of your fathers") mirrors the common Hebrew construction *ʾĕlōhê ʾăbôtêhem*, "god of your fathers."[27] Similar reasoning underlies the biblical emphasis on Yahweh as "the god of the father(s)" (Gen 26:24; 28:13, etc.; Exod 3:6, 13, 15; 2 Kgs 20:5 // Isa 38:5; Ezra 8:28; 10:11). This appeal to a tradition of submission is thus part of the rhetoric of both *Wenamun* and the Hebrew Bible.

Another keyword in *Wenamun* is the "commands/commissions" (*sḥn.w*)[28] of Amun (2/3, 6, 11, 33, 47, 61[×2]). These play a role analogous to the "commandments of Yahweh" (*miṣvôt Yhwh*) in Biblical Hebrew. The term *sḥn.w* is much more commonly used of the orders and missions of pharaohs and other human authorities,[29] and so it serves to reinforce the theme of divine suzerainty from Semitic texts. Amun and Yahweh both take on the role of a human ruler who imposes stipulations.

In considering how Wenamun's demands would have struck the ears of Zakarbaal and the rest of the Phoenician audience, one might contrast the rather different approach of Solomon when he came to the Phoenicians with a goal similar to Wenamun's: building the Jerusalem Temple.[30] Although the biblical authors were not modest about claiming broad sovereignty for Solomon—even supposedly over Phoenician Tyre[31]—they also portrayed him as far more generous and politic in requesting timber from a Phoenician king. In 1 Kgs 5, Solomon begins by explaining to Hiram why he now wishes to build, and then comes to the point: "Therefore command that cedars from

---

27. One would not want to overemphasize this normal Egyptian construction, but the previous epithet for Amun does use the preposition: *nb n pȝ ʿnḫ snb*, "Lord of life and health."
28. These are all written with the -*w* ending, though Ritner omits it.
29. There are 60 attestations of *sḥn(.w)* in *TLA*.
30. See further on this comparison López-Ruiz, *Phoenicians*, 284–85; Schipper, *Die Erzählung*, 209–11; Schipper, *Israel und Ägypten in der Königszeit*, 61–64.
31. 1 Kings 4:21, 24: "Solomon was sovereign over all the kingdoms from the Euphrates to the land of the Philistines, even to the border of Egypt; they brought tribute and served Solomon all the days of his life.... For he had dominion over all the region west of the Euphrates from Tiphsah to Gaza, over all the kings west of the Euphrates; and he had peace on all sides."

the Lebanon be cut for me. My servants will join your servants, and I will give you whatever wages you set for your servants; for you know that there is no one among us who knows how to cut timber like the Sidonians" (1 Kgs 5:6). In effect, Solomon offers to let Hiram name his price, which ends up being large amounts of grain and oil paid to Hiram every year: 20,000 kors of wheat and 20 kors of fine oil (1 Kgs 5:11).[32] He also collaboratively offers to supply some of the labor for the project, while simultaneously acknowledging the Tyrians' superior expertise in the area of timber.

Wenamun is far less politic in his approach to the Phoenicians in Byblos. Zakarbaal is immediately put off by the Egyptian's lack of documentation and haughty bearing, and asks, "On what commission have you come?" (2/3). Wenamun responds imperiously: "It is in pursuit of the timber for the great and noble bark of Amon-Re, King of the Gods, that I have come. What your father did, and what the father of your father did, you shall do also!" (2/4–5).

Zakarbaal is quite blunt: "If you pay me for doing it then I shall do it . . . what is it that you have brought to me for my part?" (2/6–8). He has the ledgers of past business between Byblos and Egypt brought to him, which shows that past pharaohs, even in their imperial glory, had previously brought payment in advance for timber (2/7–8). He goes on:

> Were the ruler of Egypt the lord of what is mine, and I his servant as well, would he have caused silver and gold to be brought to say: "Perform the commission of Amun!"? Wasn't it the delivery of royal gifts that he used to perform for my father? Now as for me myself, I am not your servant, nor am I the servant of the one who sent you either. (2/10–13)

In this speech, Zakarbaal not only reminds Wenamun of how the system of exchange is supposed to work but also explicitly rejects the idea that Wenamun or Herihor has the right to impose terms upon him as if he were a vassal—a servant.

It probably never was quite so simple as Wenamun's demand might suggest. Zakarbaal's expectations—to be paid in kind and addressed respectfully—are consistent not only with the Solomon story, but with the system of royal gifts among the Late Bronze Age powers, as reflected in the Amarna Letters.[33] There, kings whose nations were part of the "Club of Great Powers" called each other "brother," and exchanged gifts that were essentially a form of elite trade. Gerhard Herm has captured the contrast between Wenamun's expectations and Zakarbaal's reply with dry humor: "This reply must have

---

32. A kor is estimated at 350–400 liters. (See Powell, "Weights and Measures," 904.)
33. Cline and Yasur-Landau, "Nature and Destination," 127.

completely staggered Wen-Amon; it was quite unprecedented. Did this man have the effrontery to talk of payment? Where were his manners? On the Nile one never did business, one gave generously that which was due to the gods, and if one or the other of their earthly representatives profited thereby, one was tactful enough not to mention it—it was an understood thing."[34] But of course, there were always misunderstandings, even in more stable times. The Late Bronze Age exchanges were framed amicably, but they often led to gripes and complaints. A certain amount of haggling and gamesmanship seems to have been part of the royal gift exchanges. For example, Kadašman-Enlil, the king of Babylon, complains to the pharaoh, "It was just 30 minas of gold that you [sent me]. My [gi]ft [does not amoun]t to what [I have given you] every yea[r]" (EA 3:21–22). The king of Assyria writes to the pharaoh to complain that he has received less gold than other rulers: " I am the [equal] of the king of Ḫanigalbat, but you sent me [only x minas] of gold, and it is not enough [for the pay] of my messengers on the journey to and back!" (EA 16:26–31). Other letters say that the gold sent is so impure that when melted down it is only a quarter of the amount claimed (EA 7 and 10). The originally friendly agreement between Solomon and Hiram in 1 Kings also leads to hard feelings: we read that Solomon later adds twenty cities in the Galilee to Hiram's compensation, but Hiram is not happy with them (9:11–12). So perhaps Solomon got the better of the deal.

A bit of haggling seems to have been normal. So Zakarbaal might have expected to have to bargain indirectly with an Egyptian representative seeking timber, but he did not expect to have him attempt to dictate terms. He is trying to have business conversation, while Wenamun is issuing ultimatums from an imperial deity.

Wenamun picks up on Zakarbaal's rejection and answers it. He reasserts Amun's sovereignty and repeats that Amun was "lord of your fathers" (2/31). He may be sputtering a bit at this point, however, based on the repeated verbiage: "You also—! *You* are a servant of Amun!" (*mntk m-rꜣ-ꜥ mntk bꜣkỉ n ꜣImn*; 2/32). Wenamun is demanding that Zakarbaal be subject to Amun, whom he happens to represent, and serve him. The equivalent Hebrew phrase, "servant of the Lord" (*ʿbd yhwh*), is regularly used in biblical literature of human leaders who faithfully carry out divine commissions (e.g., Moses in Deut 34:5; Josh 1:1, etc.; 2 Kgs 18:12; 2 Chr 1:3; Josh 24:29; Joshua in Judg 2:8; David in Pss 18:1; 36:1; Zerubbabel in 1 Esd 6:27; and an unnamed leader in Isa 42:1, 19; 49:6).

Wenamun goes on to exhort Zakarbaal to submit to the god's demands: "If you say 'I shall act, I shall act' to Amun, and you accomplish his commission, you will live; you will prosper; you will be healthy; and you will be fortunate

---

34. Herm, *Phoenicians*, 47.

in your entire land and your people" (2/32–33; *ir iw=k dd iry sp-2 n 'Imn mtw=k 'r'r p3y=f shn iw=k 'nh mtw=k wd3 mtw=k snb mtw=k nfr n p3y=k t3 [r] dr.w=f n3y=k rmt.w*). With its allusions to blessings for the people and the land for faithfulness, this is perhaps the weightiest of the similarities to ancient Near Eastern treaties and biblical covenants.

As noted above, the repetition of the phrase "I shall act" gives the utterance a certain legal force, like a vow. Of course, vows to a god were sacrosanct, from the standpoint of ancient religions. Oaths made to Yahweh and in his name were treated seriously in the Hebrew Bible. For Yahweh: Deut 23:21 warns, "If you make a vow to Yahweh your God, do not delay to fulfill it; for Yahweh your God will surely require it of you, and you would incur guilt"; Num 30:2 says, "When a man makes a vow to Yahweh, or swears an oath to bind himself by a pledge, he shall not break his word; he shall do according to all that proceeds out of his mouth." And most famously, the commandment of Exod 20:7 dictates, "You shall not make wrongful use of the name of Yahweh your God, for Yahweh will not acquit anyone who misuses his name."

More striking still, in light of biblical covenantal rhetoric, is Wenamun's promise to Zakarbaal that if he satisfies Amun, "you will live; you will prosper; you will be healthy; and you will be fortunate in your entire land and your people" (2/32). Again, this is a core value of treaties and covenants. Returning to the Hittite treaty corpus, Hattusili III dictates as follows to Ulmi-Teššup of Tarhuntassa: "If you observe the words of this tablet ... then these oath gods shall benevolently protect your person, together with your wife, your son, your land, your house, your threshing floor, your orchard, your fields, your oxen, your sheep, and all your possessions. And you shall live to a good old age in the hand of My Majesty."[35]

Such blessings were almost always accompanied by curses: in this case, Hattusili says that if the treaty terms were broken, "then these Thousand Gods shall eradicate your person, together with your wife, your sons, your land, your house, your threshing floor, your orchard, your fields, your oxen, your sheep, and all your possessions."[36] Wenamun, too, moves directly from his promises of life and flourishing to the image of Amun as a lion, making clear the threat if Zakarbaal does not submit.

Moses's message to the people in Deuteronomy is quite similar. In fact, this choice between blessings and curses is the core message of Deuteronomic theology. Deuteronomy 30:15–19 provides a clear example:

---

35. *CTH* 106; Beckman, *Hittite Diplomatic Texts*, 107: 18B §10 (rev. 8–11).
36. *CTH* 106; Beckman, *Hittite Diplomatic Texts*, 107: 18B §9 (rev. 5–7).

See, I have set before you today life and prosperity, death and adversity. If you obey the commandments of Yahweh your God that I am commanding you today . . . then you shall live and become numerous, and Yahweh your God will bless you in the land that you are entering to possess. But if your heart turns away and you do not hear . . . I declare to you today that you shall perish; you shall not live long in the land that you are crossing the Jordan to enter and possess. I call heaven and earth to witness against you today that I have set before you life and death, blessings and curses. Choose life so that you and your descendants may live!

This same message is taken up by prophetic books in the Deuteronomistic tradition, such as Jeremiah, which repeatedly emphasizes the importance of vowing truly:

If you return, O Israel, says Yahweh,
    if you return to me,
if you remove your abominations from my presence,
    and do not waver,
and if you swear, "As Yahweh lives!"
    in truth, in justice, and in uprightness,
then nations shall be blessed by him,
    and by him they shall boast. (Jer 4:2)

And again:

If they will diligently learn the ways of my people, to swear by my name, "As Yahweh lives," as they taught my people to swear by Baal, then they shall be built up in the midst of my people. But if any nation will not listen, then I will completely uproot it and destroy it, says Yahweh. (Jer 12:17)

Thus Wenamun has cast Amun as the suzerain who sends him (2/25), who is a master with servants, and whose will must be done. And as the Hebrew prophets promise on behalf of Yahweh, Wenamun says that Zakarbaal and his people will be blessed if they do it.

The portrayal of Amun as a suzerain may seem like a subtle shift, since there was a long tradition of deities as witnesses to, guarantors of, and even participants in treaties.[37] But this effacement of the human king in Wenamun's

---

37. For examples of deities as witnesses in Late Bronze Age Hittite treaties, see Beckman, *Hittite Diplomatic Texts*, 24–25 (CTH 42); for Egyptian deities as guarantors of covenants, see Hays,

rhetoric upends some cherished conclusions of biblical scholarship about treaties and covenants. In a foundational essay, G. E. Mendenhall and Gary Herion wrote that despite biblical covenants' "continuity with age-old patterns of thought" the switch to a divine suzerain "represented a complete discontinuity from earlier ways of thinking."[38] That claim cannot be maintained in light of the evidence just presented. The tale of *Wenamun* shows, from a time before the written form of biblical covenants, that the same substitution of a divine suzerain was preached by the theocratic officials of the Theban state.

Some would argue that gods are always projections of human desires for power, and a fine-grained analysis of the relationship between the god and the human king in theocratic monarchies is beyond the scope of this book, but the claims can still be analyzed from a literary-theological perspective. From that standpoint, Wenamun's rhetoric of Amun's suzerainty goes well beyond divine witnessing to treaties. It is similar to biblical theology, and contrasts with other treaty-language. To take the Assyrian Vassal Treaties of Esarhaddon as an example: these are presented as "the treaty *of Esarhaddon* ... (which he) confirmed, made, and concluded *in the presence of* [the gods]."[39] Hittite treaties were similarly dictated in the name of the emperor, not the gods.

This was also the case in Egypt, where there was a long tradition of treaty-making. We have already noted some echoes of treaty language in the Amarna Letters, and these also include explicit references to treaties. In the Late Bronze Age, the Egyptians made multiple treaties in addition to the Treaty of Kadesh with Hatti.[40] In EA 34:42–46, the king of Alasiya asks the pharaoh to make a treaty. Tantalizingly, Rib-Hadda of Byblos also mentions making treaties or alliances on a number of occasions (EA 74:36; 83:21–27; 85:39–47; 132:30–35; 138:53 [all Akk. *kittu*]; 136:24–32 [Sum. DÙG.GA]). However, these are all references to treaties among the smaller Levantine states.

There are no surviving written treaties involving Egypt in the Third Intermediate Period, but it appears that this is an accident of preservation, and that treaties and oaths continued in use in Egypt. The Piye Victory Stela, from the eighth century (Kushite 25th Dynasty), alludes to oaths of submission taken by Hereditary Prince Padiese (ll. 110–13) and Chief of the Ma Tefnakht (ll. 126–44).[41] These similarly express the vassal's terror of Piye, offer their

---

Death in the Iron Age II, 294–99. In the Neo-Assyrian ritual/prophetic text SAA 9 3.5 iii 13–15, Ištar commands, "Keep this covenant that I have made on behalf of (*ina muḫḫu*) Esarhaddon."

38. Mendenhall and Herion, "Covenant," 1183; discussed in Hays, *Hidden Riches*, 184–85.
39. *adê ša* ᵐ*Aššur-aḫu-iddinu ... ina pān* DN *udanninuni iṣbatu iškununi*.
40. Murnane, *Road to Kadesh*. Weinfeld argued that treaty terminology originated in the Amarna Period: "Covenant Terminology," 190–99.
41. Ritner, *Libyan Anarchy*, 488–89.

wealth and horses to him, and promise a servant's faithfulness to him. The Tefnakht oath is particularly relevant in light of the language in *Wenamun*:

> When he went into the temple, he praised god and cleansed himself by a divine oath (ʿnḫ nṯr), saying: "I shall not transgress the royal command. I shall not thrust aside that which His Majesty says. I shall not do wrong to a count without your knowledge. I shall act in accordance with what the king has said. I shall not transgress what he has commanded." (ll. 142–44)

The promises to obey stipulations and to be allied with the suzerain's allies are highly characteristic of ancient Near Eastern treaties. Despite the temple context and "divine oath," it is the king who issues the commands, and to whom faithfulness is promised.

In addition to these narrative allusions in the Victory Stela, there are two fragmentary clay sealings excavated from Nineveh that bear the impressions of both Egyptian and Neo-Assyrian seals, which include the name of Shabako and have been thought to attest a treaty between the 25th Dynasty and Assyria in the late eighth century.[42] Finally, there are allusions to Judahite treaties with Egypt in Isa 20:1–6; 28:15–18; and 30:1–2.[43]

Thus in *Wenamun*'s time, treaty ideology and language would have been commonly understood tropes. But does his exchange with the Byblian ruler indicate that there was an actual treaty or oath governing relations between the nations? This has been asserted: "Given Zeker-Baʿal's stress upon his loyalty to the Egyptian king and the argumentation of the Byblian ruler's legal status as vassal to Pharaoh, it is entirely reasonable to assume that the relationship had been marked by formal oaths or a treaty.... [I]t is tempting to see Zeker-Baʿal's statement in 2, 13–14 as a paraphrase of an actual oath taken in conjunction with his acceptance of Pharaonic vassalage."[44]

However, if there had been a treaty in effect, the reader might expect one or the other party to refer to it. Byblos's poor treatment of the previous emissaries from Ramses XI, detaining them for 17 years until they died (2/51–53), strongly suggests that diplomatic relations had broken down. (As the story of Sinuhe reflects, burial outside of the homeland was not the ideal for Egyptian officials.) In this passage, Zakarbaal even repeatedly calls Ramses by his birth name, Khaemwase, denying him his royal epithets in an act of disrespect.

---

42. Ritner, *Libyan Anarchy*, 499, with further literature.
43. See further below on Isa 30:1–2. On Isa 28, see Hays, "'Those Weaned from Milk,'" 61–89.
44. Morschauser, "'Crying,'" 323, 325.

Wenamun addresses Zakarbaal *as if* he were a vassal, but far from accepting that claim, the Byblian ruler is quick to undercut it.

Thus Wenamun's language is not a reference to any existing treaty between Egypt and Byblos; rather, it is an attempt to impose a new and ambitious treaty dictated by Amun himself. Wenamun goes beyond the common ancient Near Eastern claims that a national deity was "king of the gods," and beyond rationales for warfare that depended on a sense of divine manifest destiny.[45] Again, Amun is the only one called "king" or given pharaonic titles in *Wenamun*. Although there are no existing covenant or treaty documents naming Amun as suzerain, the concept is envisioned and described in *Wenamun*. As Baines has written, Wenamun's claim that "his mission is divine and hence superior to earlier Egyptian requests" is an "escalation of traditional claims."[46]

New Kingdom hymns already described Amun as "Sovereign (l.p.h.)," "chief over mankind," "Lord of the Throne of the Two Lands" "the king who ... united the lands by the commandments he had given," and "who sends the enemy chieftains to the fire, for his Eye fells those who rebel against him."[47] These phrases all describe Amun in terms similar to those used for pharaohs, and they allude to the imposition of treaty stipulations and the punishment of unsubmissive vassals. Still, the disappearance of reference to human kingship in *Wenamun* goes a step farther.

Conclusion

The role played by Amun in *Wenamun* is strikingly similar to the role of Yahweh in the Hebrew prophets. Both are envisioned as divine kings who claim supremacy over distant lands and their produce; both Wenamun and the Hebrew prophets portray their own lords as lions possessive of their property; leonine imagery for Egypt and its pharaoh are also present in the prophets. Finally and most strikingly, both Wenamun and the prophets employed the language of treaties and oaths. Wenamun invokes Byblos's past submission as a precedent, he demands that Zakarbaal agree to the stipulations of the divine suzerain Amun, and he promises divine blessings for faithful execution—all in keeping with ancient Near Eastern treaties and biblical covenants.

Egypt and Byblos shared in a long tradition of such treaties, stretching back to the Amarna Period and extending into the Third Intermediate Period. But

---

45. Oded, *War, Peace, and Empire*.
46. Baines, "On the Background of Wenamun," 36.
47. Foster and Hollis, *Hymns*, 59, 61, 67, 60.

for various reasons, it does not appear that there was any actual treaty governing the diplomatic relationship, and indeed Wenamun's rhetoric of divine sovereignty without reference to a human ruler is an innovation compared to older and contemporaneous treaty language. Although Zakarbaal rejects Wenamun's worldview and demands, steering the conversation toward a more balanced economic negotiation via humor, insults, and threats, he is not portrayed as struggling at all to understand the theological rhetoric as such. In fact, he responds in kind, so that both men sound like prophets. Such an exchange in the eleventh or tenth century BCE has the potential to reconfigure our understanding of the roots of biblical covenants and prophecy.

CHAPTER 5

Wenamun as a Prophetic Messenger

IN KEEPING WITH THE WAY the story uses royal language for Amun, Wenamun is portrayed as a messenger of the divine king, just as the Hebrew prophets were. It was noted at the outset that the Hebrew prophets were "theopolitical commentators." This is a way of emphasizing that they often proclaimed divine perspectives on the political events of their times rather than announcing future outcomes.[1] They "supported and legitimized [the] ideology" of a nation or group.[2] Needless to say, the line between commenting and predicting was quite blurry—the judgments of mighty gods implied their own outcomes—but proclaiming the future is only a part of the content of the biblical prophetic books.

In announcing the divine will, prophets sometimes simply spoke in the voice of God; in other cases, they introduced divine messages as a messenger would. Hebrew prophecy uses messenger formulae in a way that creates an analogy between prophets as messengers of the divine King and emissaries of human kings.[3]

This messenger analogy has been the subject of extensive analysis, and has sometimes been taken as a unifying theme of biblical prophecy. As Gerhard von Rad observed, "The 'messenger formula' ... persists as a constant factor in all OT prophecy from Elisha to Malachi, and is, too, the most consistently

---

1. Nili Shupak has demonstrated that prophetic "social rebuke" is common to Hebrew and Egyptian texts ("Egyptian 'Prophecy,'" 133–44).
2. Schneider, "Land Without Prophets?," 78–79.
3. This phenomenon seems to have been studied in depth first by Köhler, *Deuterojesaja*, 102–9. Köhler identified messenger formulae such as כה אמר and נאם יהוה as analogous to the pronouncements of royal messengers, as reflected in ancient Near Eastern correspondence. See also Lindblom, *Die literarische Gattung*, 100–101; Westermann, *Basic Forms of Prophetic Speech*, 98–128. Despite doubts raised by, e.g., Greene (*Role of the Messenger*), the consensus does not seem to have been basically altered. See, more recently, Blenkinsopp, *History of Prophecy in Israel*, 48–55; Stökl, *Prophecy*, 157–200; Fox, *Message from the Great King*.

67

used of all the many different prophetic literary categories."[4] In fact, the formula "Thus says Yahweh" (כה אמר יהוה) is so pervasive in the Hebrew Bible that one could forget its derivation from human contexts, but these are relatively common as well. For example, in 2 Kgs 9:17–18: "Joram said, 'Take a horseman; send him to meet them, and let him say, "Is it peace?"' So the horseman went to meet him; he said, *'Thus says the king,* 'Is it peace?'" Or 2 Chr 36:22: "King Cyrus of Persia ... sent a herald throughout all his kingdom and also declared in a written edict: *'Thus says King Cyrus of Persia ...'*" etc. This formula also has cognates in Akkadian letters, such as *qibī-ma umma(mi)* PN ("Say, 'Thus [says] PN ...'"), which were already adapted for relaying divine messages in earlier periods (e.g., in the Mari letters).

Wenamun's Prophetic Role

Like a Hebrew prophet, Wenamun is repeatedly identified as a messenger from the divine ruler, in this case Amun, using the common Egyptian term *ipw.ty/ wpw.ty*. The ecstatic prophet at Byblos is the first to do this, when he cries out:

"Bring up the god!
Bring the messenger (*ipw.ty*) who bears him!
It is Amun who has sent him.
It is he who has caused that he come." (1/39–40)

This identification of a statue with a god is familiar. As Robert Ritner has said, in ancient Egyptian religion, "statues and reliefs are animated images of deity" just as "royal statues are embodiments of the king."[5] The statue is a manifestation of the deity. According to the worldview of the text, Wenamun has both been sent by Amun and has brought Amun to the Levant.

Wenamun himself emphasizes his special status as a messenger of a god. When Zakarbaal threatens him by pointing out that he had detained previous Egyptian messengers until they died, Wenamun refuses to be shown to their graves, and retorts: "As for Khaemwase (i.e., the earlier Pharaoh Ramses XI), *they were but men (rmṭ.w) whom he sent to you as messengers (ipw.tyw), and he himself a man (rmṭ)*!" (2/53). By contrast, Amun is not a man (cf. Balaam in Num 23:19 and Samuel in 1 Sam 15:29, which distinguish God from humans).

---

4. Von Rad, *Message of the Prophets*, 18–19. Examples of prophets being called messengers include Isa 42:19; 44:26; 52:7; Hag 1:13; Mal 2:7; 3:1; 2 Chr 36:15–16. On the fact that the preexilic prophets did not explicitly call themselves messengers, see Ross, "Prophet as Yahweh's Messenger," 98–107, esp. 106.

5. Ritner, *Mechanics*, 35–46.

Wenamun tells Zakarbaal that he should celebrate that "Amun-Re, King of the Gods, sent to [him] Amun-of-the-Road, his messenger (*ipw.ty*), l.p.h., together with Wenamun, his human messenger (*ipw.ty [n] rmṯ*)" (2/56–57). This is an interesting passage, in that it allows that Wenamun too is a human messenger, yet asserts that he is transformed into something greater thanks to the fact that he bears the divine statue of Amun.

The reader may be meant to infer from the fact that Wenamun is traveling with the statue, the embodiment of the god, that he is receiving oracles by means of it.[6] But in any case, the sending of gods in the form of statues to emphasize the message of an emissary is attested in the Amarna Letters—in EA 164, a letter from Aziru of Amurru to an Egyptian courtier named Tutu. Aziru begs Tutu and the pharaoh to hear him: "May the king, my lord, heed my words. My lord, I fear the king, my lord, and Tutu. Here are my gods and my messenger."[7] Similarly, in EA 23, Tušratta of Mitanni sends the statue of Šauška of Nineveh to the pharaoh, and in the text speaks as the goddess, via the messenger formula: "Thus Šauška of Nineveh, mistress of all lands: 'I wish to go to Egypt, a country that I love, and then return.' Now I herewith send her, and she is on her way." Although this mission is commonly said to have been to restore the pharaoh's health, William Moran associated it with ensuring that a diplomatic marriage involving Tušratta's daughter was finalized successfully.[8] In line with these examples, Wenamun is accompanied by the statue of Amun to increase his authority. And as with Šauška, Amun is said to command his own sending, with a certain inverted echo of Isa 6:8: "Amun-Re, King of the Gods—said to Herihor, my lord: 'Send me! (*i-wḏ wi*)'" (2/26).

Because of his elevated status as the messenger and bearer of a god, Wenamun is also able to demand protection. When Wenamun challenges the ruler of Alasiya to keep him safe from the mob that meets him there, he says, "If the sea rages and the wind blows me to the land where you are, will you let them greet me so to kill me, although I am a messenger of Amun?" (2/80–81). She seems to acquiesce. Furthermore, in the earlier scene when the Tjeker whom Wenamun robbed track him down in Byblos, Zakarbaal says to them: "I will not be able to imprison the messenger of Amun within my land. Let me send him off, and you go after him to imprison him" (2/73–74). This suggests that Wenamun's expectation of protection is not merely idiosyncratic, since other characters also take it for granted.

---

6. On the role of statues in divination in Egypt, see Černý, "Egyptian Oracles," 35–48; Hilber, "Egyptian Prophecy." On the solicitation of oracles in the ancient Near East, see Schroeder, *Let Us Go to the Seer!*, including pp. 129–30 on the Wenamun episode.

7. *a-nu-um-ma* DINGIR.MEŠ-*ia ù* LÚ.DUMU.KIN-*ri-ia*. Translation: Moran, *Amarna Letters*, 252. Text from Rainey, *El-Amarna Correspondence*, 812.

8. Moran, *Amarna Letters*, 62; cf. Rainey, *El-Amarna Correspondence*, 1358.

The idea that the prophets are a protected group, even when they are hated, is reflected in the biblical literature as well. For example, Jeremiah prophesies against Judah and is deemed a traitor to the nation, so that enemies seek his death. He responds:

> "Here I am in your hands. Do with me as seems good and right to you. Only know for certain that if you put me to death, you will be bringing innocent blood upon yourselves and upon this city and its inhabitants, for in truth Yahweh sent me to you to speak all these words in your ears."
>
> Then the officials and all the people said to the priests and the prophets, "This man does not deserve the sentence of death, for he has spoken to us in the name of Yahweh our God." (Jer 26:14–16)

Some of the elders then compare Jeremiah to Micah, who had also prophesied against Jerusalem in an earlier era. They ask: "Did King Hezekiah of Judah and all Judah actually put him to death? Did he not fear Yahweh and entreat the favor of Yahweh, and did not Yahweh change his mind about the disaster that he had pronounced against them? But we are about to bring great disaster on ourselves!" (Jer 26:19).

This is not to say that prophets were actually protected in all cases. Jeremiah 26 goes on to report the case of a different prophet, Uriah son of Shemaiah, who was killed for saying similar things. But where the prophets are unjustly killed by those in power, the latter are judged for it. For example, the queen Jezebel is condemned for killing prophets in 1 Kgs 18:4–13 and 19:1–10. In sum, the shared ideology of the protected status of prophets is another point of contact between *Wenamun* and the Hebrew Bible.

Other vocabulary contributes to the portrayal of the exchange between Wenamun and Zakarbaal as prophetic. The preceding chapter noted that Wenamun comes bearing the "commands/commissions" (*sḥn.w*) of Amun; that term was more customarily used of the directives of human rulers, which emphasizes the operative metaphor. It also reinforces the messenger metaphor, which can also be supported further by the story's use of the term *wḫꜣ.(w)*, "decree(s)." Zakarbaal cross-examines Wenamun and asks why he has no "decrees of Amun" (*wḫꜣ.w n 'Imn*; 1/52).[9] Like *sḥn.w*, *wḫꜣ.w* is normally used of decrees by pharaohs and other human authorities, so its use here reinforces the analogy between gods and kings.[10] One might compare *wḫꜣ.(w) n 'Imn* to

---

9. For the writing, see Schipper, *Die Erzählung*, 62. It is given as *wšḫ* by Ritner (*Libyan Anarchy*, 89), but this appears to be simply a typo.

10. Interestingly, one other text in which *wḫꜣ.(w)* in used repeatedly in the sense of messages and directives sent by a god is in The Contendings of Horus and Seth (19 times), which reinforces our earlier theory of a literary relationship between these two texts.

the common biblical expressions *dābār Yhwh* ("the word of Yahweh") and *nĕʾūm Yhwh* ("the announcement of Yahweh").

The story's reference to Zakarbaal's *mwʿd*, "assembly" (2/71), may also invite focus on the theological implications. Schipper points out that "in the Old Testament, the religious meaning of [*mwʿd*] dominates ... Against this background, one may ask whether the term *moʿed* in *Wenamun* 2/71 does not also have a cultic connotation."[11] Indeed, in the Bible, the *'ōhēl mōʿēd*, usually rendered "tent of meeting," is both the location of the Lord's prophetic revelations to Moses (Exod 33:7; Num 11:16–17) and a place where people assembled to encounter prophetic revelations and the divine words (Lev 8:4; 9:5; Num 16:19, 42; 20:6; 2 Chr 1:3). In the case of *Wenamun*, this assembly seems to be convened as witnesses to the safe departure of the "messenger of Amun."

Messenger Formulae and Metaphors

It has sometimes been argued that the origins of the biblical analogy between prophets and messengers originated from the Israelite and Judahite encounter with the Neo-Assyrian Empire. John Holladay, for example, pointed out that the Neo-Assyrians imposed loyalty oaths upon whole peoples, which involved direct addresses to entire populations instead of just rulers.[12] Thus he concluded that "the institution of the suzerain, or 'great king,' as it classically flourished in the ancient Near East, furnished an ideal theological model for Israel's understanding both of the sovereignty of God and of her peculiar relationship to him."[13] Michael R. Fox follows and augments this argument, emphasizing the Neo-Assyrian shift toward making the whole nation bear the consequences of its treaty faithfulness.[14]

It is important to note, however, that whereas this Neo-Assyrian innovation is significant in the development of national covenantal theology, it is not as relevant to the origins of the portrayal of the prophets as messengers. There are many accounts in the Bible, including in the eighth-century prophets, in which the prophets serve as messengers to the king and his elites, and not to the whole people (e.g., Amos 7:10–17, with a messenger formula in 7:17; Isa 7, with a messenger formula in 7:7; Jer 36, with messenger formulae in 36:29–30, etc.). There is no general presupposition that the prophets are messengers

---

11. Schipper, *Die Erzählung*, 215: "Dabei dominiert im Alten Testament die religiöse Bedeutung des Begriffs ... Vor diesem Hintergrund wird man fragen dürfen, ob bei dem Begriff *moʿed* in Wenamun 2,71 nicht auch eine kultische Konnotation mitschwingt."
12. Holladay, "Assyrian Statescraft," 29–51.
13. Holladay, "Assyrian Statescraft," 48.
14. Fox, *Message from the Great King*, 63–71.

from God to the whole people, so the Neo-Assyrian data (though ample) are only part of the picture. This *Sitz im Leben* and messenger formulae predated the Assyrian Empire.[15] The adaptation of the messenger formula to prophetic announcements was already present in the Old Babylon period at Mari.

If we survey the use of messengers and "messenger formulae" in the ancient Near East, it is quite clear that Egypt was an active participant in these exchanges and made extensive use of these literary forms in conversation with the Levant. The Amarna Letters pervasively use the same messenger formulae as other Akkadian letters (*qibī-ma umma* PN, "Say, 'Thus says PN,'" etc.). Similar diplomatic correspondence continued almost unabated through the Iron Age. As López-Ruiz has commented, *Wenamun* "illustrates that diplomatic conventions, including hospitality rules, had not changed much since the time of the Amarna letters in the New Kingdom."[16] When Zakarbaal's harbor-master repeatedly tells Wenamun: "Stay until morning—so says the prince! (*ḥrꜥf n pꜣ wr*)" (1/43, 46–47), this is a kind of messenger formula.

Egyptian influence on messenger formulae is just as likely as Mesopotamian, insofar as the biblical text attests to messenger activity between Egypt and Judah. Isaiah 18:2 refers to the Kushite 25th Dynasty "sending ambassadors (*ṣîrîm*)"[17] by the Nile, and says "Go, you swift messengers (*malāʾkîm*)!" And 2 Kgs 17:4 reports that Hoshea "sent messengers to King So [probably Osorkon IV[18]] of Egypt" when he rebelled against Assyria.

Levantine kingdoms of the Neo-Assyrian Period tended to be in close contact with Egypt, and used it as a foil for the Assyrians' imperial ambitions. Therefore Egypt served as a place of refuge for numerous royals whose lives were at risk in their own lands, including Hadad of Edom (1 Kgs 11:14–22) and Jeroboam, later king of Israel (1 Kgs 11:26–40).[19] The same phenomenon is attested extrabiblically in the inscriptions of Sargon II, who campaigned against Ashdod in 712 BCE and conquered it.[20] Its ruler, Yamani, fled to Egypt before Sargon arrived to take the city, only to be extradited back to Assyria by Shabitko of the 25th Dynasty, who was presumably seeking to avoid conflict with Assyria. None of these kings fleeing to Egypt would have arrived on its doorstep without some advance preparation via messengers. The nations in

---

15. In addition to the aforementioned literature, see Meier, *Messenger in the Ancient Semitic World*.
16. López-Ruiz, *Phoenicians*, 284. For an overview of Egyptian letters with further literature, see Sweeney, "Letters," 1055–71. On the continuity of the involvement of coastal Levantine cities in shipping trade with Egypt, see already Sasson, "Canaanite Maritime Involvement," 126–38.
17. Cf. Isa 57:9; Jer 49:14; Obad 1; Prov 13:17 (also parallel with מלאך); 25:13.
18. Kitchen, *Third Intermediate Period*, 372–75 (§§333–34); Schipper, "Wer war 'Sō'?," 71–84.
19. Galvin, *Egypt as a Place of Refuge*, esp. 82–117.
20. Sargon II 116:19–21; Frame, *Royal Inscriptions of Sargon II*, 441. See also Isa 20:1.

question had existing diplomatic relations with Egypt that would have laid the groundwork for the momentous decision to flee to a foreign land.

Later still, we have the evidence of the Aramaic papyri from Elephantine, showing the regular, extensive contacts between Jerusalem and a Jewish community deep in Egypt. The limitations of space prevent a thorough discussion here, but taken together, these data attest that the Egyptians would have been corresponding with the Levant throughout the period of the Hebrew prophets.

In sum, the "messenger formula" was used internationally, and prophets were not defined by their address to a wide popular audience. Neo-Assyrian models and covenantal theology are significant for the history of prophecy, but they do not account for the origins of the messenger metaphor. The conclusion to this volume revisits the question of influence and origins.

There is evidence that that messenger metaphor was operative in *Wenamun* as well. Many of Wenamun's statements to the leaders he meets are consistent with, or at least plausible oral adaptations of, the formulas in letters from officials of Amun temples in the 21st Dynasty. The senders of this relatively small collection of letters include priests, prophets, and a captain, most of whom also describe themselves as scribes. The epistolary form is relatively consistent—most of the letters begin with a greeting that wishes the recipient blessings: "In life, prosperity and health and in the favor of Amun-Re, King of the Gods! May he (Amun-Re) give you life, prosperity and health, a long lifetime, [a good ripe old age] and favors in the presence of gods and people every day."[21] These openings recall Wenamun's briefer opening words to Zakarbaal: "Amun be merciful!" (1/50). Despite the well-wishing, both this opening and the ones in the actual 21st Dynasty letter assert Amun-Re's primacy and thus implicitly the importance of the missives from his servants. Another example from a 21st Dynasty letter more overtly impresses this upon the recipient: "In life, prosperity and health and in the favor of Amon-Re, King of the Gods, *your good lord!*"[22]

Following their opening invocations of Amun, the 21st Dynasty letter-writers generally move immediately to imperatives. These are not lengthy, florid letters. Some of them concern fugitives: "You shall [seek out(?)] those servants ... [and] you shall hand them over," etc.[23] Another concerns a fowler and his birds: "As soon as he reaches you, you shall commit [the birds] to his charge, but don't let him depart. Give him men who are fit for assignment, namely, the reliable men who were in his charge once before. And dispatch

---

21. Wente, *Letters from Ancient Egypt*, 206 (#333).
22. Wente, *Letters from Ancient Egypt*, 209 (#339).
23. Wente, *Letters from Ancient Egypt*, 206 (#333).

him so as to send him on very speedily."[24] These orders are consistent with Wenamun's expectation that his status as an emissary of Amun gives him the authority to issue commands.

We also see in the 21st Dynasty letters the importance of having the written documentation in one's hand. One of them concerns a conflict over the right to till a certain piece of land:

> Now as for the person who may dispute with you, you shall go before Serdjehuty, this grain-reckoning scribe of the Temple of Osiris, *taking this letter [šʿt] in your hand*, since I have entrusted to him my holding of the fresh land and my holding of this mud flat as well. And *you shall preserve my letter so that it may serve you as testimony [mtr.t]*.[25]

As we saw in chapter 1's discussion of his title and mission, Wenamun seems to have been another Temple official who was accustomed to bearing documents as testimony. But in this case, since he had left his letters in Egypt, he had no such formal, written testimony to show for himself.

Conclusion

Wenamun is portrayed in the story as a messenger of the decrees of Amun, much as the Hebrew prophets were messengers of Yahweh's words. And as the prophets sometimes did, Wenamun embraces his special status and the protection that it affords him. The biblical "messenger metaphor" for prophets has sometimes been said to derive from the encounter with Neo-Assyrian and Persian imperialism, but the diplomatic conventions on which it depends were also operative in the long-running relationship between Egypt and the Levant.

Egyptian letters of the same period reinforce the story's own description of Wenamun as a messenger, and his sense of himself as a representative. The key difference is that these ordinary letters do not claim to report the words of Amun-Re himself, but only of his human agents. By contrast, Wenamun is portrayed as conveying Amun's own messages—as the Hebrew prophets did for Yahweh.

---

24. Wente, *Letters from Ancient Egypt*, 208 (#336).
25. Wente, *Letters from Ancient Egypt*, 209 (#339). For the Egyptian text, see Spiegelberg, "Varia: 10," 107–11.

CHAPTER 6

Is Wenamun Also Among the Prophets?

IN THE HEBREW BIBLE, JUST after Saul is anointed king of Israel, he falls in with a band of ecstatic prophets and begins prophesying and behaving like them. People see this and ask, "Is Saul also among the prophets?" (1 Sam 10:11–12). One might ask the same about Wenamun: if he speaks like a prophet and acts like a prophet, does that make him a prophet? This question leads us into the broader debate about the existence of prophecy in ancient Egypt.

It is commonly stated by leading scholars that there was no prophecy in pre-Hellenistic Egypt;[1] at a literary level, the comparisons between specific Egyptian texts to Hebrew prophecy have generally been limited in scope and not fully successful.[2] Yet we have noted above Alan B. Lloyd's judgment that prophecy "is integral and fundamental to the agenda" of a wide range of Egyptian texts,[3] and the negative conclusions about the existence of Egyptian prophecy have been challenged, notably by Thomas Schneider, Alexandra von Lieven, and John Hilber.[4] As Schneider noted, absence of evidence is not evidence of absence, and "serious consideration needs to be given to the possibility that prophecy existed but is not at present documented before the Hellenistic age."[5]

A survey of the various approaches to the question charts a path between these competing assessments and sets the stage for a fresh consideration of *Wenamun*.

---

1. Significant examples of this negative assessment include Bonnet, "Propheziehung," 608–9; Stökl, *Prophecy*, 14, 16; Assmann, *Search for God*, 6–7, 153–54; and Schipper, "'Apokalyptik,'" 38.
2. For a survey of comments in scattered literature from the first half of the twentieth century (and in addition to the more recent sources cited in this chapter), see Herrmann, "Prophetie in Israel und Ägypten," 47–65.
3. Lloyd, "*Heka*, Dreams, and Prophecy," 88.
4. Schneider, "Land Without Prophets?," 59–86; Hilber, "Prophetic Speech," 47–53; Hilber, "Prophetic Ritual," 51–62; von Lieven, "Divination," 77–126.
5. Schneider, "Land Without Prophets?," 78.

Priests as Prophets?

The older and once-default position was that some Egyptian priests functioned in ways akin to prophets. This is a view of fairly great antiquity. For example, the priests of Amun bore titles such as ḥm nṯr tpy n 'Imn, "Chief God's-Servant of Amun"; ḥm nṯr snnw n 'Imn, "Second God's-Servant of Amun," and so on, but Greek authors interpreted them as προφήτης, "prophets."[6] Wenamun is not given the title ḥm nṯr, although as chapter 1 noted, his title ("elder of the portal") does describe him as an official of the temple of Amun.

The various prophetic and oracular roles of Egyptian priests are discussed at some length in Serge Sauneron's classic study *The Priests of Ancient Egypt*,[7] including bark oracles, oracles of healing in temples, oneiromancy (prophecy by dreams), and oracles by written questions and by interpreting the movements of animals. The accounting of Egyptian divination has become significantly richer and more detailed in recent years, making clear what a large role it played in the culture.[8] And "of all the oracles, that of the Theban Amun remained by far the most prominent."[9]

It may be argued, however, that most of these fall into the category of technical or inductive divination, whereas prophecy is intuitive and noninductive.[10] As Assmann explains:

> In Egypt, deities "spoke" through movement to make their wills known. Thus, the divine image moved toward the pretender chosen to be the successor to the throne or to be high priest or the official chosen to be scribe of the granary. Questions put to oracles had to be formulated in such a way that they could be answered by a simple yes or no. A forward movement of the divine image signified assent, a backward movement disapproval. Alternative responses were written down separately and presented to the deity, and the one toward which the statue turned was the correct one.[11]

---

6. In Demotic, ḥm nṯr could also be used for "prophet," thanks to the influence of Greek, but this is later than the period in question here. Liwak, "Herrschaft zur Überwindung der Krise," 61; Erichsen, *Demotisches Glossar*, 305.
7. Sauneron, *Priests*, esp. 95–101. See also Hilber, "Prophetic Ritual," passim.
8. Von Lieven, "Divination," 77–126; von Lieven, "Das Orakelwesen im Alten Ägypten"; Ritner, "Necromancy in Ancient Egypt."
9. Assmann, *Search for God*, 35.
10. Nissinen, *Ancient Prophecy*, 14–19.
11. Assmann, *Search for God*, 35.

In other words, what we do *not* generally have are accounts of temple authorities speaking for the gods.

Diana Edelman has provocatively drawn out the analogy between the priesthoods of Egypt (including the ḥm nṯr) and the Hebrew prophets.[12] She notes that there was "direct native contact with Egyptian cultic practices" in the Levant, "particularly where Egyptians were physically present, and a possible direct adoption or adaptation," and that this situation endured at least intermittently in the Iron I and Iron II.[13] Edelman alludes to Ezekiel, who is probably both a priest and descended from a priestly lineage (Ezek 1:3), as well as to Micaiah ben Imlah and Isaiah ben Amoz as "specialized cultic specialist[s] who had undergone initiation that allowed them access to the holy of holies in the temple in Jerusalem and other Yahwistic temples throughout the kingdom."[14] Other characters in the Hebrew Bible are also described as both prophets and priests: Aaron, Moses, Samuel, and Jeremiah.[15]

We could expand on Edelman's case with reference to Haggai, who—although he is called a prophet and not a priest (Hag 1:1, 3)—makes use of specialized priestly terminology and practices[16] and has been deemed a cultic prophet.[17] His interests are strikingly similar to Wenamun's, in that he too is gathering timber for the cultic structures of his deity. Haggai commands in the voice of Yahweh: "Go up to the hills and bring wood and build the house, so that I may take pleasure in it and be honored!" (1:8). Like Amun, Yahweh claims an imperial right to the wealth of foreign countries: "I will shake all the nations, so that the treasure of all nations shall come, and I will fill this house with splendor, says Yahweh of hosts. The silver is mine, and the gold is mine" (2:7–8). Also like Wenamun, Haggai pronounces covenant curses upon those who do not perform the god's will (1:9–11). Thus we have Haggai, the priestly prophet who demands wood for his god's temple, and Wenamun the prophetic priest who demands wood for his god's bark.

Some of the denials of the comparison between Egyptian priests and Hebrew prophets end up undermining themselves and revealing much about their own presuppositions. For example, Sauneron tried to clarify for the modern reader the ways in which Egyptian priests were *not* like "prophets":

---

12. Edelman, "Of Priests and Prophets," 103–12.
13. Edelman, "Of Priests and Prophets," 104.
14. Edelman, "Of Priests and Prophets," 106.
15. Tiemeyer, "Seer and the Priest," 137–51. In general, the essays in this volume as a whole emphasize the overlap between priestly and prophetic roles in the Hebrew Bible.
16. Meyers and Meyers refer to the "arcane priestly question" and "complex priestly ruling" of Hag 2:10–19: *Haggai, Zechariah 1–8,* 76.
17. Grabbe, *Priests, Prophets, Diviners, Sages,* 112–13.

> We ought above all to guard ourselves, in using the term *priests*, against considering them as the guardians of a revelation which would make them a sect apart, living on the edge of society and only venturing to convert the crowds by impassioned sermons to a richer or more active moral life.... No, the Egyptian priests have a very precise role to play, as substitutes for the king, officiating in title only: to maintain the integrity on earth of the divine presence, in the sanctuary of the temples where this presence has consented to dwell—and this is all. Their action contributes to the essential theological role of the Pharaonic monarchy: to maintain the universe in the form in which the gods have created it. It is a work of specialists, a task of technicians. Once the necessary material acts are accomplished to obtain this result, what the priests think or do is fairly unimportant—at least in the rigorous view of the State; they have nothing of the Hebrew prophets, nothing of the Christian priests about them. These are men like any others, not profiting from any divine privilege, not having to win over the crowds, nor to convert the gentiles; "functionaries" of a sort, they are delegated by the king to perform in his place certain material rites necessary to the general welfare.[18]

The first thing that will strike the scholar of Hebrew prophecy here is the degree to which Sauneron assumes that the popular image of a prophet was shaped by the New Testament—by figures such as John the Baptist and Jesus: "a sect apart, living on the edge of society," trying "to convert the gentiles." The prophets of the Old Testament do not fall into a single category or type; rather, some of those called prophets were ecstatics, some charismatics, some sharers in divine pathos, some religious innovators, and some cultic officials. Many of them fell into more than one category.

Furthermore, significant portions of the law attributed to the prophet Moses were precisely "to maintain the integrity on earth of the divine presence, in the sanctuary of the temples where this presence has consented to dwell." For example, Moses says in Deut 23:14: "Because Yahweh your God travels along with your camp, to save you and to hand over your enemies to you, therefore your camp must be holy, so that he may not see anything indecent among you and turn away from you (cf. Lev 19:2, etc.). And many of the prophets who followed were preoccupied with exactly the same concerns; Ezekiel particularly comes to mind (e.g., Ezek 43:7–12).

Still more important for the present purpose is that the role Sauneron describes for Egyptian priests is just what Wenamun is seeking to achieve in the story: he is a "substitute" speaking for the ruling power, seeking "to

---

18. Sauneron, *Priests*, 34–35.

maintain the integrity" of Amun and his sanctuary; to maintain the universe and its order in the form in which the gods have created it. And in the story he is particularly focused on the "material acts" necessary to accomplish this result—namely, acquiring timber.

What Sauneron does not consider, because it is not a primary feature of his sources, is that "impassioned sermons"—lengthy theological speeches—were often compatible with achieving material ends. Sometimes they would have been useful. Sometimes it was necessary to assert the divinely ordained order of things, as Wenamun does (and as the Hebrew prophets did) in the process of attaining those goals with the least expenditure and bloodshed. Perhaps Sauneron is right that the priests did not normally have to "win over the crowds"—Wenamun shows himself not to be especially good at it!—but it is easy to see that, especially in an era when the actual, looming force of Egyptian power behind a priestly functionary was greatly reduced, he might have to compensate with force of words. That is what we see in the story.

Textual Interpretation as Prophecy

There are other angles of approach to prophecy in Egypt. There is evidence predating *Wenamun* and the Hebrew Bible for the interpretation of past texts as prophetic. Egyptians were, at least by the Ramesside period, searching for oracles in texts, as reflected by P.Chester Beatty IV's paean to scribes. Ritner pointed out that this passage clearly attributes a kind of "magical" foresight to past authors:

> Is there one here like Hardedef?
> Is there another like Imhotep?
> None of our kin is like Neferti
> Or Khety, the foremost among them.
> I give you the name of Ptah-emdjehuty
> Of Khakheperre-sonb.
> Is there another like Ptahhotep,
> Or the equal of Kaires?
> *Those sages who prophesied the future,*
> *What came from their mouth occurred:*
> *It is found as (their) pronouncement,*
> *It is written in their books.*
> The children of others are given to them
> To be heirs as their own children.
> They hid their magic from the masses

> (But) it is read in their Instructions.
> Death caused their names to be forgotten
> But books caused them to be remembered![19]

The italicized passage is self-explanatory; the texts attributed to legendary sages such as Imhotep and Neferti were viewed as revelatory and predictive (the verb used for "prophesied" is *sr*). The closing reference to the hiddenness of their magic is familiar both from the Mesopotamian scribal tradition and from the biblical tradition of the sealed prophecy that cannot be interpreted until the right time (Isa 8:16; 29:11; Dan 12:9).[20] Furthermore, P.Chester Beatty IV's list of the great prophetic figures from the past, and its judgment that "none of our kin is like them," is reminiscent of Deut 34:10: "Never since has there arisen a prophet in Israel like Moses." In conjunction with the widespread oracular activity of priests, this reference to text-interpretive prophecy adds to our sense that the phenomena from the two cultures are related.

But despite these provocative echoes, P.Chester Beatty IV is not a record of prophecy as such, but rather the seeking of divine knowledge in past texts. Some of the named authors, such as Hardedef and Ptahhotep, were figures to whom wisdom instructions were attributed. These have little to do with prophecy.

A text such as the "Prophecy of Neferti" seems more promising. It is a story set in the reign of the Old Kingdom pharaoh Snefru (ca. 2613–2589 BCE), in which a lector-priest named Neferti is summoned to the pharaoh to entertain him with some words about "what will come to pass." But the prophecy is *ex eventu*. Neferti "predicts" that "there shall come a king from the south," named "Ameny," who will reverse a state of chaos and destruction in the land. It appears that the text was composed as royal propaganda in the reign of Amenemhet I (1985–1956 BCE).[21] Better-attested "prophetic" texts from Hellenistic Egypt such as the Potter's Oracle originated in the same royal-propagandistic genre as Neferti and then were reinterpreted for new situations over relatively long periods. They provide interesting comparisons for the biblical prophetic books,[22] and seem to reflect an awareness of prophetism, but the lack of other examples from prior to the Hellenistic period has made Neferti appear to be an outlier. We have very few records of any kind from Egypt of prophets speaking like prophets.

---

19. This translation is basically that of Lichtheim (*AEL* 2:177), but adopts a few features of Ritner's (*Mechanics*, 38).
20. On secrecy in Mesopotamian scribal traditions, see Lenzi, *Secrecy and the Gods*.
21. On Neferti and P.Westcar, see Schlichting, "Prophetie," 1122–25.
22. For discussion and literature on Neferti and the Potter's Oracle, see Hays, *Origins*, 34–37.

Prophecy as Speech or Literature?

Wenamun presents an intriguing and unusual example, since he does speak like a prophet. But he does so not in a collection of oracles, but in a kind of novella. Some would say that the use of prophetic theological rhetoric does not make him (or Zakarbaal) a "prophet," any more than Solomon's theological speeches in 1 Kings make him one. That is to say that literary-generic considerations mean that the same theological rhetoric in a different form is not prophecy.[23]

Theological speeches may not make a person a prophet, but they do often indicate a connection with prophetic ideology. Solomon's speeches are literary products of storytellers—in this case, the Deuteronomistic historians—just as the *Wenamun* speeches are. Yet it is not accidental that those biblical "histories" are more traditionally called Former Prophets. The perspective of the Deuteronomistic History was informed by the Hebrew prophets, particularly their idea that covenant faithfulness to Yahweh was crucial to the nation's flourishing, so it is not surprising many of its characters speak like prophets. (In Jewish and Muslim tradition, of course, Solomon can be considered a prophet.[24])

Comparisons between the biblical prophetic books and Egyptian texts have sometimes been hampered by definitions of prophecy that are too narrow. Although the interpretation of prophecy has moved some distance from its roots in relatively dogmatic theological scholarship, it is hard to escape the sense that the whole conversation is still shaped by the old "apologetic" concern to distinguish biblical literature from its cognates. It is as if Hebrew prophecy were necessarily and fundamentally incomparable on theological grounds. Rüdiger Liwak criticizes this tendency to emphasize the "Unvergleichlichkeit und Analogielosigkeit israelitischer Prophetie."[25]

Often a distinction is also made between prophecy as a spoken phenomenon and as a literary product. The comparative conversation about prophecy in Egypt has focused largely on the delivery of oracles and the social roles of those who deliver them. Various ingrained biases in biblical-studies method predispose us to seek the *Sitz im Leben* of prophets and the personae and *ipsissima verba* of the prophets. The insistence on "inspiration," "performance," and "audience" as qualifiers for recognizing prophecy are essentially anthropological, and thus potentially misleading for the study of prophetic *literature*.[26]

---

23. Shupak, "Egyptian 'Prophecy' and Biblical Prophecy," 5–40.
24. Q *An-Nisa'* 4:163; b. *Soṭah* 48b; b. *Megillah* 14a; etc.
25. Liwak, "Herrschaft," 58–60.
26. See Hilber, "Egyptian Prophecy."

The spoken words and actions of past prophets are inaccessible by their nature. Although occasional brief reports of prophetic activity (such as those from the Mari letters) may create an impression of journalistic accuracy compared to the more literary prophetic books and stories, in reality we are dealing entirely with written presentations, albeit of varying literary complexities.[27] All the major Hebrew prophetic books include not only oracles as such, but stories about prophets that contain reports of their speech. And every prophetic book is a literary, scribal product, not a simple report of past events. The essentially literary character of the Hebrew prophetic books is now taken for granted by many who study them, but this has perhaps not yet been sufficiently reckoned with in comparative study.

Wenamun is a series of lengthy theological speeches built on the framework of a historical narrative. In that respect, it has more in common with highly developed literary stories about prophets such as one finds in the Hebrew Bible than the Mari or Neo-Assyrian prophetic texts. For example, it is reminiscent of Jeremiah: Both Jeremiah and *Wenamun* present main characters who get involved in theological conflicts and are entangled in the political events of their times. By contrast, the Mari accounts of prophetic words are all occasional reports in letters, and even the surviving Neo-Assyrian compilations (SAA 9.1–3) were assembled at most six years after the events that motivated them.[28] None of them includes literary narratives about prophets.

Wenamun is also a product of the scribal desk, with similarities to later "scribal prophecy."[29] It is an intertextual work with numerous allusions—to hymns, wisdom instructions, myths, epistolary forms, and so on.[30] In the Bible, sometimes this takes the form of intertextual allusion as part of a theological argument, as for example in the use of Pentateuchal traditions about Exodus and the patriarchs in postexilic portions of Isaiah. In other cases, the explicit reinterpretation of past texts came to be a feature of late Hebrew prophecy as well, as in the case of Dan 9:2's revision of the "seventy years" oracle in Jer 25:11–12. Just as described in P.Chester Beatty IV and shown in the reinterpretations of the Potter's Oracle, the composers of later Hebrew prophecies continued reading and reinterpreting the work of "sages who prophesied the future."

---

27. Weeks, "Predictive and Prophetic Literature," 25–46.
28. Parpola, *Assyrian Prophecies*, lxvii–lxx.
29. Hays, *Origins*, 250–56.
30. Moers, *Fingierte Welten*, 106–53.

Conclusion

The arguments for the existence of prophecy in Egypt merit closer consideration. The weight of the total picture is significant, but specific arguments about prophetic speech and literature have remained tentative and hypothetical because of the perceived lack of extended prophetic texts from Egypt. *Wenamun*, however, provides extensive and fascinating comparative material. It is an example of theological speech to achieve a political end, framed in a historical narrative; and so, while its uniqueness among Egyptian texts might suggest that it is merely an author's creative presentation of a foreign world, its speeches are part of a native Egyptian tradition. Furthermore, they are executed with a deftness that suggests native familiarity.

Is Wenamun among the prophets? He doesn't have a title such as ḥm nṯr that is traditionally associated with prophets—but he was a temple official, and in Egypt various priests and temple officials controlled the divinatory procedures and pronouncements on behalf of the gods.[31] This was analogous to some Hebrew cultic prophets, notably Ezekiel and Haggai, who similarly campaigned for resources to build the sacred spaces for his deity. Wenamun also traveled with a statue of Amun and may have received his messages by means of it.

Wenamun is a outlier among the Egyptian texts that are generally considered in connection with prophecy; neither the earlier (e.g., the Prophecy of Neferti) nor the later (e.g., the Dream of Nectanebo, the Potter's Oracle) demonstrate the aforementioned literary affinities with Semitic prophecy or the same close relationship between the speaker and the deity as a basis for authority. This makes *Wenamun* inconvenient for theorizing—it is a dot on the graph that cannot be fitted to the curve. But it deserves attention, and it is striking how little it gets in the arguments for or against prophecy in Egypt.

Insofar as we can recognize Wenamun as a speaker of prophetic words, he joins a very short list of ancient Near Eastern prophets about whom stories are told outside the Bible. Prophetic acts and oracles are occasionally briefly reported in letters and administrative documents.[32] But in the category of literary stories, arguably there is only Balaam.[33] But a further biblical example, discussed in the next chapter, offers the best comparison of all.

---

31. Even if Wenamun's title were not priestly, one might still think of a "lay prophet." Stökl employs the category of "lay prophet" extensively for various cultic officials in Mesopotamian culture: *Prophecy*, 9, 13, 37, 44, 50–63, 68, 76, 79, 95, 98, 117–21, 157, 173, 180, 200–201, 222, 230–31.

32. Nissinen, *References to Prophecy*.

33. Nissinen, *Ancient Prophecy*, 332: "Even the prophetic episode at Byblos recorded in the Egyptian report of Wenamun belongs to the category of literary prophecy." But again, he treats only the episode of the Byblian ecstatic as prophetic.

CHAPTER 7

Wenamun and Jonah: Foolish Prophets of Serious Gods

WENAMUN SEEMS SO SERIOUS WHEN he talks about Amun, but for all of the theologizing and politicking that goes on in the story, most readers have also perceived that it has comic aspects. To paraphrase Bedor: "Is *Wenamun* serious or is it joking?"

There has been ample analysis of the story's humorous and ironic elements.[1] It seems to me that readers have correctly recognized something in it. (The graphic-novel adaptation entitled "The Misadventures of Wenamun" is one of the funnier things on the Internet.[2]) Although the speeches have the ring of authenticity, and even sincerity, good satire hews close to its marks.[3] Wenamun himself has been called a "pseudo-Hero,"[4] and he does indeed appear to be a sort of tragicomic figure. Comparison with biblical literature brings the story's humorous aspects into better focus.

Wenamun and Balaam

One comparison that has already been well recognized is between *Wenamun*'s ecstatic-prophet episode and the story of Balaam in Num 22–24. Both episodes involve prophets for hire. The unnamed prophet at Byblos is in the employ of Zakarbaal; the Byblian ruler makes sacrifices, and his prophet would be expected to speak for Baal or another Levantine deity. Instead, the Egyptian god Amun uses him to deliver his own message, expressing his power. Translations usually say that Amun "seized" the ecstatic prophet at Byblos, but readers

---

1. See, e.g., Perotta, "Test of Balaam," 280–300; Houlihan, *Wit and Humour*; Eyre, "Irony"; Winand, "L'ironie"; Winand, "Report," 555. Schipper (*Die Erzählung*, 273–74) does not seem comfortable identifying humor and irony in the story.
2. Potts and van Tassel, "Misadventures of Wenamun."
3. For discussion of the varieties of satire and parody in relation to ancient Near Eastern literature, see Giorgetti, "Building a Parody."
4. Loprieno, *Topos und Mimesis*.

may miss the nuance: the verb used (*t3w*) means more literally "to steal," and is used of the theft of the silver throughout the story. Amun's silver has been stolen, so he steals the prophet's voice and services to help restore what he is owed!

This is analogous to the story of Balaam, who was hired by the king of Moab to curse Israel, but was instead inspired and compelled by Yahweh to speak for the "other side."[5] In each case, the king who employs the prophet sets up sacrifices that prompt the surprising proclamations (Num 23:1–4, 14, 29–30; *Wenamun* 1/38). Balaam, who is supposed to be an independent contractor, is coopted: "Must I not take care to say what Yahweh puts into my mouth?" (23:11).

There are clear comic undertones in the Balaam story, with its talking donkey and mystified prophet: Balaam is supposed to be a great seer who "sees the vision of the Almighty" (Num 24:4, 16; cf. Deir 'Alla [*KAI* 307] I:1), but the donkey can see Yahweh's angels long before he can (22:22–30). The sputterings of the frazzled Balak, king of Moab, are also reminiscent of some of the rulers in *Wenamun*: "What have you done to me? I brought you to curse my enemies, but now you have done nothing but bless them!" (23:11); "Now be off with you! Go home!" (24:11); "Do not curse them at all, and do not bless them at all!" (23:25). Zakarbaal similarly tells Wenamun repeatedly to "Get out of my harbor!" (1/37–38), and he and Bedor both react incredulously to this strange emissary of a foreign god: "Are you serious?"

Balaam also figures as a main character in the Deir 'Alla plaster inscriptions from the eighth to seventh century, one of which begins: "The account of Balaam, son of Beor, who was a seer of the gods. The gods came to him in the night, and he saw a vision like an oracle of El." Thus it appears that stories about prophets and their adventures were to some degree an international phenomenon in the Iron Age II.[6] In the biblical account of Balaam, Balak sends multiple delegations of increasing stature in his effort to hire Balaam (Num 22:5–21), and this literary portrait of the prophet's status and authority in inspiring such treatment also bears indirect witness to the fame of certain prophets.

---

5. Cody, "Phoenician Ecstatic," 105–6: "In both narratives the superior power of the foreign god, whether Amūn or Yahweh, is demonstrated by his brushing aside the local gods as it were in order to deliver a message of his own by usurping the services of a professional oracular messenger who is in the service of the local ruler."

6. It is a well-established aspect of biblical scholarship that stories (sometimes *legenda*) about the prophets were compiled and made up one of the early pieces of biblical scholarship; see Noth, *Überlieferungsgeschichtliche Studien*, 78–87; Rofé, "Classification of Prophetical Stories"; Rofé, *Prophetical Stories*; Redford, *Egypt, Canaan, and Israel*, 320–21.

Wenamun's Wisdom?

Wenamun portrays himself as an important person and a wise man. But how seriously are we to take him? In the midst of Zakarbaal's speeches, Wenamun says, "I was silent at that important moment" (*iw=i gr n tȝy wnw.t ꜥ.t*). This is a clear allusion to the longstanding Egyptian wisdom tradition that the "silent man" is wise.[7] Using the same term (*gr*), the Instruction of Ptahhotep advises that "silence is more effective for you than to speak (your) heart";[8] the Teaching of a Man for His Son says, "If you are silent/modest, a (good) ending arises for you";[9] and the Instruction of Amenemope advises, "Let [your enemy] insult/curse you while you keep quiet."[10] In the Bible, the same tradition is attested in Prov 11:12 ("a prudent man remains silent") and 17:28 ("Even a fool who keeps silent is considered wise; the one who shuts his lips, discerning").

There are signs in the text that Wenamun is not so wise, however. His seizure of the silver from another ship is a rash act rather than a diplomatic way to solve his problem, and although he is at pains to insist it is not a theft (1/30–32), it immediately goes wrong. Furthermore, his collapse into tears when the men of Tjeker catch up to him in Byblos (2/64) is not a reaction used to describe successful people in genuine Egyptian autobiographies. Weeping is common in late Egyptian stories,[11] where it apparently had entertainment value, but more generally in Egyptian culture it expressed emotional weakness and failure.[12] Moers has described Wenamun's experience as one of being "humiliated and cast out," and experiencing the "doubtfulness of his Egyptian existence."[13]

Wenamun arguably brings his suffering upon himself. Zakarbaal's secretary says more concisely what a number of the characters seem to have been thinking: "What's wrong with you?" (2/65).[14] This creates a contrast with the late Egyptian story that was found with *Wenamun*; the Tale of Woe also addresses the struggles of a temple official living in chaotic times, but its protagonist Wermai seems to suffer innocently.

---

7. Moers, *Fingierte Welten*, 271.
8. 6,6: *ȝḫ n=k gr r pri.t ib* (lit., "bring forth your heart").
9. §20,6: *[i]r gr=k ḫpr n=k pḥ[.wy]*.
10. 26,3: *imm iri=f shwr=k iw=k gr*.
11. Winand, "Report," 545.
12. Hsu, "'I Wish I Could Die,'" 81–82.
13. "erniedriegt und verstoßen"; "die Fragwürdigkeit seiner ägyptischen Existenz"; Gerald Moers, "Die Reiseerzählung des Wenamun," 913.
14. Ritner's rendering of the phrase *iḫ r=k* ("What's with you?") is refreshingly colloquial; this is only a slight clarification.

The Byblians capitalize on Wenamun's existential crisis by taunting him as soon as the agreement is complete. Even Zakarbaal's cupbearer, Penamun, mocks Wenamun, saying: "The shadow of Pharaoh, l.p.h., your lord, has fallen upon you." Penamun's point is that the new pharaoh is Zakarbaal, and "the shadow" represents his favor and protection.[15] An illuminating biblical comparison comes from Isa 30:1–2, where the prophet condemns those

> who make an alliance, but against [Yahweh's] will,
>   adding sin to sin;
> who set out to go down to Egypt
>   without asking for my counsel,
> to take refuge in the protection of Pharaoh,
>   and to seek shelter in the shadow of Egypt.[16]

Penamun's further identification of Zakarbaal to Wenamun as "your lord" reverses the language of the 21st Dynasty letters discussed in chapter 5, which called Amun "your good lord."[17] And Penamun's reference to the standard l.p.h. formula ("life-prosperity-health," *'nḫ wḏȝ snb*) undermines Wenamun's previous claim that earlier pharaohs had been the sources of "life and health" for Byblian rulers (*'nḫ snb*; 2/29–30). Practically speaking, Zakarbaal is now in a position of power comparable to the one that the pharaohs had been accustomed to occupy. Since Penamun seems to be an Egyptian name (*p[ȝ-]n-'Imn*, "the one of Amun"), presumably he knows just how to twist the knife through this rhetoric.[18]

Penamun's mocking comment has some resonance with prophetic rhetoric. Taunts concerning the reduced powers of various empires were standard fare for the Hebrew prophets. Perhaps the most famous of these is Isa 14's mock

---

15. Ritner, *Libyan Anarchy*, 99n13. As Egberts insightfully comments, "The butler Penamun had gone abroad and found a new Pharaoh in Zekerbaal; the homesick envoy Wenamun, on the other hand, had given his heart to Amun. These two Egyptians symbolise the options one has when living in a land on the decline: outward and inward emigration" ("Hard Times," 103). This exchange has been subject to various other interpretations, but these are generally less cogent. For a survey, see Jackson, "'Shadow of Pharaoh,'" 273–86; cf. Meltzer, "Wenamun 2, 46," 86–88; Oppenheim, "Assyriological Gleanings IV," 7–11; Schipper, *Die Erzählung*, 15–16.

16. The context of Isaiah's oracle is the late eighth century, when Judah, under pressure from Assyrian imperial expansion, did indeed seek protection in an alliance with Egypt. For discussion and further literature, see Hays, *Death in the Iron Age II*, 288–315; and Hays, "'Those Weaned from Milk,'" 61–89.

17. Wente, *Letters*, 209 (#339).

18. Schipper (*Die Erzählung*, 205) notes that there is various evidence of Egyptians in the service of foreign courts at this time.

dirge for a fallen Mesopotamian king, but Egypt also figures prominently in these. Isaiah says, "Egypt's help is worthless and empty, therefore I have called her, 'Rahab who sits still'" (Isa 30:7). Jeremiah also gets in a similar dig at Egypt: "Give Pharaoh, king of Egypt, the name, 'Braggart who missed his chance'" (Jer 46:17). And Ezekiel says to the pharaoh, "Which among the trees of Eden was like you in glory and in greatness? Now you shall be brought down" (Ezek 31:18).

These are not purely prophetic tropes; indeed, they were part of a broader "diplomatic" discourse that sought to undermine the credibility of other nations. A similar taunt against Egypt in the Third Intermediate Period is reported in an Assyrian representative's speech to the officials of Hezekiah during the 701 siege of Jerusalem. As part of his effort to convince Jerusalem to submit without a fight, he says: "Look, you're relying on that broken reed of a staff, Egypt? It will pierce the hand of anyone who leans on it!" (Isa 36:6).

Returning to *Wenamun*: Zakarbaal cuts off Penamun, saying, "Leave him alone!" He is not ready to give his servant the privilege of insulting his newly indebted "vassal." Instead, he directs an even more pointed barb at Wenamun, telling him that he should be grateful he escaped with his life, that "I have not done to you what was done to the messengers of Khaemwase (i.e., Ramses XI)," who were kept in Byblos until their deaths (2/51–53). He suggests that Wenamun should go visit their tomb (*mʿḥʿ.t*; 2/52). Claiming power over life and death was a common way to assert royal and divine power in the ancient Near East.[19]

Wenamun's grandiosity, however, knows no bounds, and he has a different idea about monuments: he responds that Zakarbaal ought to make himself a stela (*wḏy*; 2/55) to commemorate his visit, praising "Amun-Re, King of the Gods [who] sent to me Amon-of-the-Road, his messenger, l.p.h., together with Wenamun," telling the story of the mission, and beseeching "50 years of life from Amon over and above my allotted fate" (2/55–58). He even tells him that in the future an Egyptian visitor may "read your name on the stela, you will receive water in the west like the gods who are there," promising him nothing less than a happy afterlife (2/59–60).

Like much of what Wenamun proposes, this is not sheer fantasy so much as an outdated expectation. Previous rulers of the Levantine coastal states had, once upon a time, credited pharaohs and Egyptian gods with giving life, and thanked them for it. In EA 136, Rib-Hadda of Byblos implored the pharaoh,

---

19. Hays, *Origins*, 68–94.

"May the king, my lord, give life to (his) servant!"[20] And the king of Ugarit sent a letter to the pharaoh that seeks "length of days for my lord before Amun, and before the gods of Egypt, that they might protect the soul/life of the Sun, the great king, my lord."[21] (Indeed, there is some indication that Amun was worshiped at Ugarit, even alongside Baal in his temple.[22])

However, as the stela inscriptions of the first-millennium Byblian kings Abibaal and Elibaal (*KAI* 5–6) reflect, by this time they were seeking the same thing from their own goddess, the Lady (Baalat) of Byblos, even on a stela seemingly made in Egypt (*KAI* 5:2). They no longer relied on Egypt in the same way.

When Wenamun has finished admonishing Zakarbaal, the Byblian ruler says to him: "This is a great testimony of words that you have said to me" (*iw≠f ḏd n≠i mtr.[t] ʿ3.t n.[t] md.t tȝy [i]-ḏd≠k n≠i*). Ritner's restrained, literalistic translation that is quoted here seems to me to render perfectly a quiet sarcasm on Zakarbaal's part. He is saying, drily, that this is a bunch of hot air. Or, as Baines put it: "The envoy of Amun offers nothing apart from fine words and spiritual benefits."[23] Even Wenamun realizes that his speech has fallen flat, and so reassures Zakarbaal that he will be paid (2/60–62).[24]

In support of this inference that Wenamun's "great testimony of words" is judged negatively, there are cautions in the Egyptian instruction literature about who should and should not write such a testimony. For example, in the Instruction of Any, from this same period: "A youth (*ʿḏdi*) does not write an instruction (or) testimony" (*bw iri ʿḏdi sbȝ.yt mtr.t*).[25] Zakarbaal may be saying that Wenamun is not mature or wise enough to instruct him. He has violated the wisdom tenets by creating a big heap of prophetic words. Or, as Antonio Loprieno rendered it, "ein großartiges Zeugnis von Predigt": "a great testimony of preaching"![26]

Thus, although Wenamun's theological rhetoric shows continuity with earlier totalizing claims for Amun, it rings differently in the Third Intermediate Period context. There is an increasingly large gap between rhetoric and reality.

---

20. LUGAL EN-ia ⌈TI⌉.⌈LA⌉ ÌR‹-šu›: EA 136:43. Rainey, *Amarna Correspondence*, 696–97. And see also EA 141–44, 147, 155, 198, etc.
21. *urk ym bʿly l pn amn w l pn il mṣrm dt tǵrn npš špš mlk rb bʿly*: KTU 2.23:20–24.
22. Eßbach, "Amun," 28.
23. Baines, "On the Background of Wenamun," 36.
24. Emphasized by Wilson in his review of *Untersuchungen zu Stil*, 229.
25. Instruction of Any, Version G, 5,1; cf. B, 22,17. Interestingly, the term *ʿḏdi* is the same one used for "ecstatic prophet" earlier in the story. There is also the Instruction of Amenemope, 16,1–2: *m-iri iri mt(r.t) n.(t) mdw(.t) n ʿḏȝ mtw≠k rmni ky m ns{.t}≠k*, "Do not make a testimony of false words, and do not carry away another with your tongue."
26. Loprieno, *Topos*, 72.

The Levantine rulers repeatedly bring the Theban back into line, and down a few notches, by reorienting him to the degrading realities of his actual political context.[27]

These conclusions help inform the long-running debate about *Wenamun*'s intended message. The most basic point is that Wenamun expresses a fairly radical view of Amun's primacy, one that resonates in various ways with biblical Yahwism. But since these also had significant continuities with traditional theologies of Amun-Re, it is not immediately apparent to all readers that Wenamun would have sounded foolish or extreme to an Egyptian audience. Perhaps the author was using a literary conceit to present Wenamun as a skilled spokesman, one who was able to convey Amun's theology in ways that a Levantine audience would be able to understand?

Much would depend upon the end of the story. It is sometimes argued that the story cannot be meant to undermine Amun, since in the end his will is done[28]—but one does not know this since the ending is lost. Wenamun receives the timber (2/47–49), but does he gets it home? Are his gambits, in the end, fully successful?[29] The reappearance of the Tjeker in pursuit of the silver that he stole (2/62–63) is an example of the story's use of delayed retribution, and it indicates the story did not simply end happily with the securing of the timber from Byblos. Zakarbaal makes it clear that he is not going to do anything more to protect Wenamun than he has to, telling the Tjeker that they can arrest him as soon as he is away from Byblos.

Further doubts about Wenamun's success arise at the port of call at which the story breaks off. Alasiya (Cyprus) greets him in an even less friendly way than the earlier ones: a mob tries to kill him. Wenamun seeks out the ruler, Ḥatiba, but does not even speak her language, and so requires an interpreter. When one volunteers, Wenamun immediately confronts the ruler with a pointed question: "Is injustice done daily even here?" She responds, "Really, what is the meaning of your saying that?" (*yꜣ iḫ m pꜣy⸗k ḏd.t⸗f*; 2/79–80). The introductory phrase has a negative connotation—basically, "Oy, what are you talking about?" It is in the vein of Bedor's "Are you serious or are you joking?"

---

27. Loprieno, *Topos*, 69: "es besteht eine eindeutige Kluft zwischen den von Wenamun vorgebrachten religiösen Argumenten und der Erniedrigung des politischen Kontextes, auf die der Byblosfürst ihn immer (direkt oder indirekt) hinweist." Also Schipper, *Die Erzählung*, 330: "Die faktische Macht in Syrien/Palästina liegt—so muß der menschliche Gesandte Wenamun schmerzvoll erfahren—nicht mehr bei den ägyptischen Pharaonen, sondern bei den lokalen Stadtfürsten"; Moers, "Travel as Narrative," 54–58. On the New Kingdom backdrop of Egyptian expectations, see Cornelius, "Ancient Egypt and the Other," 322–40.

28. Schipper (*Die Erzählung*, 15–16) traces this approach to Wiedemann (*Ägyptische Geschichte* [1884], 94–95) and Maspero ("Contes populaires" [1906], 214–15). More recently, examples of this include Baines ("On *Wenamun* as a Literary Text," 230) and Assmann (*Mind of Egypt*, 294).

29. Winand, "Report," 541, 559.

and the Byblian secretary's "What's wrong with you?" Things are, if anything, going downhill for Wenamun.

Moers argues that Wenamun's character undergoes development in the course of the surviving story, and that, having been forced by Zakarbaal to realize that "he is not who he thought he was, and also that the world does not function as he thought," he learns to be more cagey with Ḥatiba.[30] It is not clear to me that the text supports this conclusion. What does seem likely, given his ongoing struggles, is that still other things befell him in subsequent parts of the story that are lost.

One could catalogue more comic elements. For example, even the names in the story reflect a certain Dickensian quality of being a bit too spot-on to be real,[31] starting with Wenamun's name ("Amun exists!") and Zakarbaal's ("Baal remembers!" or "Remember Baal!"). The ruler of Dor is named "the one in Dor," and another ruler is perhaps called "Great One of the Crown" (*wr-ktr*). Wenamun has an interlocutor with a name that rhymes with his (Penamun). All of these seem like the stuff of literature, even fairy tales. But what is the purpose of the comedy?

The Target of the Satire

Even among interpreters who perceive a satirical edge to the story, there is disagreement about who or what is being satirized. According to Assmann, it is Theban theocracy itself: "The Tale of Wenamun makes it clear that contemporary Thebans regarded [this theocratic governing style] as a curiosity that clearly flouted tradition and that was very difficult if not impossible to make plausible to outsiders like the Prince of Byblos."[32] Yet, as we have seen, the perspectives expressed about Amun do not, for the most part, flout theological tradition; rather, it is Wenamun's diplomatic skills that are problematic.

We might return to the circumstances of *Wenamun*'s discovery. The fact that it was collected with the Onomasticon of Amenope and the Tale of Woe suggests (to speak loosely) a "wisdom" milieu and a scribal school.[33] *Wenamun* is not a monumental or official document. So although the author certainly

---

30. Moers, *Fingierte Welten*, 265.
31. Among Charles Dickens's characters are the scrounging Scrooge, the bumptious Mr. Bumble, and Mr. Merdle, who is full of *merde*.
32. Assmann, *Mind of Egypt*, 295–96.
33. Caminos, *Tale of Woe*, 3: "There can be little doubt that the three texts, though each written by a different hand, are products of the same scribal school or copying office and very much of the same age." See also Winand, "Report," 541; Muhs, "Wenamun's Bad Trip," 7.

seems to have been conversant with Amun theologies, he was not merely restating them. Rather, *Wenamun* may have been a "view from the margins." It reads as a wisdom tale that entertains while teaching its audience. It maintains a sense of humor and a critical distance from its main character, but it is not intended to undermine Amun.

It may, however, be intended to undermine Wenamun and those like him. As discussed in chapter 1, the latest arguments for the tenth-century origins of *Wenamun* argue that its composition was influenced by the effort of the new Pharaoh Sheshonq to undermine the Theban priesthood of Amun. Of course, one could not get rid of Amun—or Thebes, where Karnak had long been the most important religious center in Egypt. The disastrous reign of Akhenaten had amply demonstrated that. But by founding a new Amun temple and undercutting the priestly power of the older one, one could fragment its authority. While this remains inferential, it is certainly an appealing argument, in that it would explain why the Theban priesthood is satirized while the god is respected.

Wenamun and Jonah

How should one assess Schipper's hypothesis that an Egyptian author basically sympathetic with Amun-worship wrote a story about a foolish representative sent on a divine mission, and that one of the chief goals of the story was to show that Amun's will would be done despite the foibles of his human representatives? Is it plausible that the author would have explored the comic potential of this situation as much as *Wenamun*'s author did? The humorous aspects of ancient prophetic stories have already been noted above in connection with Balaam, but there is another biblical tale that is even more similar to *Wenamun* as a whole: that of Jonah.

In the book of Jonah, a man is charged to deliver a message from his deity in a foreign land (Jonah 1:1–2); he goes on a voyage to an exotic locale (1:3), and the ship is blown off course (1:4, 13). In much the same way, Wenamun is sent on a divine mission, and immediately meets with trouble. He too is blown off course into dangerous circumstances (2/74).

Like Wenamun, Jonah does not behave as one might expect a hero and a spokesman for a deity to behave. While the storm rages, and the sailors frantically labor to save the ship, Jonah goes below deck and takes a nap (Jonah 1:5). In fact, he somehow manages to fall into a deep sleep despite the ship threatening to break apart around him. And like those whom Wenamun meets, the captain's reaction to Jonah leaves no doubt how he was perceived by others: "The captain came and said to him, 'What are you doing sound asleep?'" (Jonah 1:6). Basically a version of "What's with you?" (2/65). There is even the suggestion that Wenamun might be thrown into the sea by his ship's crew (1/56), just as Jonah was (1:11–15).

Like Wenamun, however, when this foolish Jonah opens his mouth, theological poetry comes out. He is told by the captain to "Get up, call on your god!," and so he proclaims to the seafaring foreigners that he serves "the God of heaven, who made the sea and the dry land" (1:9). The reader is led to conclude that their efforts to call on their own gods (1:5) are pointless. Thus, as with Amun in *Wenamun*, the primacy, authority, and power of Yahweh is asserted at the very outset. Even though Jonah turns out to be the problem, Yahweh is the solution.

Like Wenamun, Jonah gets second chances despite his failures; although he is threatened with death, he is saved by divine intervention (2:11–3:1 MT). He eventually proclaims the message to Nineveh, and does so in a way that would be completely implausible to actual Mesopotamian audiences: "Forty days more, and Nineveh shall be overthrown!" (3:4). And yet, despite him, the Ninevites believe and repent, and the divine will is achieved (3:5–9). In Wenamun's case, it is the ecstatic prophet's invocation of Amun that convinces Zakarbaal to give him a chance. In both cases, the turning point is portrayed as the work of the deity.

One might also compare the sudden about-faces of the foreign rulers in the court tales of Joseph (Gen 41:39–45) and Daniel (Dan 2:46–48; 3:28–30; 4:34–37). As in *Wenamun* and Jonah, these followed prophetic or divinatory revelations. Furthermore, all of these biblical tales are from the postexilic period and responding (like *Wenamun*) to the challenges of the encounter with powerful foreign courts in distant, exotic locales.

Throughout the story, Jonah, like Wenamun, shows himself to be foolish, impetuous, and moody. He is told to go to Nineveh, but immediately flees far away (1:3). He gets angry about Yahweh's mercy and wishes to die (4:2–3). God gives him a mere shade-bush, which makes him happy, but when it withers he immediately wants to die again (4:8–9). The reader is given to understand that Jonah is intemperate and inconstant. And yet, in the midst of this, Jonah proves himself capable of enunciating traditional ideas about Yahweh with attractive rhetorical force: "O Yahweh! Is not this what I said while I was still in my own country? That is why I fled to Tarshish at the beginning; for I knew that you are a gracious God and merciful, slow to anger, and abounding in steadfast love, and ready to relent from punishing" (4:2). All these aspects of Jonah are broadly comparable to Wenamun. Schipper remarks on the transformation of Wenamun as soon as he begins "preaching" (to use Loprieno's term again): "Here suddenly a completely different Wenamun emerges than the clumsy commercial traveler. Wenamun appears rhetorically skilled, theologically versed and argues in such a way that he achieves his goal."[34]

Indeed, the ideological outlooks and goals of the two stories are extremely similar, even though Jonah is written in a simpler literary register. Both allow the reader to laugh about the weaknesses of a god's prophetic representatives while simultaneously absorbing positive messages about the god himself. (As Baines noted, "*Wenamun* is more likely to show that human beings cannot serve Amun as befits him than to question his efficacy."[35]) In both cases, this would have been a potentially promising rhetorical strategy for an author who wanted to promote the authority of a deity at a moment when weakened national circumstances meant that the god's actual human agents looked rather unimpressive. The book of Jonah is postexilic, from a period when Judah's monarchy had been crushed by foreign powers and confidence in prophets had waned; although Egypt was not in quite as dire straits in the time of *Wenamun*'s composition, power and confidence are relative, and both would have ebbed significantly.

Both Judah and Egypt were in moments of great anxiety about their status as nations and about the roles of the gods who had long been thought to underwrite that status. Jonah was also written in a period during which Yahwistic prophecy no longer enjoyed the prominence that it had before and during the Babylonian Exile.[36] It may have been intended to supply a rationale for the passing away of the prophetic institution that had defined Yahwism, while seeking to preserve faith in the god for whom the Hebrew prophets had spoken. Arno Egberts has argued that *Wenamun* was doing something similar: "'Wenamun' showed its audience a way of coping with the harsh realities of their age, which included the collapse of the traditional monarchy and its outdated decorum. By transforming Amun into the infallible king of the universe, the ancient Egyptians could regain in religion what they had lost in politics."[37] The arguments of Egberts and Schipper, that *Wenamun* maintains (or even amplifies) reverence for Amun himself while humbling his Theban representatives, makes the best sense of the text. By the postexilic period when Jonah was written, Judah had suffered an even greater reversal of political fortunes, having lost its independence. Like *Wenamun*, it asserts the dominance of its god in the face of contradictory historical facts.

---

34. Schipper, *Die Erzählung*, 269–70: "Dabei liegt das eigentlich Bemerkenswerte darin, daß hier auf einmal ein ganz anderer Wenamun zutage tritt als der ungeschickte Handelsreisende. Wenamun erscheint rhetorisch beschlagen, theologisch versiert und argumentiert so, daß er sein Ziel erreicht."
35. Baines, "On *Wenamun* as a Literary Text," 230.
36. On the decline of Hebrew prophecy, see, e.g., Blenkinsopp, *History of Prophecy*, 226–29.
37. Egberts, "Hard Times," 108.

One might demur from Schipper's argument about the authorizing power behind the text, however, in that he implies at times that it was propagated by Sheshonq I himself in support of his new Amun temple at el-Hiba: "On the one hand, Amun's (and thus Egypt's) claim to Syria/Palestine is to be expressed and on the other hand, the Theban priesthood is to be made aware of the fact that Amun is on the side of the ruling pharaohs and that they have all real political power.... It is precisely through the interaction between the Theban god and the power-political authorities, i.e., the ruling pharaoh, that the fate of Egypt can be guided."[38] I cannot see that *Wenamun* makes a strong argument in favor of pharaonic power, and it is difficult to see it as a royal product. The rulers of Egypt are scarcely present in the text, and they do nothing but send payments and sign off on Amun's wishes. Rather, it is in a scribal/wisdom vein—a reflection on theological themes and priestly behavior. As such, one could infer that it was written by priests, for priests.[39]

It is telling that *Wenamun* was found with the Tale of Woe / Letter of Wermai; as is often observed, these represent two different perspectives on the experience of chaos in the postimperial world. Both report negative repercussions of the unrest in Egypt; the Tale of Woe focuses on the experience internal to Egypt, while *Wenamun* focuses on the external experience. As Gerald Moers has noted, "Fictional travel-literature is the only place where in pharaonic Egypt the apparently problematic interface of cultural and individual identity is openly discussed."[40] That sort of reflection does not happen in official literature, even in the Third Intermediate Period. In its reflection, *Wenamun* does indeed seem to take the inflated Theban priesthood as a negative example, and offers the main character's series of errors and misfortunes as lessons in what the wider world outside the walls of the temple and the boundaries of Egypt is like, and what not to do when you encounter it.

It is unwarranted to imagine any direct literary connection between the earlier *Wenamun* and the later book of Jonah. The longstanding tradition of tales about prophets and wise men such as Balaam and Ahiqar, which reached across national boundaries in the ancient Near East, leaves open the

---

38. Schipper, *Die Erzählung*, 317: "Es soll zum einen der Anspruch Amuns (und damit Ägyptens) auf Syrien/Palästina zum Ausdruck gebracht und zum zweiten die thebanische Priesterschaft darauf eingestellt werden, daß Amun auf Seiten der regierenden Pharaonen ist und diese über alle realpolitische Macht verfügen.... Dabei kann gerade durch das Zusammenspiel des thebanischen Gottes und der machtpolitischen Instanzen, sprich dem regierenden Pharao, das Geschick Ägyptens geleitet werden." He strikes a different note a few pages later, however: "Die faktische Macht in Syrien/Palästina liegt—so muß der menschliche Gesandte Wenamun schmerzvoll erfahren—nicht mehr bei den ägyptischen Pharaonen, sondern bei den lokalen Stadtfürsten" (330).
39. Cf. Fischer-Elfert in his review of *Die Erzählung*, 224.
40. Moers, "Travel as Narrative," 58.

possibility, but it seems more likely that these were parallel developments within each culture on the basis of the older theologies. As the conclusion to this volume discusses in more detail, the crucial cultural contacts were probably in an earlier period for Israel, when its imagery of Yahweh as a divine king emerged.

Conclusion: Amun Theocracy and Biblical Monotheism

THIS BRIEF STUDY HAS IDENTIFIED similarities between the theological rhetoric of *Wenamun* and that of the Hebrew Bible, especially the prophetic literature. It reviews the ample existing scholarship on *Wenamun*'s use of Semitic loanwords and other linguistic features as part of its literary efforts to portray the foreign flavor of the Levant for an Egyptian audience. Within the historical context of Mediterranean shipping and international trade in the tenth century BCE, Wenamun's totalizing claims about Amun's absolute lordship over everything stand out as not merely aggressive but somewhat fantastical, for a nation whose power and international reach were reduced. This bore comparison to the similarly ambitious theological rhetoric of the biblical texts indigenous to Israel and Judah, which made similar claims for Yahweh.

As the story goes on, Wenamun's claims lead to a theological confrontation between him and Zakarbaal of Byblos over which nation's god is really most powerful and has authority over the Lebanon. The Byblian ruler answers that Amun is not really so powerful without Seth/Baal at his side: it is the Levantine storm god who really thunders in the heavens. This dispute between Amun and Baal is analogous to the prophetic contests over the powers of Baal and Yahweh in the Hebrew Bible, and just as the representatives of Amun and Baal seem to share a certain amount of theological language, there are numerous examples of Yahwistic authors in conversation with Baalistic rhetoric. Amun thus plays a similar role in *Wenamun* to the role of Yahweh in the biblical prophets. Although some efforts to compare Amun and Yahweh theologies have been noted by both Egyptologists and biblical scholars, very few of the specific comparisons discussed here have been identified, nor have the historical channels of transmission that they suggest.

The study also offers a new analysis of the crucial exchange at the end of Zakarbaal's longest speech, in which he mocks Wenamun for being on a "foolish mission" (*mšʿ śwgꜣ*). It demonstrates that *śwgꜣ* is related to a group of Hebrew and Akkadian roots that are also used to mock prophets deemed crazy or drunken. In sum, Zakarbaal impugns Wenamun's claims by suggesting that he is a fool or a madman who is speaking falsely of the gods.

In response, Wenamun reasserts that Amun is sovereign over the Lebanon and its timber, and will fight like a lion for his property. This too is phraseology with close cognates in the Hebrew Bible, as well as other Egyptian texts; the Bible asserts Yahweh's ownership of the Lebanon, and even the Nile, as well as his divine kingship and leonine qualities. Furthermore, glyptic evidence shows that leonine imagery for deities was common to Egypt and the Levant in the Iron I–IIA.

According to Wenamun, Amun's sovereignty leads to suzerainty: the right to dictate terms to supposedly lesser powers. Using language that is very reminiscent of Hittite treaties and biblical covenants, Wenamun enjoins Zakarbaal and Byblos to submit to Amun's demands as previous generations had, so as to be good "servants of Amun." Comparison with the similar efforts of Solomon to get help from the Phoenicians for his temple-building project brings into sharper focus the impolitic aspects of Wenamun's approach. Since Egypt no longer dominated the Phoenician seacoast in this period, Wenamun's efforts would have appeared out of touch or even comic. Nevertheless, like the authors of biblical covenants, Wenamun grandiosely promises that Zakarbaal and his people will flourish in the land if they are faithful to his deity, and he invokes oath language that is also familiar from biblical literature. This casting of Amun as the divine suzerain in a diplomatic context has not been adequately recognized in scholarship on biblical covenants and has the potential to shift our understanding of their influences and origins.

In the story, Wenamun is also portrayed as a messenger of Amun. This is an unusually direct theological relationship for Egyptian texts, which more typically portray such officials as messengers of the pharaoh. However, it is directly analogous to biblical prophetic literature, which regularly characterizes prophets as messengers of Yahweh. This invites comparison with Egyptian letters concerning Amun temple officials from the period of the story, who speak similarly to Wenamun, albeit in a less extreme and literary manner. This may also shift the discussion about the origins of the prophetic "messenger metaphor" away from the typical Mesopotamian and Persian sources toward a consideration of Egyptian messengers as well.

We have also asked whether Wenamun ought to be considered "among the prophets." Priests and other temple officials in Egypt played important roles in divination and were called "prophets" by the Greeks. Egyptian texts both before and after *Wenamun* describe predictive speeches, but these are usually *vaticinium ex eventu* for the purpose of royal propaganda. There is also evidence in Egypt that the consultation of older texts was seen as an ongoing source of revelation, much like scribal prophecy in the Hebrew Bible, and

Wenamun shows evidence of this intertextual quality. A thorough analysis of the issue of Egyptian prophecy was not feasible, but the fact that the proclamations of priests and other officials about Amun have such significant and diverse similarities with those of Yahweh ought to invite further discussion.

Wenamun's speeches proclaiming the will and status of the gods are set in a narrative context; it has this in common with various Hebrew prophetic books as well. Even more specifically, Wenamun's maritime journey to an exotic location, his misfortunes along the way, his extreme theological claims, and his sometimes comically foolish behavior all bear a close similarity to aspects of the book of Jonah. Both stories seem to sincerely assert the supremacy of a deity while undermining certain of the deity's representatives, for reasons plausibly related to crises of religious authority in changing socio-historical contexts.

Channels of Transmission

These numerous points of comparison between *Wenamun* and the Hebrew prophets invite fresh reflection on the cultural and religious relationships among Egypt, Phoenicia, and Israel/Judah. While many of the rhetorical features of *Wenamun* described here can be found in various ancient Near Eastern texts across a wide range of times and places, the overall impression that they create, of a prophetic debate akin to those of the Hebrew Bible, is not to be ignored. The entire story is arguably a meditation on prophecy, its foundations, and its claims.

As with most instances of cultural influence, these ideas would not have been simply transmitted all at one time. Cultures absorb ideas from the world around them gradually, and in a variety of ways. They also tend to take on ideas for which a receptive matrix already exists in the receiving culture; ideas that seem completely foreign are difficult to convey and to accept. In the case of Egypt and the Levant, the contact was almost aboriginal; the beginning point in the cultural conversation was prehistoric.[1] Nevertheless, in the periods under discussion, Egypt was the greater power, and the wealthier and more prestigious culture; and as far as we can tell, it recorded these ideas about theocracy and world dominion long before Israel, Judah, or Phoenicia did.

---

1. As Liwak ("Herrschaft," 57) commented specifically in connection with prophecy: "Beziehungen zwischen Ägypten und Syrien-Palästina bestanden seit dem 4. Jt. v. Chr., über weite Strecken mit kultureller Dominanz Ägyptens. Deshalb ist die Frage nach einer Rezeption ägyptischer Literatur über einen allgemeinen kultur- und religionsgeschichtlichen Einfluss hinaus berechtigt und sinnvoll."

Focusing on the period of *Wenamun*'s composition in the early first millennium BCE, there is ample evidence for the closeness of the connections between Egypt and the Levant. More specifically, Shirly Ben-Dor Evian has helped to fill in some of the gaps in that story during the Iron I–II/Third Intermediate Period by means of material data from the archaeological record.[2] She particularly emphasizes "the role of trading systems in spreading the Amun name in the Levant."[3] In connection with the glyptic finds from Jerusalem published by Keel and noted in chapter 2, these studies bring into focus the broad cultural networks through which these theological ideas would have flowed along with so much other information. In keeping with its power and prestige, Egypt can be seen as one of the major sources of ideas for various biblical authors.

The new studies of material culture are all the more important since older assumptions about the historicity of biblical stories are now weakened. Previous generations of Egyptologists had (unknowingly) all but written the history of the transmission of Theban Amun-theocracy to the Solomonic court when they suggested that the daughter of pharaoh whom the Bible repeatedly claims Solomon married (1 Kgs 3:1; 7:8; 9:24; 11:1) was a daughter of Siamun[4]—the same Siamun who reinterred Princess Neskhons, and to whose reign the Amun hymn, the official "credo" of the theocratic Amun state, is credited (see chapter 1).[5] While it is certainly intriguing to imagine Siamun's daughter introducing Solomon to Amun—as it is said his other wives introduced him to their gods (1 Kgs 11:1–10)—there is no extrabiblical attestation of such a marriage.[6]

Considered from a more strictly historical perspective, there are at least two ways to think of ongoing Egyptian influence in Israel and Judah throughout the Iron I–IIA. The first, which the story of *Wenamun* particularly invites reflection on, was via mediation through the coastal trading powers, especially the Phoenicians, who had extensive contact with both Egypt and the mostly inland Levantine nations. The second is not to be overlooked, however: Egyptian culture deeply imbued that of the southern Levant via Egypt's imperial domination of the region in the late Bronze Age. Egyptian culture may have faded and become intermingled with that of the autochthonous population during the Iron Age, but it certainly did not disappear. Each of these vectors is discussed in turn.

---

2. Ben-Dor Evian, "Egypt and Israel," 30–39; Ben-Dor Evian, "Egypt and the Levant."
3. Ben-Dor Evian, "Amun-of-the-Road," 59.
4. E.g., Shaw, *Ancient Egypt*, 327.
5. Ritner, *Libyan Anarchy*, 145; Broekman, "21st Dynasty," 13–19.
6. Ben-Dor Evian, "Past and Future," 1–11.

The role of the Phoenicians as a conduit of indirect Egyptian influence on Israel and Judah should also not be underestimated. The links between Israel, Judah, and the coastal city-states are sketched briefly above. Some would advocate more caution about connecting *Wenamun* to the biblical literature by this channel of influence—Byblos, of course, was not Jerusalem, but both were part of a closely linked network of cities. The lack of documentation for their correspondence is a result of their use of soft media for writing; it is especially clear in this case that absence of evidence is not evidence of absence. Byblos and other Phoenician cities were at the center of a network. As Monroe has observed, "In a *longue durée* view of Phoenician identity, one may plausibly suggest that by 1000 BCE residents of Byblos, Sidon, and Tyre had two thousand years of training in the politics of the middle ground. They were the perfect 'people' to create a Mediterranean small world."[7] Provocative similarities between Phoenician and biblical religion are already well recognized in that they share aniconic tendencies,[8] but the comparative conversation could be expanded.

Ideas about the gods were regularly translated to and from different cultures in the ancient Near East.[9] Itamar Singer wrote that a "basic knowledge of foreign pantheons was not just an intellectual asset of Hittite theologians, but rather an essential requirement for the Hittite 'Foreign Office'"[10]—and this was not only true of imperial courts of the Late Bronze Age but also (and perhaps especially) of smaller states throughout ancient history. They had a strong interest in understanding empires' ideology in order to interact successfully with them. Although one cannot assume that *Wenamun* is a historical account or biography, it is reasonable to take it as a rumination on a realistic state of affairs, reflecting potential problems that might be faced by Egypt's international representatives at the time.

It is apparent in the Amarna correspondence of the Late Bronze Age that claims about Amun were already being transmitted by New Kingdom Egyptians and absorbed by Levantine royal courts. A king of Tyre quoted Egyptian hymnic language to the pharaoh, in Akkadian.[11] A king of Ugarit wrote to the pharaoh: "I am [your servant] who begs [for life to] the Sun, the great king, my lord. Then do I not pray for the life of his soul before Baʻal Saphon my lord, and length of days for my lord before Amun and before the gods of Egypt

---

7. Monroe, "Marginalizing Civilization," 268.
8. Doak, *Phoenician Aniconism*.
9. Smith, *God in Translation*, passim.
10. Singer, "'Thousand Gods of Hatti,'" 93.
11. Albright, "Egyptian Correspondence," passim.

who protect the soul of the Sun, the Great King, my lord?"[12] The sensitivity of Levantine rulers to Egyptian theology is also demonstrated by their *ceasing* to refer to Amun during the Amarna Period when his worship was suppressed in favor of Aten,[13] and this same sensitivity would have allowed later Levantine rulers and their scribes to absorb the sort of theocratic language about Amun that Wenamun spoke, and that later found its way into the Bible.

Turning to the second vector, the Gaza Amun temple has brought into focus the apparent perseverance of Egyptian culture in the southern Levant after the recession of its imperial rule in the Third Intermediate Period. The direct Egyptian presence decreased, but Levantine culture in the Iron I–II continued to be a composite made up of all the cultures that had influenced the region over millennia, including Egypt's. Iconographic analysis points to the way that "during the formative Middle Bronze Age both Egyptian and Syrian/Anatolian traditions flowed together into the pool of Canaanite motifs."[14] Aaron Burke has recently called attention to the wide array of Egyptian officials who populated Canaan at the end of the Late Bronze Age, and argues cogently that many of these officials would have formed family and other connections in the region—so that even as the imperial support apparatus collapsed, a number of them stayed behind.[15] Among them were early Iron Age scribes who represented a "community of practice" transmitting knowledge about everything from "the material to the ideological, from tools to routines, stories, training, and symbols."[16]

Furthermore, there were always particular nodes of more intense contact with Egypt. Byblos, as discussed above, was one of these. Another was the temple to Amun in Gaza, which was built or rebuilt as late as the reign of Ramses III (r. 1183–1152), just a few decades before the end of Egyptian rule there.[17] It has been hypothesized for some time that the worship of Amun continued in the southern Levant, and even that the Gaza temple continued to serve as a workshop for Amun paraphernalia.[18] Amun and Amun-Re were the second most popular gods on Southern Levantine seals during the Iron I,

---

12. *KTU* 2.23 (RS 16.078+.15–24). Another possible reference to Amun is found in *KTU* 5.11; see Pardee, "New Readings," 45.
13. Galan, "EA 164 and the God Amun," 287–91; Rainey, *El-Amarna Correspondence*, 23.
14. Schroer, "Continuity of the Canaanite Glyptic Tradition," 482–502.
15. Burke, "Left Behind," 50–66.
16. Burke, "Left Behind," 60.
17. This is recounted in Papyrus Harris I; for the text and further references, see Wimmer, "Egyptian Temples," 1086–87. On the dating of the Egyptian withdrawal in general, see Burke, "Left Behind," 51–52.
18. This suggestion originated with Uehlinger, "Der Amun-Tempel Ramses' III," 11–15, and it is carried forward into his later work, including with Keel. An updated discussion of the theory is presented by Koch, *Colonial Encounters*, 124.

reflecting the ongoing footprint of Egyptian religion there.[19] Amun was not forgotten in his former imperial territory. The lion iconography noted in chapter 4 is another example. Münger deems artifacts such as these examples of "direct and unbiased access to the past societies' belief systems and their participation in the cultural exchange with neighboring civilizations."[20] It is not even quite right to speak of Egyptian and Levantine culture as if they were entirely discrete or pure entities. The exchange of ideas is fairly inevitable for neighboring regions, and elements of cultures flowed in all directions.

It is surely not an either-or question. Rather, we see Egyptian influence from various directions. There is ample evidence of the influence of the existing Amun theology on the Semitic cultures that formed the backdrop for early Yahwistic theologies.

Egypt and Semitic Prophecy

Thus the Levant absorbed Amun theologies from Egypt, but is it also possible to speak of an Egyptian appropriation of Levantine prophetic ideas? Is *Wenamun* a record of Egyptian prophetic proclamation? Were the Egyptians impressed by the potential of this bombastic theological rhetoric that took the claims of temple hymns and proclaimed it aloud in practical and political situations? Or was *Wenamun* merely a skillful portrait (and perhaps even a send-up) of prophetic practices and ideologies?

Past scholarship has generally concluded that what we see in *Wenamun* is an Egyptian reaction to the foreign phenomenon of making prophetic speeches in public, political contexts. And indeed, it must be granted that, as far as we can tell, *Wenamun* was not part of a native Egyptian genre of prophetic texts. Other similar texts are scarce in Egypt, and a number of *Wenamun*'s terms and phrases for prophets and their messages were borrowed from secular usage or from Semitic languages.

And yet, the author of *Wenamun* recognizes in the classic tropes and metaphors of prophetic speech a kinship between the two cultures that he exploits. Wenamun makes a fool of himself, by Egyptian standards, by shouting at nearly every ruler he meets; yet he is shouting the same claims that Egyptian theologians had made for Amun for generations—and in the strange, foreign world of the Levant, this uncouth and abrasive technique seems to have met with a certain kind of success. Thus the author is able to bring across what he

---

19. Ben-Marzouk, "Some Highlights," 292–301.
20. Münger, "References to the Pharaoh," 40. See also Strawn, *What Is Stronger?*, 87–109.

regarded as true claims about Amun's authority while simultaneously undermining the unreliable main character and poking fun at the relatively uncivilized Wild West Asia (as Egyptians would have seen it).

The Egyptians were not unaffected by the encounter with Semitic prophecy. *Wenamun* is only part of the picture; we can safely infer that they were not meeting it for the first time in the Third Intermediate Period. Prophecy was incorporated into political discourse centuries earlier at Mari; and so Egypt, which was deeply involved in Bronze Age Syria, will have known of it. Martti Nissinen has rightly observed, "Whatever 'really' happened in Byblos, the report of Wenamon tells us how an Egyptian writer would have interpreted a prophetic performance, and the way he does it is compatible in every respect with the cuneiform evidence he could not possibly have been familiar with. This speaks for a common, long-term Near Eastern understanding of the divine–human communication by means of the prophetic activity."[21] Nissinen is speaking only about the ecstatic-prophet episode, but the rest of the story demonstrates that the observation holds for prophetic rhetoric in much more detailed ways. The momentary befuddlement of Bedor or Zakarbaal is not because of Wenamun's theological claims or the way they are made, but only because they don't correspond with their understanding of the power dynamics. The Semitic speakers clearly comprehend the rhetoric, because they rise to meet it with their own. There is a shared understanding of the "rhetorical moment," particularly in Zakarbaal's responses.

It would appear that what is foreign to Egypt about prophecy is more the performance than the rhetoric: it does not seem to have been common for an Egyptian official to issue ambitious monologues about Amun's greatness to unsympathetic audiences. That would have been inconsistent with the classic Egyptian ideal of the wise courtier as a "silent one." And real power, of the sort that Egypt consistently had during the New Kingdom, doesn't need to announce itself with blustery verbiage. Yet in case after case, we have seen that the claims that Wenamun makes echo those of Egyptian religious hymns or the missives of temple officials. We know that this is true of the Hebrew prophets as well, that they (and the scribes who recorded or invented their words) creatively used existing literary and cultural forms, tropes, and motifs to suit their rhetorical purposes. That is perhaps why Wenamun's "prophetic rhetoric" sounds so much like theirs—it is theological rhetoric *in extremis*, proclaimed under the pressure of adverse historical circumstances.

It is unfortunate that the early records of Semitic prophecy are not more revealing about the nature of the prophets' rhetoric. The Mari texts do not

---

21. Nissinen, *Ancient Prophecy*, 181–82. This understanding is affirmed by Schroeder, *Let Us Go to the Seer!*, 130.

include extended prophetic speeches (unlike the later biblical and Neo-Assyrian prophetic texts), Ugarit does not offer evidence of prophecy,[22] and scant textual records survive from Phoenicia. With more information, it might be possible to determine whether the Egyptians absorbed certain theological ideas or tropes from the Levant. For example, we know that the Hyksos brought certain features of material culture with them to Egypt, and we know that Egypt was impacted by their religion (for example, the changes in Egyptian views of Seth/Baal discussed in chapter 3). To investigate such questions, however, would take us into a much earlier period, and away from the task at hand.

Theocracy and Kingship

As the introduction lays out, theocracy and summodeism are, respectively, political and theological ways to describe claims for the sole power of a deity. They are not equivalent with monotheism, but they do employ extravagant rhetoric that is easily adapted to a monotheistic worldview. These ideas are intertwined, and a clearer recognition of their histories might reconfigure some common assumptions about biblical rhetoric.

Levantine nations absorbed theocratic ideas oriented toward Amun at least from the New Kingdom onward. Amun theologies, including their theocratic aspects, have been shown to be a part of Israel's Canaanite heritage. Scribes employed by the rulers of Late Bronze Age Byblos, Ugarit, and Tyre could allude to and even quote Egyptian theology. These theologies would have been reinforced for Israel and Judah during the monarchic period by the extensive diplomatic contacts with Egypt, and no doubt experts at the later Davidic court in Jerusalem were aware of Egyptian religion as well. This provides a context in which priests, scribes, and other Hebrew elites such as international traders could absorb and propagate ideas.

In fact, the socio-rhetorical conditions of Wenamun's proclamations of Amun and the Bible's proclamations of Yahweh were strikingly analogous: both were produced by theocratic representatives of cultures that had more ambition than actual power. Much like Egypt in the Third Intermediate Period, Israel and Judah had limited capacities to impose their will on other nations; even in their periods of flourishing, they were not imperial powers. And even before the theological rhetoric of the Mesopotamian empires of the era made their impression on Israel and Judah, one sees an exchange of universalizing rhetoric between Egypt and the Levant.

---

22. Del Olmo Lete, *Canaanite Religion*, 290.

Wenamun portrays Amun as a divine king who claims dominion and demands submission, implicitly to stipulations akin to those of treaties and covenants. Although the story goes further than most Egyptian texts in effacing human kingship, theocratic ideas such as these coexisted with human kingship in various configurations; they were propagated not only by the Theban priest-kings but by a succession of pharaohs from the Ramessides to the Kushites. The idea of Amun's kingship was essentially compatible with human kingship.

This has implications for the history of Israelite religion, especially for the image of Yahweh as king. Within biblical studies, the idea that theocracy was only advanced by priests after the end of the Davidic dynasty is a cherished axiom that manifests itself in various ways. It is now commonly argued that theocratic biblical covenants would only have sprung up after the end of the Davidic monarchy and the imposition of Persian rule that forbade the reestablishment of native, human monarchy.[23]

Wellhausen's influential *Prolegomena to the History of Israel* played a significant role in normalizing that idea. Theocracy is a major focus of the *Prolegomena*, and in general it is discussed as a hierocracy created by the priestly law. But even Wellhausen grants in passing that the Davidic monarchy itself could be seen as a manifestation of theocracy: "The kingship of Yahweh, in the political sense in which it is conceived, is the religious expression of the founding of the kingdom by Saul and David. The theocracy was the state itself; the ancient Israelites regarded the civil state as a miracle, or, in their own words, a divine help. In their view of theocracy, later Jews always took the state for granted as already there, and so they could build theocracy on the top of it as a specially spiritual entity."[24] As this reflects, the kingship of Yahweh and the Davidic kingship could be seen as complementary. Theocracy and human kingship easily coexist, as Assyrian justifications for war demonstrate;[25] it is hierocracy that flourishes in the absence of monarchy. Thus, it does not seem safe to theorize that the kingship of Yahweh developed only in a period without a king in Israel/Judah; nor is it justifiable to assume that when a deity was portrayed

---

23. Levin, "Israel," 79–80: "The Second Temple community . . . overcame the desire of the restitution of the monarchy with the notion that Yahweh himself was the king over Israel."

24. "Das Königtum Jahve's, in der politischen Bestimmtheit wie es gedacht wird, ist der religiöse Ausdruck der Staatsgründung durch Saul und David. Die Theokratie war eben der Staat selber; den bürgerlichen Staat sahen die alten Israeliten als ein Wunder oder, wie sie sich ausdrückten, als eine Hülfe Gottes an. Die späteren Juden setzten bei ihrer Anschauung von Theokratie den Staat immer schon als bestehend voraus und konnten darum die Theokratie als ein besonderes geistliches Wesen darüber zimmern." Wellhausen, *Prolegomena zur Geschichte Israels*, 439. Translation adapted from Black and Menzies (p. 414).

25. Oded, *War, Peace, and Empire*, esp. 9–36, 97–98, 121–37, 169–73.

as personally making covenant demands, there must not have been a human ruler on the throne.

Both monarchy and hierocracy can be seen as expressions of theocracy. Divine and human kingship coexisted regularly in the ancient Near East, in various permutations. In some cases, the king functioned as the chief priest. And often, instead of functioning in the absence of a king, the priests *represented* the king—in temple worship, and in other administrative roles as well.[26] The priestly hierarchies of Yahweh in Jerusalem and Amun in Thebes appear to have functioned similarly, and in concert with human kingship, long before the Persian Period.[27]

Theocracy and Monotheism

The comparison of biblical literature with *Wenamun* also adds another data point in our outline of the development of monotheism. What follows is only a sketch of how it fits into that larger conversation, leaving ample room for additional work.

One reason biblical rhetoric often sounds so similar to Amun rhetoric is that most of the Hebrew Bible is not much more monotheistic than *Wenamun*. Rather, it is monolatrous or henotheistic; it advocates a more or less permanent adherence to Yahweh, without denying the existence of other gods. As Nathan MacDonald has observed in his analysis of the modern origins of the idea of monotheism, "A yawning gap exists between 'monotheism' and the Old Testament."[28] Much of what is popularly considered monotheistic rhetoric does not require the ontological rejection of other gods—for example, the idea of a sovereign and all-encompassing deity who knows the hearts of humankind and requires ethical conduct. Amun was such a deity: a "transcendant world-god and helper of the needy."[29]

Even those biblical expressions of monotheism that are regarded as the "purest," those of Second Isaiah, are part of larger compositions that actually reflect polytheistic assumptions in certain ways. That is to say, however much they press toward monotheism, they do so out of a worldview in which polytheism is taken for granted. So Yahweh is God, "and there is no other"

---

26. Sauneron, *Priests*, 43, 180. The assumption that priests were everywhere and at all times delegates of the king exceeds the evidence, though this has generally been the starting point for conversation; see Baines, "Ancient Egyptian Kingship," 103–8.
27. The literature on the date of the priestly law is much too large to summarize here, but the most effective response to the old idea that it must be late is Weinfeld, *Place of the Law*.
28. MacDonald, *Deuteronomy*, 52.
29. Assmann, *Search for God*, 221–44.

(Isa 45:22), partly because "Bel bows down" and "Nebo stoops" (46:1). Although biblical anti-idol polemics pursue the logic of the point further, the overall picture in Second Isaiah is not far from Ps 82, in which Elohim sentences the other gods of the divine council to death. Is that a monotheistic text? Not exactly, but it is a monothe*izing* one. Texts like these are elucidated and brought into better focus by Egyptian models of summodeism.[30]

Past discussions of the origins of biblical monotheism among historians of religion have largely revolved around two comparative connections.[31] One theory is that monotheism was an adaptation of the Atenism of the Amarna Period in Egypt.[32] Sometimes Moses himself is said to be the one who brought it to Israel, as classically seen in Sigmund Freud's *Moses and Monotheism*.[33] The rhetoric of a text like the Great Hymn to the Aten ("O Sole God beside whom there is none!"[34]) resonates with biblical literature. The correlations between imagery of the sun-disk Aten and solar images of Yahweh in the Hebrew Bible (e.g., Pss 19; 104; 2 Kgs 23:11) and material culture (e.g., the Taanach Cult Stand) have also made this a provocative suggestion. However, attempts to draw specific historical connections between Israel as it emerged in the early first millennium BCE and Akhenaten's court in the fourteenth century are tenuous at best. This is a gap of centuries. We have seen that Egyptian culture and religion left their mark on the Levant during the Late Bronze Age and Iron I. But there is no extrabiblical evidence for Israel's direct connection to Egypt at its origins—no record of a figure such as Moses—so mechanisms of direct literary influence are not discernible.

The second theory about biblical monotheism, which has been more influential, is that it was a reaction against the universalizing theological rhetoric of the Mesopotamian empires of the first millennium: the Neo-Assyrian

---

30. A new article that was in press at the same time as this book (Smoot, "Egyptian View") draws the comparison between Israelite and Egyptian religion in a more philosophical manner, contrasting Assmann's "monotheism of perspective" with past scholarship that has essentially argued for a "monotheism of ontology." Smoot rightly calls attention to past studies that argue that Second Isaiah was *not* ontologically monotheistic, and he adduces various Egyptian texts for comparison, including some of those discussed above. Though the "monotheism of perspective" is arguably just a different way of emphasizing monotheizing as a form of rhetoric, as David L. Petersen and Mark S. Smith had already done with respect to the Hebrew prophets, the article is a welcome synthetic contribution to the scholarship on Isaiah.

31. The significance of developments internal to Israel and Judah has recently been emphasized by Schaper, *Media and Monotheism*. Yet the importance of intercultural dialogue is not to be underestimated.

32. For a review of such theories, see Assmann, *From Akhenaten to Moses*, 61–78. For a critical and accessible assessment of these theories, see Redford, "Monotheism of Akhenaten," 11–26. Somewhat distinct is the theory of Yahweh's solar nature; see Taylor, *Yahweh and the Sun*; Sarlo, *Solar Nature of Yahweh*.

33. Freud, *Moses and Monotheism*, 41, etc.

34. *AEL* 1:98.

emphasis on a sort of imperial Manifest Destiny commanded by the god Aššur,[35] or the Neo-Babylonian summodeism that rhetorically assimilated the whole pantheon as aspects of Marduk (discussed in the introduction).[36] The idea in either case is that when faced with these totalizing and hegemonic theological claims of their imperial neighbors, biblical authors were pressed to make larger, more global claims about Yahweh in response. The prominence of henotheistic ideas in Josiah's (seventh-century) Deuteronomistic exhortations, and of a stricter monotheism in the (late sixth-century) prophecies of Second Isaiah, fits well with this theory's timeline. Compared to the theory of Atenist influence, this approach has the distinct advantage that it correlates with the actual era in which the Hebrew Bible was being written and biblical monotheism was coming into focus.

I do not intend to argue that either of those theories is incorrect—historical developments often result from a confluence of multiple factors[37]—but to call attention to an additional factor: Egyptian theological rhetoric in the early first millennium also provides interesting material for comparison to biblical monotheism, especially in the rhetoric of prophets. It is better to look not at Amarna, but at this later period, for channels through which these ideas were directly shared. Before the biblical authors received messages from the Mesopotamians about the imperial dominance of foreign deities, in the period during which the Israelite state was nascent, Egyptian and Phoenician interlocutors were even more significant in the intercultural formation of theological ideas. This was the period in which Hebrew scribal culture developed—at the origins of the Hebrew Bible's composition in the early Iron Age II. When the earliest biblical authors were developing ways to write about God, they were probably hearing rhetoric about Amun similar to what Wenamun expounded.[38]

This cultural interaction might be described as the assimilation and rejection of Amun theologies, much as Mark S. Smith explained the biblical authors' handling of the Levantine ("Canaanite") pantheon. As noted in the introduction, Smith models the development of monotheism as a rhetorical process in which authors assimilated to Yahweh some characteristics of other deities, while rejecting others.[39] Over time, the other gods came to be excluded entirely. Smith's rhetorical approach to monotheizing (in contrast to ontological or evolutionary approaches) enables us to make the historical connection

---

35. E.g., Levine, "Assyrian Ideology."
36. E.g., Smith, *God in Translation*, 168–74; Lemaire, *Birth of Monotheism*, 105–8.
37. On complexity theory, see Cline, *1177 B.C.*, 167–80.
38. Keel (*Jerusalem and the One God*, 62–63) notes in passing certain similarities between *Wenamun* and the narratives of the Davidic Succession Narrative in 1 Sam 9–20 and 1 Kgs 1–2.
39. Smith, *Early History of God*, 1–18. Smith describes this process as the "convergence and differentiation" of divine attributes.

between Amun and Yahweh that Assmann denies because he is focused on what he perceives as the differing essences of the two theological systems.[40]

The rejection of Amun is implicit in the oracles against Egypt, especially a text that impugns its counselors and sages such as Isa 19:1–15. The solar-religion paraphernalia that Josiah removed from the Temple, though it was surely "native," may also have been associated by some with Amun-Re. Certainly by the time of Isa 45's polemic, which contrasts Amun's hiddenness and chaotic origins with Yahweh's proclaimed openness and ordering (45:18–19), we see a rejection of Amun.[41] It is to be expected to find Amun on the "hit list" of major foreign deities, along with Marduk and Nabû (46:1–2), in the section of the Bible best known for its monotheizing rhetoric.[42] Yet Isa 45 does not reject everything that could be connected with Amun; strikingly, Isa 45:9 reasserts Yahweh as a Divine Potter—a role that Amun had absorbed from Khnum much earlier in Egypt, but which had long been claimed for Yahweh by this time. Much as Hos 2 credits Yahweh with the agricultural and economic productivity that was elsewhere attributed to Baal, so Isaiah and many other biblical texts claimed for Yahweh the role of potter-creator that was attributed to Amun in Egypt.

Isaiah 45 is a relatively late example that reflects a much longer-running comparison and competition between deities. It is difficult to say how far back and how directly Amun and Yahweh were associated. Sethe's old claim that Amun was "the original from whom Yahweh was derived" (chapter 2) was certainly too flatly stated. Furthermore, the analogy between Yahweh and Amun is not based on wind, as he thought. But there is nonetheless something to his claim that merits more extensive examination.

Given the limitations of the present project, I make this suggestion only briefly: that hiddenness—the very quality that Isa 45 so vociferously disavows—was the clearest point of analogy between Amun and Yahweh. Amun's name means "Hidden One," and in various ways he was seen as a mysterious figure, the counterpoint to the highly visible Re with whom he was syncretized. A significant strain of Israelite religion portrayed Yahweh as mysterious or hidden (Exod 24:15–16; 33:20; Isa 6:5; 8:17; Prov 25:2; Job 34:29, etc.), and he was generally not portrayed iconographically.

This association between Amun and the aniconic Yahweh, whose presence was symbolized by an empty cherubim throne, is suggested also by a specific late Egyptian representation of Amun called the "veiled Amun"—basically an

---

40. E.g., Assmann, *Of God and Gods*, 74–75.
41. Hays, "Hidden God," passim.
42. The degree to which Isa 40–55 is actually monotheistic has rightly come under scrutiny, which demonstrates the difficulty of "radical" monotheistic thinking in an ancient Near Eastern context. E.g., Olyan, "Is Isaiah 40–55 Really Monotheistic?," 190–201 (and see 108n30 above).

enthroned abstract representation of Amun that was not anthropomorphic except for his head with the Min-crown.[43] It appears around the end of the first millennium BCE, and rises in popularity throughout these later periods. It is understandable that someone might compare this semianiconic version of Amun with the aniconic portrayal of Yahweh enthroned in the Jerusalem temple. Both even had similar theriomorphic thrones. Again the Phoenician data helpfully connect Amun and Yahweh, since Phoenicia was well known for its aniconic religious expressions—which did not programmatically avoid all symbolization of deities, but rather avoided anthropomorphic images.[44] Some of these are comparable with the "veiled Amun."

Much work remains to be done on the religious connections between Egypt, Phoenicia, and Israel/Judah, but it is not hard to see how the results of the analysis will one day be incorporated into histories of Israelite religion. The origins of biblical monotheism are often traced to the Atenism of the Amarna Period, and there is a significant kernel of truth in this; but given the later period of the Hebrew Bible's formation, it is more accurate to say that the biblical authors were influenced by Atenism's descendant, the theocratic and universalizing Amun theology of the Third Intermediate Period. In this way, one can cogently incorporate Aten and Amun into the conversation about Yahweh's origins, along with El and Baal, Aššur and Marduk. The story of *Wenamun* offers rare, detailed vignettes from this ongoing ancient exchange of ideas.

---

43. Doresse, "Le dieu voilé." See previously Wainwright, "Aniconic Form of Amon," 173–89.
44. Doak, *Phoenician Aniconism*, 29–34.

BIBLIOGRAPHY

Albright, W. F. "The Egyptian Correspondence of Abimilki, Prince of Tyre." *JEA* 23 (1937): 190–203.
Allon, Niv. "Seth Is Baal—Evidence from the Egyptian Script." *Ägypten und Levante/Egypt and the Levant* 17 (2007): 15–22.
Assmann, Jan. *Ägypten: Theologie und Frömmigkeit einer frühen Hochkukltur*. Stuttgart: Kohlhammer, 1984.
———. "Amun." Pages 28–32 in *Dictionary of Deities and Demons in the Bible*. Edited by Karel van der Toorn, Bob Becking, and Pieter W. van der Horst. 2nd ed. Leiden: Brill, 1995.
———. *Death and Salvation in Ancient Egypt*. Ithaca: Cornell University Press, 2005.
———. *Egyptian Solar Religion in the New Kingdom: Re, Amun and the Crisis of Polytheism*. London: Kegan Paul International; New York: Columbia University Press, 1995.
———. *From Akhenaten to Moses: Ancient Egypt and Religious Change*. Cairo: American University in Cairo Press, 2016.
———. *Of God and Gods: Egypt, Israel, and the Rise of Monotheism*. Madison: University of Wisconsin Press, 2008.
———. *The Mind of Egypt: History and Meaning in the Time of the Pharaohs*. Translated by Andrew Jenkins. New York: Metropolitan Books, 2002.
———. "Monotheism and Polytheism." Pages 17–31 in *Religions of the Ancient World: A Guide*. Edited by Sarah Iles Johnston. Harvard University Press Reference Library. Cambridge, MA: Harvard University Press, 2004.
———. *Re und Amun: Die Krise des polytheistischen Weltbilds im Ägypten der 18.–20. Dynastie*. Freiburg: Universitätsverlag; Göttingen: Vandenhoeck & Ruprecht, 1983.
———. *The Search for God in Ancient Egypt*. Ithaca, NY: Cornell University, 2001.
Ayad, Mariam F. *God's Wife, God's Servant: The God's Wife of Amun (c. 740–525 BC)*. London: Routledge, 2009.
Azzoni, Annalisa. "Amon." Page 133 in vol. 1 of *New Interpreter's Dictionary of the Bible*. Edited by Katharine Doob Sakenfeld. 5 vols. Nashville: Abingdon, 2006–9.
Baines, John. "Ancient Egyptian Kingship." *Annuaire de l'École pratique des hautes études (EPHE), Section des sciences religieuses* 121 (2014): 103–8.

———. "On the Background of Wenamun in Inscriptional Genres and in Topoi of Obligations Among Rulers." Pages 27–36 in *Texte—Theben—Tonfragmente: Festschrift für Günter Burkard*. Edited by Dieter Kessler and Burkard Günter. ÄAT 76. Wiesbaden: Harrassowitz, 2009.

———. "On *Wenamun* as a Literary Text." Pages 209–33 in *Literatur und Politik im pharaonischen und ptolemäischen Ägypten: Vorträge der Tagung zum Gedenken an Georges Posener, 5.–10. September 1996 in Leipzig*. Edited by J. Assmann and E. Blumenthal. Bibliothèque d'Étude 127. Cairo: Institut francais d'archéologie orientale, 1999.

Bardinet, Thierry. *Relations économiques et pressions militaires en Méditerranée orientale et en Libye au temps des pharaons: Histoire des importations Égyptiennes des Résines et des conifères du Liban et de la Libye depuis la période archaïque jusqu'à l'époque Ptolémaïque*. Études et mémoires d'égyptologie 7. Paris: Cybele, 2008.

Basch, Lucien. "Le navire *mnš* et autres notes de voyage en Egypte." *The Mariner's Mirror* 64 (1978): 99–123.

Becker, Meike, Anke Ilona Blöbaum, and Angelika Lohwasser. *"Prayer and Power": Proceedings of the Conference on the God's Wives of Amun in Egypt During the First Millennium BC*. ÄAT 84. Münster: Ugarit-Verlag, 2016.

Beckman, Gary M. *Hittite Diplomatic Texts*. SBLWAW 7. Atlanta: Scholars Press, 1996.

Ben-Dor Evian, Shirly. "Amun-of-the-Road: Trade and Religious Mobility Between Egypt and the Levant at the Turn of the First Millennium BCE." *Welt des Orients* 47 (2017): 52–65.

———. "Egypt and Israel: The Never-Ending Story." *NEA* 80 (2017): 30–39.

———. "Egypt and the Levant in the Iron Age I–IIA: The Ceramic Evidence." *TA* 38 (2011): 94–119.

———. "The Past and Future of 'Biblical Egyptology.'" *JAEI* 18 (2018): 1–11.

Ben-Marzouk, Nadia. "Some Highlights in Local Versus Regional Glyptic Consumption in the Southern Levant During the Iron I." *NEA* 86 (2023): 292–301.

Blenkinsopp, Joseph. *A History of Prophecy in Israel*. Rev. ed. Louisville: Westminster John Knox, 1996.

Bonnet, Hans, "Propheziehung." Pages 608–9 in *Reallexikon der agyptischen Religionsgeschichte*. Berlin: de Gruyter, 1952.

Bordreuil, Pierre. "Flèches phéniciennes inscrites: 1981–1991 I." *Revue Biblique* 99 (1992): 205–13.

Breasted, J. H. "The Report of Wenamon." *American Journal of Semitic Languages and Literatures* 21 (1905): 100–109.

Breyer, Francis. "Kleinasiatisches Lokalkolorit in der Geschichte des Wenamun." *Lingua Aegyptia* 18 (2010): 33–40.

Brinker, Christopher. "'Are You Serious? Are You Joking?': Wenamun's Misfortune at Dor in Its Ancient Near Eastern Legal Context." Pages 89–101 in *Egypt and the Near East: The Crossroads Proceedings of an International Conference on the Relations of Egypt and the Near East in the Bronze Age, Prague, September 1–3, 2010*. Edited by Jana Mynářová. Prague: Czech Institute of Egyptology, 2011.

Broekman, Gerard P. F. "The Leading Theban Priests of Amun and Their Families under Libyan Rule." *JEA* 96 (2010): 125–48.

———. "The 21st Dynasty: The Theocracy of Amun, and the Position of the Theban Priestly Families." Pages 13–19 in *The Coffins of the Priests of Amun: Egyptian*

Coffins from the 21st Dynasty in the Collection of the National Museum of Antiquities in Leiden. Edited by Lara Weiss. Papers on Archaeology of the Leiden Museum of Antiquities 17. Leiden: Sidestone; Rijksmuseum van Oudheden, 2018.

Broodbank, Cyprian. *The Making of the Middle Sea: A History of the Mediterranean from the Beginning to the Emergence of the Classical World*. Oxford: Oxford University Press, 2013.

Bryan, Betsy M. "Hatshepsut and Cultic Revelries in the New Kingdom." Pages 93–123 in *Theban Symposium: Creativity and Innovation in the Reign of Hatshepsut*. Edited by J. M. Galán, B. M. Bryan, and P. F. Dorman. Studies in Ancient Oriental Civilization 69. Chicago: Oriental Institute, University of Chicago, 2014.

Bunnens, Guy. "La mission d'Ounamon en Phénicie: Point de vue d'un non-égyptologue." *Rivista di Studi Fenici* 6 (1978): 1–16.

Burke, Aaron A. "Left Behind: New Kingdom Specialists at the End of Egyptian Empire and the Emergence of Israelite Scribalism." Pages 50–66 in *"An Excellent Fortress for his Armies, a Refuge for the People": Egyptological, Archaeological and Biblical Studies in Honor of James K. Hoffmeier*. Edited by R. E. Averbeck and K. L. Younger. Winona Lake, IN: Eisenbrauns, 2020.

Caminos, R. A. *A Tale of Woe from a Hieratic Papyrus in the A. S. Pushkin Museum of Fine Arts in Moscow*. Oxford: Griffith Institute, 1977.

Campbell, James Elliott. "Cuneiform Legal Presence in 'The Report of Wenamun'?" *JAEI* 3 (2009): 1–10.

Černý, Jaroslav. "Egyptian Oracles." Pages 35–48 in *A Saite Oracle Papyrus from Thebes*. Edited by Richard A. Parker. Providence: Brown University Press, 1962.

―――. *Paper and Books: An Inaugural Lecture Delivered at University College, London, 29 May 1947*. London: H. K. Lewis, 1952.

Cline, Eric H. *1177 B.C.: The Year Civilization Collapsed*. Rev. ed. Princeton: Princeton University Press, 2021.

Cline, Eric H., and Assaf Yasur-Landau. "Musings from a Distant Shore: The Nature and Destination of the Uluburun Ship and Its Cargo." *TA* 35 (2007): 126–41.

Cody, Aelred. "The Phoenician Ecstatic in Wenamūn: A Professional Oracular Medium." *JEA* 65 (1979): 99–106.

Cornelius, Izak. *The Many Faces of the Goddess: The Iconography of the Syro-Palestinian Goddesses Anat, Astarte, Qedeshet, and Asherah c. 1500–1000 BCE*. Fribourg: Academic Press; Göttingen: Vandenhoeck Ruprecht, 2008.

Cornelius, Sakkie. "Ancient Egypt and the Other." *Scriptura* 104 (2010): 322–40.

Davis, Stacy. "Unapologetic Apologetics: Julius Wellhausen, Anti-Judaism, and Hebrew Bible Scholarship." *Religions* 12 (2021): 560. https://doi.org/10.3390/rel12080560.

Di Biase-Dyson, Camilla. *Foreigners and Egyptians in the Late Egyptian Stories: Linguistic, Literary and Historical Perspectives*. Probleme der Ägyptologie 32. Leiden: Brill, 2013.

―――. "Linguistic Insights into Characterisation: The Case Study of Wenamun." *Lingua Aegyptia* 17 (2009): 51–64.

Doak, Brian R. *Phoenician Aniconism in Its Mediterranean and Ancient Near Eastern Contexts*. Atlanta: SBL, 2015.

Dodson, Aidan. "Some Notes Concerning the Royal Tombs at Tanis." *Chronique d'Égypte* 63 (1988): 221–33.

Doresse, Marianne. "Le dieu voilé dans sa châsse et la fête du début de la décade." *Revue d'Égypotologie* 23 (1971): 113–36; 25 (1973): 92–135; 31 (1981): 36–65.

Ebach, J., and U. Rüterswörden. "Der byblitische Ekstatiker im Bericht des *Wn-Imn* und die Seher der Inschrift des ZKR von Hamath." *GM* 20 (1976): 17–22.

Edelman, Diana. "Of Priests and Prophets Interpreting the Past: The Egyptian *Ḥm-Nṯr* and *Ḥry-Ḥbt* and the Judahite *Nāḇîʾ*." Pages 103–12 in *The Historian and the Bible: Essays in Honour of Lester L. Grabbe*. Edited by P. R. Davies and D. V. Edelman. London: T&T Clark, 2010.

Egberts, Arno. "Double Dutch in The Report of Wenamun?" *GM* 172 (1999): 17–22.

———. "Hard Times: The Chronology of 'The Report of Wenamun' Revised." *ZÄS* 125 (1998): 93–108.

———. "Wenamun." In *OEAE* 3:495–96.

Erichsen, Wolja. *Demotisches Glossar*. Kopenhagen: Ejnar Munksgaard, 1954.

Eßbach, Nadine. "Amun—die verborgene Gott in Ugarit." *Ugarit-Forschungen* 53 (2024): 19–33.

Eyre, Christopher J. "Irony in the Story of Wenamun: The Politics of Religion in the 21st Dynasty." Pages 235–52 in *Literatur und Politik im pharaonischen und ptolemäischen Ägypten: Vorträge der Tagung zum Gedenken an Georges Posener, 5.–10. September 1996 in Leipzig*. Edited by Jan Assmann and Elke Blumenthal. Cairo: Institut français d'archéologie orientale, 1999.

Faust, Avraham, and Ehud Weiss. "Judah, Philistia, and the Mediterranean World: Reconstructing the Economic System of the Seventh Century BCE." *BASOR* 338 (2005): 71–92.

Fischer-Elfert, H.-W. Review of *Die Erzählung*, by Bernd U. Schipper. *Welt des Orients* 36 (2006): 219–26.

Foster, John L., and Susan T. Hollis. *Hymns, Prayers, and Songs: An Anthology of Ancient Egyptian Lyric Poetry*. SBLWAW 8. Atlanta: Scholars Press, 1995.

Fox, Michael R. *A Message from the Great King: Reading Malachi in Light of Ancient Persian Royal Messenger Texts from the Time of Xerxes*. Siphrut 17. Winona Lake, IN: Eisenbrauns, 2015.

Frame, Grant, ed. *The Royal Inscriptions of Sargon II, King of Assyria (721–705 BC)*. Royal Inscriptions of the Neo-Assyrian Period 2. University Park, PA: Eisenbrauns, 2021.

Freedman, Sally M. *Tablets 41–63*. Vol. 3 of *If a City Is Set on a Height: The Akkadian Omen Series Šumma Alu ina Mele Šakin*. Philadelphia: University of Pennsylvania Museum; Winona Lake, IN: Eisenbrauns, 2017.

Freud, Sigmund. *Moses and Monotheism*. Translated by Katherine Jones. London: Hogarth Press, 1939.

Galan, Jose M. "EA 164 and the God Amun." *JNES* 51 (1992): 287–91.

———. *Four Journeys in Ancient Egyptian Literature*. LASM 5. Göttingen: Seminar für Ägyptologie und Koptologie, 2005.

Galvin, Garrett. *Egypt as a Place of Refuge*, FAT 2/51. Tübingen: Mohr Siebeck, 2012.

Gardiner, Alan H. *The Library of A. Chester Beatty: Description of a Hieratic Papyrus with a Mythological Story, Love-Songs, and Other Miscellaneous Texts*. London: Emery Walker; Oxford: Oxford University Press, 1931.

Gilboa, Ayelet. "Dor and Egypt in the Early Iron Age: An Archaeological Perspective of (Part of) the Wenamun Report." *Ägypten und Levante/Egypt and the Levant* 25 (2015): 247–74.

———. "The Southern Levantine Roots of the Phoenician Mercantile Phenomenon." *BASOR* 287 (2022): 31–53.

Gilboa, Ayelet, Ilan Sharon, and Elizabeth Bloch-Smith. "Capital of Solomon's Fourth District? Israelite Dor." *Levant* 47 (2015): 51–74.

Giorgetti, Andrew. "Building a Parody: Genesis 11:1–9, Ancient Near Eastern Building Accounts, and Production-Oriented Intertextuality." PhD diss., Fuller Theological Seminary, 2017.

Goedicke, Hans. *The Report of Wenamun*. Baltimore: Johns Hopkins University Press, 1975.

———. "Seth as a Fool." *JEA* 47 (1961): 154.

Golub, Mitka R. "Personal Names on Iron Age I Bronze Arrowheads: Characteristics and Implications." *Jerusalem Journal of Archaeology* 2 (2021): 16–40.

Gordon, Cyrus H. "He Is Who He Is." *Berytus* 23 (1974): 27–28.

Goren, Yuval. "International Exchange During the Late Second Millennium B.C.: Microarchaeological Study of Finds from the Uluburun Ship." Pages 54–61 in *Cultures in Contact: From Mesopotamia to the Mediterranean in the Second Millennium B.C.* Edited by Joan Aruz, Sarah B. Graff, and Yelena Rakic. New York: Metropolitan Museum of Art, 2013.

Görg, Manfred. "Der Ekstatiker von Byblos." *GM* 23 (1977): 31–33.

———. "Fremdformen im Wenamun." Pages 69–72 in *XX. Deutscher Orientalistentag, vom 3. bis 8. Oktober 1977 in Erlangen*. Edited by Wolfgang Voigt. Wiesbaden: Franz Steiner, 1980.

———. "Zu einem semitischen Personennamen in der Erzählung des Wenamun." *Biblische Notizen* 74 (1994): 24–26.

Grabbe, Lester L. *Priests, Prophets, Diviners, Sages: A Socio-Historical Study of Religious Specialists in Ancient Israel*. Valley Forge, PA: Trinity Press, 1995.

Green, Michael. "Wenamun's Demand for Compensation." *ZÄS* 106 (1979): 116–20.

Greene, John T. *The Role of the Messenger and Message in the Ancient Near East*. Brown Judaic Studies 169. Atlanta: Scholars Press, 1989.

Gressmann, Hugo. "Hadad und Baal: Nach den Amarnabriefen und nach ägyptischen Texten." Pages 191–216 in *Abhandlungen zur semitischen Religionskunde und Sprachwissenschaft*. BZAW 33. Berlin: de Gruyter, 1918.

Hays, Christopher B. "A Hidden God: Isaiah 45's Amun Polemic and Message to Egypt." *Vetus Testamentum* 72 (2022): 1–17.

———. *Hidden Riches: A Sourcebook for the Comparative Study of the Hebrew Bible and Ancient Near East*. Louisville, KY: Westminster John Knox, 2014.

———. *The Origins of Isaiah 24–27: Josiah's Festival Scroll for the Fall of Assyria*. Cambridge: Cambridge University Press, 2019.

———. "'Those Weaned from Milk': The Divine Wet Nurse Motif in Isaiah 28's Ceremony of the Covenant with Mut." *Journal of Hebrew Scriptures* 19 (2019): 61–89.

Herm, Gerhard. *The Phoenicians: The Purple Empire of the Ancient World*. Translated by Caroline Hillier. New York: Morrow, 1975.

Herrmann, Siegfried. "Prophetie in Israel und Ägypten: Recht und Grenze eines Vergleichs." Pages 47–65 in *Congress Volume Bonn 1962*. Vetus Testamentum Supplements 9. Leiden: Brill, 1963.

Hilber, John W. "Egyptian Prophecy: Clarifying Some Issues." Forthcoming in *Ancient Egypt and Hebrew Prophecy*. Edited by Christopher B. Hays, John Huddlestun, and Thomas Schneider. ÄAT. Münster: Ugarit-Verlag.

———. "Prophetic Ritual in the Egyptian Royal Cult." Pages 51–62 in *Prophecy and Its Cultic Dimensions*. Edited by Lena-Sofia Tiemeyer. Journal of Ancient Judaism Supplements 31. Göttingen: Vandenhoeck & Ruprecht, 2019.

———. "Prophetic Speech in the Egyptian Royal Cult." Pages 47–53 in *On Stone and Scroll: Essays in Honour of Graham Ivor Davies*. Edited by J. K. Aitken, K. J. Dell, and B. A. Mastin. Berlin: de Gruyter, 2011.

Hoch, James E. *Semitic Words in Egyptian Texts of the New Kingdom and Third Intermediate Period*. Princeton: Princeton University, 1994.

Hoffmeier, James K. "Some Thoughts on Genesis 1 and 2 and Egyptian Cosmology." *Journal of Ancient Near Eastern Studies* 15 (1983): 39–49.

Holladay, John S., Jr. "Judeans (and Phoenicians) in Egypt in the Late Seventh to Sixth Centuries B.C." Pages 405–38 in *Egypt, Israel, and the Ancient Mediterranean World: Studies in Honor of Donald B. Redford*. Edited by G. N. Knoppers and A. Hirsch. Leiden: Brill, 2004.

Hornung, Erik. "Bedeutung und Wirklichkeit des Bildes im alten Ägypten." Pages 35–46 in *Kunst und Realität*. Edited by E. Schmidt et al. Akademische Vorträge gehalten an der Universität Basel 8. Basel: Helbing und Lichtenheim, 1973.

———. *Conceptions of God in Ancient Egypt: The One and the Many*. Translated by John Baines. Ithaca: Cornell University Press, 1982.

Houlihan, Patrick F. *Wit and Humour in Ancient Egypt*. London: Rubicon Press, 2001.

Hsu, Shih-Wei. "'I Wish I Could Die': Depression in Ancient Egypt." Pages 52–87 in *The Expression of Emotions in Ancient Egypt and Mesopotamia*. Edited by Shih-Wei Hsu and Jaume Llop Raduà. CHANE 116. Leiden: Brill, 2020.

Hundley, Michael B. *Yahweh Among the Gods: The Divine in Genesis, Exodus, and the Ancient Near East*. Cambridge: Cambridge University Press, 2022.

Jackson, Howard M. "'The Shadow of Pharaoh, Your Lord, Falls Upon You': Once Again Wenamun 2.46." *JNES* 54 (1995): 273–86.

James, Peter, and Robert Morkot. "Herihor's Kingship and the High Priest of Amun Piankh." *Journal of Egyptian History* 3 (2010): 231–60.

Jansen-Winkeln, Karl. "Das Ende des Neuen Reiches." *ZÄS* 119 (1992): 22–37.

Janssen, J. J. *Two Ancient Egyptian Ship's Logs, Papyrus Leiden I 350 verso and Papyrus Turin 2008 + 2016*. Oudheidkundige Mededelingen uit het Rijksmuseum van Oudheden te Leiden Supplement 42. Leiden: Brill, 1961.

Jay, Jacqueline E. "Examining the 'Literariness' of Wenamon from the Perspective of the Grammar of Narrative." Pages 287–303 in *Narratives of Egypt and the Ancient Near East: Literary and Linguistic Approaches*. Edited by Fredrik Hagen et al. OLA 189. Leuven: Peeters, 2011.

Katzenstein, H. J. "The Phoenician Term *ḥubūr* in the Report of Wen-Amon." Pages 599–602 in vol. 2 of *Atti del I Congresso Internazionale di Studi Fenici e Punici: Roma, 5–10 Novembre 1979*. Edited by P. Bartoloni et al. Rome: Consiglio Nazionale delle Ricerche, 1983.

Keel, Othmar. *Jerusalem and the One God: A Religious History*. Edited by Brent A. Strawn. Translated by Morven McClean. Minneapolis: Fortress, 2017.

———. "Paraphernalia of Jerusalem Sanctuaries and Their Relation to Deities Worshiped Therein During the Iron Age IIA-C." Pages 315–42 in *Temple Building and Temple Cult: Architecture and Cultic Paraphernalia of Temples in the Levant (2.–1.*

Mill. B.C.E.). Edited by Jens Kamlah and Henrike Michelau. Abhandlungen des Deutschen Palästina-Vereins 41. Wiesbaden: Harrassowitz, 2012.

———. *Studien zu den Stempelsiegeln aus Palästina / Israel IV.* OBO 135. Freiburg: Universitätsverlag; Göttingen: Vandenhoeck Ruprecht, 1994.

Keel, Othmar, and Christoph Uehlinger. *Gods, Goddesses, and Images of God in Ancient Israel.* Translated by T. H. Trapp. Minneapolis: Fortress, 1998.

Keel, Othmar, Christoph Uehlinger, and Florian Lippke. *Göttinnen, Götter und Gottessymbole: Neue Erkenntnisse zur Religionsgeschichte Kanaans und Israels aufgrund bislang unerschlossener ikonographischer Quellen.* 7th ed. Tübingen: Universitätsbibliothek Tübingen, 2015

Kees, Hermann. *Das Priestertum im ägyptischen Staat vom Neuen Reich bis zur Spätzeit.* Probleme der Ägyptologie 1. Leiden: Brill, 1953.

Kilani, Marwan. *Byblos in the Late Bronze Age: Interactions Between the Levantine and Egyptian Worlds.* Studies in the Archaeology and History of the Levant 9. Leiden: Brill, 2020.

———. "A New Tree Name in Egyptian: *rbrn*='juniper' in the Tale of Wenamun." *JNES* 75 (2016): 43–52.

Kitchen, Kenneth A. *The Third Intermediate Period in Egypt (1100–650 B.C.).* London: Aris & Phillips, 1973.

Klotz, David. *Adoration of the Ram: Five Hymns to Amun-Re from Hibis Temple.* Yale Egyptological Studies 6. New Haven: Yale Egyptological Seminar, 2006.

Koch, Ido. *Colonial Encounters in Southwest Canaan during the Late Bronze Age and the Early Iron Age.* CHANE 119. Leiden: Brill, 2021.

Köhler, Ludwig. *Deuterojesaja (Jesaja 40–55).* BZAW 37. Berlin: Töpelmann, 1923.

Korostovtsev, Michail A. *Puteshestvie Un-Amuna v Bibl. Egipetskij ieraticheskij papirus no. 120 Gosudarstvennogo museya izobrazitel'nykh iskusstv im. A. S. Pushkina.* Moscow: Gosudarstvennii Musei, 1960.

Krahmalkov, Charles R. *Phoenician-Punic Dictionary.* Leuven: Uitgeverij Peeters, 2000.

Kuniholm, Peter Ian. "Wood." *Oxford Encyclopedia of the Ancient Near East* 5:347–49.

Lacau, Pierre, and Henri Chevrier. *Une chapelle d'Hatchepsout à Karnak.* Vol. 1. Cairo: Le Service des Antiquités de l'Égypte / Institut français d'archéologie orientale, 1977.

Lambert, W. G. *Babylonian Creation Myths.* Winona Lake, IN: Eisenbrauns, 2013.

Leitz, Christian, ed. *Lexikon der Ägyptischen Götter und Götterbezeichnungen.* OLA 110. Leuven: Peeters, 2002.

Lemaire, André. *The Birth of Monotheism: The Rise and Disappearance of Yahwism.* Washington, DC: Biblical Archaeology Society, 2007.

Lenzi, Alan. *Secrecy and the Gods: Secret Knowledge in Ancient Mesopotamia and Biblical Israel.* SAA 19. Helsinki: Neo-Assyrian Text Corpus Project, 2008.

Leprohon, R. J. "What Wenamun Could Have Bought: The Value of His Stolen Goods." Pages 167–77 in *Egypt, Israel, and the Ancient Mediterranean World: Studies in Honor of Donald B. Redford.* Edited by G. N. Knoppers and A. Hirsch. Leiden: Brill, 2004

Levin, Christoph, "Israel, the People of God, as Theocracy." Pages 65–83 in *Theokratie: Exegetische und wirkungsgeschichtliche Ansätze.* Edited by Peter Juhás, Róbert Lapko and Reinhard Müller. Berlin: de Gruyter, 2021.

Levine, Baruch A. "Assyrian Ideology and Biblical Monotheism." *Iraq* 67 (2005): 411–27.
Lewis, Theodore J. "Amun." *ABD* 1:197.
Lichtheim, Miriam. *Ancient Egyptian Autobiographies Chiefly of the Middle Kingdom: A Study and an Anthology*. OBO 84. Freiburg: Universitätsverlag; Göttingen: Vandenhoeck Ruprecht, 1988.
Lieven, Alexandra von. "Divination in Ägypten." *Altorientalische Forschungen* 26 (1999): 77–126.
———. "Das Orakelwesen im Alten Ägypten." *Mythos*, n.s., 10 (2016): 17–30.
Lindblom, Johannes. *Die literarische Gattung der prophetischen Literatur: Eine literargeschichtliche Untersuchung zum Alten Testament*. Uppsala: Lundquist, 1924.
Lindenberger, J. M. "Ahiqar: A New Translation and Introduction." Pages 479–507 in vol. 2 of *Old Testament Pseudepigrapha*. Edited by James H. Charlesworth. New York: Doubleday, 1985.
Liverani, Mario. *Prestige and Interest: International Relations in the Near East Ca. 1600–1100 B.C.* History of the Ancient Near East / Studies 1. Padua: Sargon SRL, 1990.
Liwak, Rüdiger. "Herrschaft zur Überwindung der Krise: Politische Prophetie in Ägypten und Israel." Pages 57–83 in *Die unwiderstehliche Wahrheit: Studien zur alttestamentlichen Prophetie: Festschrift für Arndt Meinhold*. Edited by R. Lux and E.-J. Waschke. Arbeiten zur Bibel und ihrer Geschichte 23. Leipzig: Evangelische Verlagsanstalt, 2006.
———. *Israel in der altorientalischen Welt: Gesammelte Studien zur Kultur- und Religionsgeschichte des Antiken Israel*. BZAW 444. Berlin: de Gruyter, 2013.
Lloyd, Alan B. "*Heka*, Dreams, and Prophecy in Ancient Egyptian Stories." Pages 71–94 in *Through a Glass Darkly: Magic, Dreams and Prophecy in Ancient Egypt*. Edited by Kasia M. Szpakowska. Swansea: Classical Press of Wales, 2006.
López-Ruiz, Carolina. *Phoenicians and the Making of the Mediterranean*. Cambridge, MA: Harvard University Press, 2021.
Loprieno, Antonio. *Topos und Mimesis: Zum Ausländer in der ägyptischen Literatur*. Wiesbaden: Harrassowitz, 1988.
Lorton, David. *The Juridical Terminology of International Relations in Egyptian Texts Through Dynasty XVIII*. John Hopkins Near Eastern Studies 4. Baltimore: Johns Hopkins University Press, 1974.
MacDonald, Nathan. *Deuteronomy and the Meaning of "Monotheism."* 2nd ed. Tübingen: Mohr Siebeck, 2012.
Manassa, Colleen. *Imagining the Past: Historical Fiction in New Kingdom Egypt*. New York: Oxford University Press, 2013.
Markoe, Glenn. *Phoenicians*. London: Folio Society, 2007.
Massa, Viviana. "Temple Oaths in Ptolemaic Egypt: A Study at the Crossroads of Law, Ethics and Religion." PhD diss., Leiden University, 2018.
Mathieu, Bernard. "Études de métrique égyptienne. IV: Le tristique ennéamétrique dans l'Hymne à Amon de Leyde." *Revue d'Égypotologie* 48 (1997): 109–63.
Matić, Uroš. "Why Were the Leaders of the Sea Peoples Called ꜥ.w and Not wr.w? On the Size and Raiding Character of the Sea Peoples Groups." *BASOR* 388 (2022): 73–89.
Mazar, Amihai. *10,000–586 B.C.E.* Vol. 1 of *Archaeology of the Land of the Bible*. New York: Doubleday, 1990.

Meier, Samuel A. *The Messenger in the Ancient Semitic World*. Harvard Semitic Monographs 45. Atlanta: Scholars Press, 1989.
Meltzer, E. S. "Wenamun 2, 46." *Journal of the Society for the Study of Egyptian Antiquities* 17 (1987): 86–88.
Mendenhall, G. E., and Gary A. Herion. "Covenant." *ABD* 1:1188–92.
Mettinger, Tryggve N. D. *No Graven Image? Israelite Aniconism in Its Ancient Near Eastern Context*. Stockholm: Almqvist & Wiksell International, 1995.
Meyers, Carol L., and Eric M. Meyers. *Haggai, Zechariah 1–8*. AB 25B. Garden City, NY: Doubleday, 1987.
Moers, Gerald. *Fingierte Welten in der ägyptischen Literatur des 2. Jahrtausends v. Chr.: Grenzüberschreitung, Reisemotiv und Fiktionalität*. Probleme der Ägyptologie 19. Leiden: Brill, 2001.
———. "Travel as Narrative in Egyptian Literature." Pages 43–61 in *Definitely: Egyptian Literature: Proceedings of the Symposium "Ancient Egyptian Literature: History and Forms." Los Angeles, March 24–26, 1995*. LASM 2. Göttingen: Seminar für Ägyptologie und Koptologie, 1999.
———. "Vom Verschwinden der Gewissheiten." Pages 3–69 in *Dating Egyptian Literary Texts*. Edited by Gerald Moers. LASM 11. Hamburg: Wildmaier, 2013.
Möller, Georg. *Hieratische Lesestücke für den akademischen Gebrauch*. Leipzig: J. C. Hinrich, 1910.
Monroe, Christopher M. "Marginalizing Civilization: The Phoenician Redefinition of Power ca. 1300–800 BCE." Pages 231–87 in *Trade and Civilisation: Economic Networks and Cultural Ties, from Prehistory to the Early Modern Era*. Edited by Kristian Kristiansen, Thomas Lindkvist, and Janken Myrdal. Cambridge: Cambridge University Press, 2018.
———. *Scales of Fate: Trade, Tradition, and Transformation in the Eastern Mediterranean ca. 1350–1175 BCE*. Alten Orient und Altes Testament 357. Münster: Ugarit-Verlag, 2009.
———. "Sunk Costs at Late Bronze Age Uluburun." *BASOR* 357 (2010): 19–33.
Morschauser, Scott N. "'Crying to the Lebanon': A Note on Wenamun 2,13–14." *Studien zur Altägyptischen Kultur* 18 (1991): 317–30.
Muchiki, Yoshiyuki. *Egyptian Proper Names and Loanwords in North-West Semitic*. Society of Biblical Literature Dissertation Series 173. Atlanta: Scholars Press, 1999.
Muhs, Brian. "Wenamun's Bad Trip." *Oriental Institute News and Notes* 241 (Spring 2019): 6–9.
Müller, Max. "Der Papyrus Golenischeff." Pages 14–29 in *Studien zur vorderasiatischen Geschichte II*. Mitteilungen der Vorderasiatischen Gesellschaft 5/1. Berlin: Wolf Peiser, 1900.
Münger, Stefan. "Egyptian Stamp-Seal Amulets and Their Implications for the Chronology of the Early Iron Age." *TA* 30 (2003): 66–82.
———. "References to the Pharaoh in the Local Glyptic Assemblage of the Southern Levant during the First Part of the 1st Millennium BCE." *JAEI* 18 (2018): 40–62.
———. "Stamp-Seal Amulets and Early Iron Age Chronology." Pages 381–403 in *The Bible and Radiocarbon Dating: Archaeology, Text and Science*. Edited by Thomas E. Levy and Thomas Higham. Oxford: Oxford University, 2005.

Murnane, William J. *The Road to Kadesh: A Historical Interpretation of the Battle Reliefs of King Sety I at Karnak*. 2nd rev. ed. Chicago: Oriental Institute, 1990.

Nissinen, Martti. *Ancient Prophecy: Near Eastern, Biblical, and Greek Perspectives*. Oxford: Oxford University Press, 2017.

———. *Prophets and Prophecy in the Ancient Near East*. 2nd ed. SBLWAW 41. Atlanta: SBL Press, 2019.

———. *References to Prophecy in Neo-Assyrian Sources*. SAAS VII. Helsinki: Neo-Assyrian Text Corpus Project, 1998.

Noonan, Benjamin J. *Non-Semitic Loanwords in the Hebrew Bible: A Lexicon of Language Contact*. Linguistic Studies in Ancient West Semitic 14. University Park, PA: Eisenbrauns, 2019.

Noth, Martin. *Überlieferungsgeschichtliche Studien*. Tübingen: M. Niemeyer, 1957.

Oded, Bustenay. *War, Peace, and Empire: Justifications for War in Assyrian Royal Inscriptions*. Wiesbaden: Dr. Ludwig Reichert Verlag, 1992

Oden, Robert A., Jr. "'The Contendings of Horus and Seth' (Chester Beatty Papyrus No. 1): A Structural Interpretation." *History of Religions* 18 (1979): 352–69.

Olmo Lete, Gregorio del. *Canaanite Religion: According to the Liturgical Texts of Ugarit*. Translated by W. G. E. Watson. 2nd ed. Alten Orient und Altes Testament 408. Münster: Ugarit-Verlag, 2014.

Olyan, Saul M. "Is Isaiah 40–55 Really Monotheistic?" *Journal of Ancient Near Eastern Religions* 12 (2012): 190–201.

Oppenheim, A. Leo. "Assyriological Gleanings IV." *BASOR* 107 (1947): 7–11.

Osing, Jürgen. "Die Beziehungen Ägyptens zu Vorderasien unmittelbar nach dem Neuen Reich." Pages 33–39 in *Nubia et Oriens Christianus: Festschrift für Detleff G. Müller zum 60. Geburtstag*. Edited by P. O. Scholz and R. Stempel. Bibliotheca Nubica 1. Cologne: Jürgen Dinter, 1987.

Pardee, Dennis. "New Readings in the Letters of ʿzn bn byy." Pages 39–53 in *Vorträge Gehalten auf Der 28. Rencontre Assyriologique Internationale in Wien, 6.–10. Juli 1981*. Archiv für Orientforschung Beihefte 19. Horn: Berger, 1982.

Parker, Simon B. "Possession Trance and Prophecy in Pre-Exilic Israel." *Vetus Testamentum* 28 (1978): 282–83.

Parpas, Andreas P. *The Maritime Economy of Ancient Cyprus in Terms of the New Institutional Economics*. Oxford: Archaeopress Archaeology, 2022.

Parpola, Simo. *Assyrian Prophecies*. SAA 9. Helsinki: Helsinki University Press, 1997.

Peckham, Brian. *Phoenicia: Episodes and Anecdotes from the Ancient Mediterranean*. Winona Lake, IN: Eisenbrauns, 2014.

Perotta, Anthony J. "A Test of Balaam: Locating Humor in the Biblical Text." Pages 280–300 in *Probing the Frontiers of Biblical Studies*. Edited by J. H. Ellens and J. T. Greene. Eugene, OR: Pickwick, 2009.

Petersen, David L. *The Prophetic Literature: An Introduction*. Louisville: Westminster John Knox, 2002.

Potts, Rolf, and Cedar van Tassel. "The Misadventures of Wenamun." *The Common*, December 19, 2013. https://www.thecommononline.org/the-misadventures-of-wenamun/. Accessed February 4, 2023.

Powell, Marvin A. "Weights and Measures." *ABD* 6:897–908.

Power, Cian J. *The Significance of Linguistic Diversity in the Hebrew Bible: Language and Boundaries of Self and Other*. FAT/2 138. Tubingen: Mohr Siebeck, 2022.

Pulak, Cemal. "The Uluburun Shipwreck and Late Bronze Age Trade." Pages 289–385 in *Beyond Babylon: Art, Trade, and Diplomacy in the Second Millennium B.C.* Edited by J. Aruz, J. K. Benzel and J. M. Evans. New York: Metropolitan Museum of Art, 2008.

———. "The Uluburun Shipwreck: An Overview." *The International Journal of Nautical Archaeology* 27 (1998): 188–224.

Quack, Joachim. "Ein neuer Versuch zum Moskauer literarischen Brief." ZÄS 128 (2001): 167–81.

———. Review of *Egyptian Proper Names*, by Yoshiyuki Muchiki. *Review of Biblical Literature*, April 24, 2000. https://www.sblcentral.org/API/Reviews/408_983.pdf.

Quinn, Josephine Crawley. *In Search of the Phoenicians*. Princeton: Princeton University Press, 2018.

Rad, Gerhard von. *The Message of the Prophets*. Translated by David M. G. Stalker. New York: Harper & Row, 1967.

Rainey, Anson F. *The El-Amarna Correspondence: A New Edition of the Cuneiform Letters from the Site of El-Amarna Based on Collations of All Extant Tablets*. Edited by William M. Schniedewind. Handbook of Oriental Studies 110. Leiden: Brill, 2015.

Redford, Donald B. *Egypt, Canaan, and Israel in Ancient Times*. Princeton: Princeton University, 1992.

———. "The Monotheism of Akhenaten." Pages 11–26 in *Aspects of Monotheism*. Edited by Hershel Shanks. Washington, DC: Biblical Archaeology Society, 1996.

———. *Pharaonic King-Lists, Annals, and Day-Books: A Contribution to the Study of the Egyptian Sense of History*. Mississauga: Benben, 1986.

Reymond, Eric D. *Intermediate Biblical Hebrew Grammar: A Student's Guide to Phonology and Morphology*. Resources for Biblical Study 89. Atlanta: SBL, 2017.

Ritner, Robert K. *The Libyan Anarchy: Inscriptions from Egypt's Third Intermediate Period*. Edited by Edward Wente. SBLWAW 21. Atlanta: Society of Biblical Literature, 2009.

———. *The Mechanics of Ancient Egyptian Magical Practice*. Chicago: The Oriental Institute, 1993.

———. "Necromancy in Ancient Egypt." Pages 89–96 in *Magic and Divination in the Ancient World*. Edited by Leda Ciraolo and Jonathan Seidel. Ancient Magic and Divination 2. Leiden: Brill, 2002.

Roberts, J. J. M. "Double Entendre in First Isaiah." *Catholic Biblical Quarterly* 54 (1992): 39–48.

Rofé, Alexander. "Classification of Prophetical Stories." *JBL* 89 (1970): 427–40.

———. *The Prophetical Stories: Narratives about the Prophets in the Hebrew Bible, Their Literary Types and History*. Jerusalem: Magnes, 1988.

Römer, Malte. *Gottes- und Priesterherrschaft in Ägypten am Ende des neuen Reiches: Ein religionsgeschichtliches Phänomen und seine Sozialen Grundlagen*. ÄAT 21. Wiesbaden: Harrassowitz, 1994.

Ross, J. F. "The Prophet as Yahweh's Messenger." Pages 98–107 in *Israel's Prophetic Heritage: Essays in Honor of James Muilenburg*. Edited by B. W. Anderson and W. Harrelson. New York: Harper, 1962.

Roth, Martha T. *Law Collections from Mesopotamia and Asia Minor*. 2nd ed. Atlanta, GA: Scholars Press, 1997.

Sader, Hélène S. *The History and Archaeology of Phoenicia*. Archaeology and Biblical Studies 25. Atlanta: SBL Press, 2019.

Sanders, Seth L. *The Invention of Hebrew*. Urbana: University of Illinois Press, 2009.

Sarlo, Daniel. *The Solar Nature of Yahweh: Reconsidering the Identity of the Ancient Israelite Deity*. Coniectanea Biblica. Lanham: Lexington Books; Minneapolis: Fortress Academic, 2022.

Sass, Benjamin. "Wenamun and His Levant: 1075 BC or 925 BC?" *Ägypten und Levante/Egypt and the Levant* 12 (2002): 247–55.

Sasson, Jack M. "Canaanite Maritime Involvement in the Second Millennium B.C." *Journal of the American Oriental Society* 86 (1966): 126–38.

Satzinger, Helmut. "How Good Was Tjeker-Baʿl's Egyptian? Mockery at Foreign Diction in the Report of Wenamūn." *Lingua Aegyptia* 5 (1997): 171–76.

Satzinger, Helmut, and Danijela Stefanović. *Egyptian Root Lexicon*. LASM 25. Hamburg: Widmaier, 2021.

Sauneron, Serge. *The Priests of Ancient Egypt*. Translated by A. M. Davidon. New York: Grove Press, 1960.

Schaeffer, C. F. A. *Ugaritica III*. Mission de Ras Shamra 8. Paris: Paul Geuthner, 1956.

Schaper, Joachim. *Media and Monotheism: Presence, Representation, and Abstraction in Ancient Judah*. Orientalische Religionen in der Antike 33. Tübingen: Mohr Siebeck, 2019.

Scheepers, Ann. "Anthroponymes et toponymes du récit d'Ounamon." Pages 17–83 in *Phoenicia and the Bible*. Edited by E. Lipiński. OLA 44. Leuven: Peeters, 1991.

Schipper, Bernd U. "'Apokalyptik,' 'Messianismus,' 'Prophetie'—eine Begrifsbestimmung." Pages 21–40 in *Apokalyptik und Ägypten: Eine kritische Analyse der relevanten Texte aus dem griechischrömischen Ägypten*. Edited by Bernd U. Schipper and A. Blasius. OLA 107. Leuven: Peeters, 2002.

———. *Die Erzählung des Wenamun: Ein Literaturwerk im Spannungsfeld von Politik, Geschichte und Religion*. Göttingen: Vandenhoeck & Ruprecht, 2005.

———. *Israel und Ägypten in der Königszeit: Die kulturellen Kontakte von Salomo bis zum Fall Jerusalems*. Freiburg: Universitätsverlag; Göttingen: Vandenhoeck Ruprecht, 1999.

———. "Wer war 'Sōʾ, König von Ägypten' (2 Kön 17,4)?" *Biblische Notizen* 92 (1998): 71–84.

Schlichting, Robert, "Prophetie." Pages 1122–25 in vol. 4 of *Lexikon der Ägyptologie*. Edited by Wolfgang Helck, Eberhard Otto, and Wolfhart Westendorf. Wiesbaden: Harrassowitz, 1972.

Schneider, Thomas. *Asiatische Personennamen in ägyptischen Quellen des Neuen Reiches*. OBO 114. Freiburg: Universitätsverlag; Göttingen: Vandenhoeck Ruprecht, 1992.

———. "A Land Without Prophets? Examining the Presumed Lack of Prophecy in Ancient Egypt." Pages 59–86 in *Enemies and Friends of the State: Ancient Prophecy in Context*. Edited by Christopher A. Rollston. University Park, PA: Eisenbrauns, 2017.

Schroeder, Ryan D. *Let Us Go to the Seer! Prophecy, Scribal Culture, and the Invention of Hebrew Scripture*. BZAW 563. Berlin: de Gruyter, 2024.

Schroer, Silvia. "The Continuity of the Canaanite Glyptic Tradition into the Iron Age I–IIA." *Jerusalem Journal of Archaeology* 1 (2021): 482–502.

Sethe, Kurt. *Amun und die acht Urgötter von Hermopolis: Eine Untersuchung über Ursprung und Wesen des ägyptischen Götterkönigs*. Berlin: Verlag der Akademie der Wissenschaften, 1929.

———. *Eine ägyptische Expedition nach dem Lebanon im 15. Jahrhundert v. Chr.* Berlin: Königlichen Preussischen Akademie der Wissenschaften, 1906.

Shaw, Ian. *The Oxford History of Ancient Egypt*. Oxford: Oxford University Press, 2000.

Shupak, Nili. "Egyptian 'Prophecy' and Biblical Prophecy: Did the Phenomenon of Prophecy, in the Biblical Sense, Exist in Ancient Egypt?" *Journal of the Ancient Near Eastern Society Ex Oriente Lux* 31 (1989–90): 5–40.

———. "The Egyptian 'Prophecy'—A Reconsideration." Pages 133–44 in *Von Reichlich Ägyptischem Verstande: Festschrift für Waltraud Guglielmi zum 65. Geburtstag*. Edited by K. Zibelius-Chen. Wiesbaden: Harrassowitz, 2006.

Simpson, William K. *The Literature of Ancient Egypt*. 3rd ed. New Haven: Yale University, 2003.

Singer, Itamar. "'The Thousand Gods of Hatti': The Limits of an Expanding Pantheon." Pages 81–102 in *Concepts of the Other in Near Eastern Religions*. Edited by I. Alon, I. Gruenwald and I. Singer. Israel Oriental Studies 14. Leiden: Brill, 1994.

Smith, Mark S. *The Early History of God: Yahweh and the Other Deities in Ancient Israel*. 2nd ed. Grand Rapids: Eerdmans, 2002.

———. *God in Translation: Deities in Cross-Cultural Discourse in the Biblical World*. FAT 57. Tübingen: Mohr Siebeck, 2008.

———. *The Origins of Biblical Monotheism: Israel's Polytheistic Background and the Ugaritic Texts*. Oxford: Oxford University Press, 2001.

Smoak, Jeremy D. *The Priestly Blessing in Inscription and Scripture: The Early History of Numbers 6:24–26*. New York: Oxford University Press, 2015.

Smoot, Stephen O. "An Egyptian View of the Monotheism of Second Isaiah." *Catholic Biblical Quarterly* 86 (2024): 15–36.

Spalinger, Anthony. "Wenamun: Directions in Palaeography and Structure. A Preliminary Survey." Pages 187–218 in *Observing the Scribe at Work: Scribal Practices in the Ancient World*. Edited by Rodney Ast et al. Leuven: Peeters, 2021.

Spens, Renaud de. "Droit internationale et commerce au début de la XXIe dynastie: Analyse juridique de Rapport d'Ounamon." Pages 105–26 in *Le commerce en Egypte ancienne*. Edited by Nicolas Grimal and Bernadette Menu. Cairo: Institut français d'archéologie orientale, 1998.

Spiegelberg, Wilhelm. "Varia: 10: Eine zurückgezogene Pachtkundigung." *ZÄS* 53 (1917): 107–11.

Starcky, Jean. "La flèche de Zakarba'al, roi d'Amurru." Pages 179–86 in *Archeologie au Levant: Receuil Roger Saidah*. Lyon: Maison de l'Orient et de la Méditerranée Jean Pouilloux, 1982.

Stauder-Porchet, Julie, Elizabeth Frood, and Stauder Andréas, eds. *Ancient Egyptian Biographies: Contexts, Forms, Functions*. Wilbour Studies in Egyptology and Assyriology 6. Atlanta: Lockwood Press, 2020.

Stieglitz, Robert R. "Long-Distance Seafaring in the Ancient Near East." *Biblical Archaeologist* 47.3 (1984): 134–42.

Stökl, Jonathan. *Prophecy in the Ancient Near East: A Philological and Sociological Comparison*. CHANE 56. Leiden: Brill, 2012.

Strawn, Brent A. *What Is Stronger Than a Lion? Leonine Image and Metaphor in the Hebrew Bible and the Ancient Near East.* Fribourg: Academic Press; Göttingen: Vandenhoeck & Ruprecht, 2005.

Sweeney, Deborah. "Letters." Pages 1055–1071 in *The Oxford Handbook of Egyptology.* Edited by Ian Shaw and Elizabeth Gambier Bloxam. Oxford: Oxford University Press, 2020.

Tattko, Jan. "Amun." Pages 1066–67 in vol. 1 of *Encyclopedia of the Bible and Its Reception.* Edited by Hans-Josef Klauck et al. Berlin: de Gruyter, 2009.

Tawil, Hayim. *An Akkadian Lexical Companion for Biblical Hebrew.* Jersey City, NJ: Ktav, 2009

Taylor, Glen. *Yahweh and the Sun: Biblical and Archaeological Evidence for Sun Worship in Ancient Israel.* Journal for the Study of the Old Testament Supplements 111. Sheffield: JSOT, 1993.

Te Velde, Herman. "Seth." In *OEAE* 3:269–71.

———. *Seth, God of Confusion: A Study of His Role in Egyptian Mythology and Religion.* Leiden: Brill, 1967.

Tiemeyer, Lena-Sofia. "The Seer and the Priest: The Case of the So-called Linen Ephod." Pages 137–51 in Lena-Sofia Tiemeyer. Edited by *Prophecy and Its Cultic Dimensions.* Journal of Ancient Judaism Supplements 31. Göttingen: Vandenhoeck & Ruprecht, 2019.

Uehlinger, Christoph. "Der Amun-Tempel Ramses' III. in *p3-Kn'n*, seine sudpalästinischen Tempelgüter und der Ubergang von der Ägypter-zur Philisterherrschaft: Ein Hinweis auf einige wenig beachtete Skarabaen." *Zeitschrift des Deutschen Palästina-Vereins* 104 (1988): 11–15.

Vernus, Pascal. "Choix des textes illustrant le temps des rois tanites et libyens." Pages 102–11 in *Tanis: L'or des pharaons.* Paris: Ministère des Affaires Étrangères / Association Française d'Action Artistique, 1987.

Vinson, Steve. "Boats (Use of)" (13 pages). Available from *UCLA Encyclopedia of Egyptology.* Edited by Willeke Wendrich. Los Angeles, 2013. https://digital2.library.ucla.edu/viewItem.do?ark=21198/zz002gw1hs.

Wainwright, G. A. "The Aniconic Form of Amon in the New Kingdom." *Annales du service des antiquités de l'Égypte* 28 (1928): 173–89.

———. "Some Aspects of Amūn." *JEA* 20 (1934): 139–53.

Ward, William A. "Late Egyptian 'r.t: The So-Called Upper Room." *JNES* 44 (1985): 329–35.

———. "Trade, Foreign." Pages 842–45 in *Encyclopedia of the Archaeology of Ancient Egypt.* Edited by K. A. Bard. New York: Routledge, 1999.

Weeks, Stuart. "Predictive and Prophetic Literature: Can Neferti Help Us Read the Bible?" Pages 25–46 in *Prophecy and Prophets in Ancient Israel.* Edited by John Day. Library of Hebrew Bible and Old Testament Studies 531. London: T&T Clark, 2010.

Weinfeld, Moshe. *The Place of the Law in the Religion of Ancient Israel.* Vetus Testamentum Supplements 100. Leiden: Brill, 2004.

Weinstein, James M. "Lebanon." In *OEAE* 2:285.

Wellhausen, Julius. *Prolegomena to the History of Israel.* Translated by J. S. Black and A. Menzies. Edinburgh: A. & C. Black, 1885. German original: Berlin: Georg Reimer, 1883.

Wente, Edward F. *Late Ramesside Letters.* Studies in Ancient Oriental Civilization 33. Chicago: University of Chicago Press, 1967.

———. *Letters from Ancient Egypt.* SBLWAW 1. Atlanta: Scholars Press, 1990.

Winand, Jean. "L'ironie dans Ounamon: Les emplois de *mk* et de *ptr*." *GM* 200 (2004): 105–10.

Westbrook, Raymond. "International Law in the Amarna Age." Pages 28–41 in *Amarna Diplomacy: The Beginnings of International Relations.* Edited by R. Cohen and R. Westbrook. Baltimore: Johns Hopkins University Press, 2000.

Westermann, Claus. *Basic Forms of Prophetic Speech.* Translated by H. C. White. Philadelphia: Westminster, 1967.

Wilson, John A. "The Oath in Ancient Egypt." *JNES* 3 (1948): 129–56.

———. Review of *Untersuchungen zu Stil und Sprache neuägyptischer Erzählungen*, by Fritz Hintze. *JNES* 3 (1952): 227–30.

Wimmer, Stefan J. "Egyptian Temples in Canaan and Sinai." Pages 1065–106 in *Studies in Egyptology: Presented to Miriam Lichtheim.* Edited by Sarah Israelit-Groll. Jerusalem: Magnes, 1990.

———. "The Report of Wenamun: A Journey in Ancient Egyptian Literature." Pages 541–59 in *Ramesside Studies in Honour of K. A. Kitchen.* Edited by Mark Collier and Steven R. Snape. Bolton: Rutherford, 2011.

———. *Le voyage d'Ounamon: Index Verborum, Concordance, Relevés grammaticaux*, Aegyptiaca Leondiensia 1. Liège: Centre Informatique de Philosophie et Lettres, 1987.

Zandee, Jan. "Seth als Sturmgott." *ZÄS* 90 (1963): 144–88.

SUBJECT INDEX

Akkadian, 25n33, 26, 47–48, 63, 68, 72, 97, 101
Amarna Period, 8, 17, 50, 65, 72, 101–2, 108–9, 111. See also Amarna Letters in the ancient source index
Assmann, Jan, 4, 8, 16–17, 20, 49, 76, 91, 110
Aššur, 2, 21, 109, 111
Assyria, 15, 29, 35, 40, 56, 60, 63–64, 71–74, 82, 88, 105–6, 108. See also Nineveh
Aten and Atenism, 16–17, 20, 102, 108–9, 111
autobiography, 5, 14, 17–18, 86, 101

Baal (/Hadad), 2, 4, 21, 24–25, 39–44, 50, 62, 84, 89, 91, 97, 105, 110–11
Babylon, 3, 47, 60, 72, 109
Baines, John, 9, 13–14, 65, 89, 94
Balaam, 3, 68, 83–85, 92, 95, 98, 106–7
blessings, 37–40, 44, 61–62, 65, 73, 85
Byblos, 1–2

comedy, 3, 16, 27, 33, 46, 50, 59, 66, 84–85, 90–92, 98–99
covenants, 3, 47, 56–66, 71, 73, 77, 81. See also oaths; treaties
curses, 47, 77, 85–86
Cyprus, 1, 11, 27, 90

David, 7, 9, 21, 60, 105–6
Deuteronomism, 61–62, 81, 109

diplomacy, 31, 33, 37–38, 56, 64, 66, 69, 72–74, 86, 88, 91, 98, 105
Dor, 1–2, 26–27, 29, 32–34, 36, 91
Dynasty, Egyptian
3, 9
18, 10
19, 41
20, 1, 41–42
21, 5, 8, 16, 41, 53–54, 73–74, 87
22, 7, 15–17, 41, 53–54
25, 17, 63–64, 72, 106

economics, 30–33, 50, 59–60, 66, 110. See also trade
Elijah, 2, 39, 43
Elisha, 47, 67
Exile, Babylonian (and postexilic texts) 82, 93–94

fiction, 13–15, 95

Hatti and Hittites, 10, 41, 56–57, 61–63, 98, 101
hierocracy, 3, 6, 106–7
High Priest of Amun, 16, 76
Herihor, 6–9, 17, 32, 34, 59, 69
humor. See comedy

insult. See mockery

Judaism, 8, 73, 81, 106

129

Subject Index

Karnak, 9–10, 15, 92

Late Bronze Age, 1, 20, 34, 36, 39, 53, 56–57, 59–60, 63, 100–102, 105, 108
Lebanon, 1, 9–10, 16–17, 25, 38–40, 45, 50, 52, 59, 87, 97–98
letters, 8, 10, 12, 36–38, 68, 72–74, 82–83, 87, 89, 95, 98. *See also* Amarna Letters
Lichtheim, Miriam, 13–14, 22, 44
lions, 53–54, 61, 65, 98, 103
loanwords, 19, 25–27, 47, 49

Marduk, 3, 21, 109–111
Mesopotamia, 3, 9, 11, 29, 72, 80, 88, 93, 98, 105, 108–9. *See also* Assyria; Babylon; *and others*
messengers, 3, 37, 60, 67–74, 88, 98
mockery, 39–40, 47, 49, 66, 86–88, 97
Moers, Gerald, 15, 50, 86, 91, 95
monotheism, vii, 3–4, 8, 17, 55, 97–111
Moses, 32, 60, 71, 77–78, 80, 108

networks, 10, 21, 28, 30, 100–101
Nile River, 46, 51, 54, 60–61, 72, 98
Nissinen, Martti, 22, 104

oaths, 31–32, 50, 56–66, 71, 98
oracles, 7, 17, 20–21, 31, 43, 54, 69, 76, 79–83, 85, 110

Persia, 21, 52, 68, 74, 98, 106–107
pharaohs, 5, 7, 26, 34, 37–38, 41–42, 53–54, 58–50, 63–65, 69–70, 87–89, 95, 98, 100–101, 106
  Akhenaten, 11, 17, 92, 108
  Amenemhet I, 80
  Hatshepsut, 8, 31
  Ramses II, 9, 41
  Ramses III, 36, 102
  Ramses V, 38, 42
  Ramses XI, 5, 8, 64, 68, 88
  Sheshonq I, 15–16, 92, 95
  Smendes, 5–6, 11, 17, 31–32, 34
  Snefru, 80
  Thutmose III, 7, 9–10, 16
Phoenicia, 4, 10, 15, 21, 28–30, 40, 48, 57–59, 98–101, 105, 109, 111

Priests and priesthood, 3, 7, 12, 16–17, 37, 47–48, 70, 73, 76–80, 83, 92, 95, 98–99, 105–107. *See also* hierocracy; High Priest of Amun
Prophecy
  ecstatic, 2, 22–26, 31, 37, 46–49, 68, 75, 78, 84–85, 93, 104
  at Mari, 2, 29, 47, 68, 72, 82, 104
  at Nineveh, 2, 29, 47, 64, 69, 93

Ritner, Robert, xiii, 68, 79, 89

satire. *See* comedy
Saul, 52, 75, 106
Schipper, Bernd, xiii, 16, 23, 35, 71, 92–95
scribes and scribal culture, 8, 12, 52, 73–74, 76, 79–82, 91, 95, 98, 101–2, 104–5, 109
seals and glyptic art, 11, 20–21, 30, 64, 98, 100, 102–3
Seth, 38, 41–42. *See also* Baal
Smith, Mark S., 4, 21, 109
solar theology, 8, 16–17, 89, 101–2, 108, 110
Solomon, 9, 28–29, 58–60, 81, 98, 100
statues, 11, 22n17, 36–37, 50, 68–69, 76, 83, 111
Summodeism, 3–4, 17, 105, 108–109

Tanis, 1, 5, 31, 41
taunting. *See* mockery
Temples and temple officials, 17, 38, 41, 64, 73, 76–78, 83, 86, 103–4, 107
  of Amun in Gaza, 102
  of Amun at el-Hiba, 16, 92, 95
  of Amun at Hibis, 52
  of Amun at Karnak, 1, 8–10
  of Baal at Ugarit, 89
  of Osiris, 74
  of Re-Atum at Heliopolis 12
  of Yahweh at Jerusalem 28, 58, 77, 98, 110–11
Thebes, 1, 4, 6, 8, 10, 12, 16–17, 34, 41, 44, 63, 76, 90–92, 94–95, 100, 106–7
Theocracy, 3–4, 6–8, 16–17, 31–45, 52, 63, 91, 97–111
timber. *See* wood
trade and traders, 9–11, 17, 28, 30, 41, 51, 59, 97, 105

treaties, 39, 50, 56–66, 71, 98, 106. *See also* diplomacy; oaths
Tyre, 1, 28–29, 41, 57–58, 101, 105

Ugarit and Ugaritic texts, 10, 12, 24, 27, 39, 57, 89, 101, 105

Voegelin, Eric, 3–4

wood, 9–10, 16–17, 28, 32, 35–36, 40, 56, 58–60, 77, 79, 87, 90, 98

ANCIENT SOURCE INDEX

Wenamun
1/1   8
1/2–4   31
1/3–6   5
1/4   6
1/5–6   31
1/7   25
1/8–9   36
1/10   32
1/10–32   31
1/14–16   32
1/15–16   6
1/17   33
1/18–20   33
1/21–22   25
1/21–23   34
1/23   25
1/25–26   6
1/25–30   36
1/30–32   36, 86
1/34–38   37
1/37–38   85
1/38–39   24
1/38–40   46
1/39–40   37, 68
1/43   72
1/46–47   72
1/46   25
1/48   26
1/50   37
1/50–51   38
1/52   70
1/54–2/2   40

1/55   25
1/56   93
1/57–2.2   31
1/58   25
1/59   25
2/2   27
2/3   58–59
2/4–5   56, 59
2/6   58
2/6–8   59
2/6–13   31
2/7   34
2/10   34
2/11   58
2/10–13   59
2/10–37   46
2/12   26
2/12–14   38
2/18   40
2/19   40
2/20–22   44
2/22–23   46
2/23–28   50
2/25   62
2/25–30   55
2/26   69
2/27   25
2/28   52
2/29   34
2/29–30   87
2/31–32   56, 60
2/32–33   60–61
2/33   58

Ancient Source Index

Wenamun (*continued*)
2/33–34   52–53
2/40–45   11–12
2/45   25
2/47   58
2/47–49   90
2/51–53   5, 64, 88
2/53   68
2/55–60   88
2/56–57   69
2/60   9
2/60–62   89
2/61   6, 58
2/62–63   90
2/64–65   86
2/65   93
2/68   26
2/71   26, 71
2/74   92
2/76   27
2/77   26
2/78   38
2/73–74   69
2/79–80   90
2/80–81   69

Other Texts from Egypt
Amarna Letters   10, 36–37, 41, 56, 59, 72, 101
   EA 3:21–22   60
   EA 7   60
   EA 8:8–12   57
   EA 10   60
   EA 16:26–31   60
   EA 23   69
   EA 27:9–12   57
   EA 74:36   63
   EA 83:21–27   63
   EA 85:39–47   63
   EA 118:39–44   57
   EA 132:30–35   63
   EA 136:24–32   63
   EA 136:43   88–89
   EA 138:53   63
   EA 147:13–15   41
   EA 150:33–37   57
   EA 164   69

Book of the Dead   7

Cairo Hymns to Amun (P.Boulaq 17)   52

The Capture of Joppa   15

Chester Beatty Papyri   42
   IV   79–80, 82

The Contendings of Horus and Seth   41–42, 70

The Doomed Prince   15

Dream of Nectanebo   83

Elephantine Papyri   73

Funerary Decree for Princess Neskhons   16–17, 100

Gebel Barkal Stela of Thutmose III   10, 16

Great Amun Hymn from Hibis   43, 52

Great Hymn to the Aten   108

Hymn to Amun (P.Leiden I 350)   51

Hymn to Amun-Re (P.Cairo 58032)   55

Hymn to Ramses V   38

Instruction of Amenemope
   16.1–2   89
   22.5–7   8
   26.3   86

Instruction of Any
   G, 5.1   89
   B, 22.17   89

Instruction of Ptahhotep
   6,6   86

Letters from Ancient Egypt (Wente)
  #333   73
  #339   73–74
  #336   74

Memphite Theology   4

Onomasticon of Amenope   12

Piye Victory Stela   63–64

Potter's Oracle   80, 82–83

Prophecy of Neferti   22, 79–80, 83

Setna Cycle   23

The Shipwrecked Sailor   15

Sinuhe   15

Tale of Woe / Letter of Wermai   12, 15, 86, 95

The Teaching of a Man for His Son
  §20,6   86

Other Ancient Near Eastern Texts
Ahiqar   15, 95
  137   48

Amman Citadel Inscription   29

CTH
  106   61
  131   57
  41   57
  42   62
  46   57
  62   57

Deir 'Alla inscriptions   29
  I:1   26, 85

Enuma Elish   3

KAI
  1   28
  5–6   89
  5:2   89
  10:7–8   39

KTU³
  1.0 i:12   38
  2.23   102
  2.23:20–24   89, 101–102
  5.11   102

Mari letters   2, 29, 47, 68, 82, 104–5
ARM
  3 18:15   47
  26 207   47

SAA
  9.1–3   82
  9 3.5 iii 13–15   63

Vassal Treaties of Esarhaddon   63

Zakkur Stela   24–25, 29

Hebrew Bible
Genesis
  26:24   58
  28:13   58
  41:39–45   93

Exodus
  3:6   60
  3:13   60
  3:15   60
  9:23–34   43
  12:12   56
  20:7   61
  24:15–16   110
  33:7   71
  33:20   110

Leviticus
  6:25   37–38
  8:4   71

Leviticus (continued)
9:5 71
19:2 78
11:1 43
11:16–17 71
16:19 71
16:42 71
20:6 71
22–24 84–85
23:19 68
30:2 61
33:4 56

Deuteronomy 56
1:11 58
1:21 58
4:1 58
5:32 32
6:1–3 58
10:17 55
12:1 58
23:21 61
27:3 58
28:12 40
28:28 47
28:31 47
30:15–19 61–62
34:5 60
34:10 80

Joshua
1:1 60
1:7–8 32
3:11 54
3:13 54
7 52–53
18:3 58
22:22 55
24:2 58
24:6 58
24:29

Judges
2:8 60
2:10 43
10:11–12 75
12:7 58
14:41–42 7

1 Samuel
15 52
15:29 68
16:7–13 7

2 Samuel
5:11 9

1 Kings 81
1:50–52 7
3:1 100
5 58–59
5–7 28
5:6–10 9
5:18 28
7:8 100
9:11–12 60
9:24 100
9:26–28 28
10:11 28
11:1–10 100
11:14–40 72
14:25–26 15
18 2, 39
18:4–13 70
18:27–28 39
18:38 43
19:1–10 70
20:3 54

2 Kings
1:12 43
9:11 47
9:17–18 68
17:4 72
17:13 32
18:12 60
20:5 58
23:11 108

Isaiah 24, 48, 77, 82, 107–110
2:14 52
6:3 54
6:5 110
6:8 69
7:7 71
8:16 80
8:17 110

9:13–17 2
10:33 52
14 87
19:1 43
19:1–15 110
19:11–15 2
19:18–25 44
20:1–6 64
22:17 43
24:1 43
26:21 43
28:7 48–49
28:15–18 64
29:8–11 2
29:11 80
30:1–2 64, 87
30:7 88
31:4 53
35:2 52
36:6 88
36:8–9 40
37:16 54
37:20 54
38:5 58
42:1 60
42:19 60
45 110
45:8 40
45:9 110
45:15–19 21, 110
45:22 108
46:1–2 108, 110
48:13 44
49:6 60
51:13 44
51:16 44
60:13 53
62:11 43
66:1–2 55
66:15 43

Jeremiah 2, 77, 82, 88
4:2 62
10:12 44
12:17 62
14:13–16 2
14:13–15 2
25:11–12 82

26:14–19 70
29:26 47
33:2 44
36:29–30 71
46:17 88
46:25 56
49:19 53
50:21 32
50:44 53
51:5 44

Ezekiel 83
1:3 77
13 2
18:4 54
29:3–10 54
31:15–16 52
31:18 88
32:2 53
43:7–12 78

Hosea
2 2, 110
5:14 53
9:7 47
11:10 53
13:7–8 53

Amos
1:2 53
3:8 53
6:11 43
7:10–17 71
9:6–7 44

Jonah 3, 35, 84–96, 99
1:1–15 92–93
2:11–3:1 93
3:4–9 93
4:2–9 93

Micah
1:3 43
4:13 54

Zephaniah
2:11 56

Haggai 83
   1:1–11 77
   2:7–8 77

Zechariah
   1:1 24
   4:14 54
   6:5 54
   12:1 44
   14:9 54

Malachi
   3:10 40

Psalms
   18:1 60
   19 108
   29:3 43
   29:5–6 52
   36:1 60
   50:9–10 54
   78:23 40
   82 55–56, 108
   95:3 55
   97:5 54
   104 108
   104:16 52

Job
   1:16 43
   34:29 110
   40:9 43

Proverbs
   25:2 110

Daniel
   2:46–48 93
   3:28–30 93
   4:34–37 93
   9:2 82
   12:9 80

Ezra
   8:28 58
   10:11 58

2 Chronicles
   1:3 60, 71
   12:2–9 15
   15:1 24
   15:8 24
   28:9 24
   36:22 68

1 Esdras
   6:27 60